USING AND ENJOYING
BIBLICAL GREEK

READING THE NEW TESTAMENT
WITH FLUENCY AND DEVOTION

RODNEY A. WHITACRE

Baker Academic

a division of Baker Publishing Group
Grand Rapids, Michigan

Online resources for this book are available at
www.bakeracademic.com/UEBGeSources.

© 2015 by Rodney A. Whitacre

Published by Baker Academic
a division of Baker Publishing Group
P.O. Box 6287, Grand Rapids, MI 49516-6287
www.bakeracademic.com

Printed in the United States of America

Library of Congress Cataloging-in-Publication Data
Whitacre, Rodney A., author.
    Using and enjoying Biblical Greek : reading the New Testament with fluency and devotion
/ Rodney A. Whitacre.
        pages cm
    Includes bibliographical references and index.
    ISBN 978-0-8010-4994-1 (pbk.)
    1. Greek language, Biblical—Textbooks. 2. Greek language, Biblical—Grammar. I. Title.
PA817.W54 2015
487'.4—dc23   2015020883

15 16 17 18 19 20 21   7 6 5 4 3 2 1

To the faculty, staff, students, board, alums, and friends of
Trinity School for Ministry, Ambridge, Pennsylvania

CONTENTS

Preface

This book is primarily a response to requests over the years from former students to help them get back into Greek. While writing this book, I have had in mind the vast number of folks who have taken Greek and fallen by the wayside, as well as those who have kept up their Greek and want to go deeper. Accordingly, along with review of the basic data, I have tried to offer ways for students to go much further with Greek than they often manage and thereby to discover for themselves its joys and benefits. My rallying cry is "Work toward fluency one passage at a time!" While fluency requires time and effort, there does not need to be a delay in the gratification that comes from studying Greek.

Individual Use

This book can be used by individuals and small groups (meeting either locally or online) to review the basic data and explore some favorite passages. For me, such exploration includes historical-grammatical exegesis as well as approaches practiced in the ancient church. In chapter 6 I offer an introduction to meditating on the text using both modern and ancient approaches. For those using the book on their own, I suggest reading chapters 1 and 5 and then beginning to read a favorite text, applying the knowledge gained from these chapters. The sections on basic data and mapping can be skimmed initially and then reviewed as needed. Chapter 4 on sentence structure will probably be of particular help, since this topic is seldom covered in detail in basic Greek courses. Chapter 6 (meditation) and appendix 5 (verbal analysis) offer ways to reflect more deeply on a passage and can be added in at any point.

Course Use

Much of the material in this book was developed in teaching fairly ordinary courses in basic Greek and Greek exegesis. I have also offered advanced courses based specifically on the approaches to fluency and meditation presented in this book. Since most schools do not have room in their curriculum for a special, advanced course, this book can easily serve as a supplemental text in an existing course to further enrich and challenge students.

In particular, the material on learning vocabulary nicely supplements basic Greek methods, and the discussion on sentence patterns would add material lacking in most methods. The approach to morphology varies with different methods. Thus the material in chapter 3 would probably be difficult to use in conjunction with a basic Greek text, but I have found it works well in an exegesis course for reviewing some of the basic patterns and deepening students' ability to recognize forms in a passage. Many exegesis courses include work on sentence mapping (also called "sentence flows," "phrasing," and other terms), so the chapter and appendix on mapping could be used for that section of a course. The approach to mapping offered here has a number of particular virtues. It (1) is simpler than some other methods, (2) does not require special symbols beyond those readily available in most fonts, (3) enables one to see the original Greek order, and (4) works well in both Greek and English. The list of labels provided in appendix 2 may also be useful in the exegetical analysis associated with sentence mapping.

Most important, chapter 5, on developing familiarity and fluency, could easily supplement any method used in either basic or advanced Greek courses. The guidelines I provide can be practiced right from the outset of a person's study of Greek and continued thereafter.[1]

Additional Resources

Additional suggestions and material for the use of this book by individuals and in courses are available at the website for this book. Further resources are also provided, including a list of vocabulary used in the GNT 30 times or more, parsing practice exercises based on the approach in chapter 3, and short videos that introduce the material on parsing and mapping, material

---

1. I am preparing a book for beginners based on the approaches offered in this book, a "prequel," as it were.

that can be very dense in written form! In chapter 3 I claim that all the patterns needed for parsing the vast majority of forms can fit on a single sheet of paper (8.5 x 11 in.) without microscopic print. For proof, see the website.

Acknowledgments

I am thankful for those who taught me Greek, my colleagues in teaching Greek (those I know personally and those known only through their writings), and all the Greek students I have taught, beginning at Gordon-Conwell in 1973 and especially at Trinity School for Ministry since 1983. Since 2009 I have led an online Greek Reading Circle composed of people who have lost their Greek and want to regain it or who have retained it and want to go further with it—the very sort of folks this book is for. I value the encouragement and input I have received from those in the GRC. I am grateful to James Ernest for his encouragement and expertise in shepherding this book along, as he did my earlier book, *A Patristic Greek Reader*. I am also grateful to Wells Turner and the other editors and designers at Baker who saw the book through the production process and added to its clarity, accuracy, and attractiveness. I appreciate the feedback from two anonymous readers who enabled me to improve the book considerably. One of these readers suggested that I include discussion of verbal aspect, which I was happy to do since this has been a keen interest since I read an article by K. L. McKay in 1972.[2]

I am thankful for the support of my wife, Margaret; our son Seth; and our son Chad and his wife, Jessica, both of whom majored in ancient languages in college and encouraged me in this project. Chad also helped me make appendix 5 more intelligible. Our grandchildren Leah, Miriam, Samuel, and Ruth added much support in their own wonderful and life-giving ways.

Εὐλογητὸς ὁ θεὸς καὶ πατὴρ τοῦ κυρίου ἡμῶν Ἰησοῦ Χριστοῦ

(2 Cor. 1:3; Eph. 1:3; 1 Pet. 1:3)

---

2. K. L. McKay, "Syntax in Exegesis," *Tyndale Bulletin* 23 (1972): 39–57. Available online (see bibliography).

ABBREVIATIONS

▣	indicates a core pattern
a./act.	active
Abbott-Smith	G. Abbott-Smith, *A Manual Greek Lexicon of the New Testament*
acc.	accusative
adv.	adverb
ANF	*Ante-Nicene Fathers*
aor.	aorist
app.	appendix
BDAG	Frederick William Danker, Walter Bauer, William F. Arndt, and F. Wilbur Gingrich, *A Greek-English Lexicon of the New Testament and Other Early Christian Literature*
BDF	Friedrich Blass, Albert Debrunner, and Robert W. Funk, *A Greek Grammar of the New Testament and Other Early Christian Literature*
cf.	*confer*, compare
CGEL	Frederick William Danker, with Kathryn Krug, *The Concise Greek-English Lexicon of the New Testament*
chap(s).	chapter(s)
conj.	conjunction
dat.	dative
dir. obj(s).	direct object(s)
ERV	English Revised Version (1885)
esp.	especially

ESV	English Standard Version (2011)
fem.	feminine
fr.	from
Funk	Robert W. Funk, *A Beginning-Intermediate Grammar of Hellenistic Greek*
fut.	future
gen.	genitive
GNT	Greek New Testament
impf.	imperfect
impv.	imperative
ind.	indicative
inf.	infinitive
LS	Henry George Liddell and Robert Scott, *An Intermediate Greek-English Lexicon: Founded upon the Seventh Edition of Liddell and Scott's Greek-English Lexicon*
LSJ	Henry George Liddell, Robert Scott, and Henry Stuart Jones, *A Greek-English Lexicon*. 9th ed. with revised supplement
LXX	Septuagint
m./mid.	middle
masc.	masculine
MT	Masoretic Text
NA[27]	Nestle-Aland, *Novum Testamentum Graece*, 27th ed.
NA[28]	Nestle-Aland, *Novum Testamentum Graece*, 28th ed.
NABRE	New American Bible, Revised Edition (2010)
neg.	negative
NET	The NET Bible
NETS	*A New English Translation of the Septuagint*, ed. Albert Pietersma and Benjamin G. Wright
neut.	neuter
NIV	New International Version (2011)
NLT	New Living Translation (2007)
nom.	nominative
NPNF[2]	*Nicene and Post-Nicene Fathers*, Series 2
opt.	optative
p./pass.	passive
pf.	perfect
pl.	plural
plpf.	pluperfect
prep.	preposition
pres.	present
ptc.	participle

rel.	relative
SBLGNT	*The Greek New Testament: SBL Edition*
sg.	singular
subj.	subject
subjn.	subjunctive
TLG	*Thesaurus Linguae Graecae*
UBS	United Bible Societies
UBS[4]	*The Greek New Testament*, 4th rev. ed. (United Bible Societies)
voc.	vocative
w.	with
Wallace	Daniel B. Wallace, *Greek Grammar beyond the Basics*
Young	Richard A. Young, *Intermediate New Testament Greek*

INTRODUCTION

A knowledge of the basics of Greek opens to you the greatest mental and spiritual adventure, the most edifying study. With Greek you have unique access to some of the world's greatest literature and, most significantly, the power and beauty of God's Scriptures, the very oracles of God (τὰ λόγια τοῦ θεοῦ, Rom. 3:2).[1]

The question "Why study Greek?" was raised some years ago in an internet discussion group devoted to Greek. The six reasons given by a woman who had studied Greek in a class at her church sum it up very nicely:

1. I love the language. I did not anticipate this when I started it. 2. I do get nuances out of the text that I don't get in English. 3. Reading from the Greek slows me down and makes me think. 4. I now know enough to recognize faulty arguments made by other speakers. 5. I find reading from the Greek more moving. I was gripped by reading the Passion passages in the Gospels, something I don't think I get from reading English. 6. I am a resource for the Bible study I am in. I don't answer a question every week, but there's an interpretation

1. I am applying this expression to the entire Bible, though Paul, of course, would not be including the New Testament. Most likely he is referring to "the OT as a whole with special reference, perhaps, to the promises" (Douglas J. Moo, *The Epistle to the Romans*, New International Commentary on the New Testament [Grand Rapids: Eerdmans, 1996], 182).

question I can answer, or get the answer to, with some frequency. Sometimes it's as simple as whether "you" is in the singular or plural.[2]

Would that all students of Greek had such an experience! I want to help you engage Greek texts in ways that will bring such benefits. In this introduction I will give you an overview of what I have in mind.

"Before we sip the Scriptures, we should guzzle them." This is great advice for how all Christians should approach the Scriptures. Augustine spends most of his time in *On Christian Doctrine* explaining how to interpret Scripture, and his first step is to "read them all and become familiar with their contents" (II.12 [chap. 8]). He encourages believers "to read them so as to commit them to memory, or at least so as not to remain wholly ignorant of them" (II.14 [chap. 9]).

Such extensive reading is all the more important for teachers and preachers. I remember Harold John Ockenga, when he was president of Gordon-Conwell Theological Seminary, saying that before he began to preach through a book of the Bible he read it forty times. He guzzled the book before sipping individual passages and preaching them to others.

In this book I want to encourage you to guzzle and sip the text in Greek. The methods I share in this book for gaining an ability to engage the text in these ways are neither complex nor difficult. You can use these two approaches right from the outset in basic Greek and then continue them throughout your life. It certainly takes time to become fluent, but there are ways to move toward fluency that are very enjoyable and valuable. I will not focus on exegesis,[3] though these approaches complement exegetical study of texts and can deepen your ability to do exegesis. As we will see, fluency and meditation have their own values.

Fluency

Reading extensively, guzzling, requires some level of fluency in reading a text in Greek. Fluency is often understood as the ability to read, write, and speak a language with a high level of accuracy and without stumbling over words, forms, or constructions. Rosetta Stone language courses, for example, are designed for such fluency.[4] An ability to speak and write Greek

2. Karen Pitts, message on the online discussion forum *B-Greek* (see bibliography), posted December 14, 1999.

3. There are many good guides to exegesis. See in particular, Gordon D. Fee, *New Testament Exegesis: A Handbook for Students and Pastors*, 3rd ed. (Louisville: Westminster/John Knox, 2002). For a brief review or overview, see David Alan Black, *Using New Testament Greek in Ministry: A Practical Guide for Students and Pastors* (Grand Rapids: Baker, 1993).

4. Rosetta Stone does not have courses in Biblical Greek and Hebrew, but Randall Buth has produced material for fluency in speaking and writing as well as reading Biblical Greek and Hebrew as part of immersion courses. See his Biblical Language Center (see bibliography).

is certainly a deeper level of familiarity with the language than just the ability to read. But fluency in reading can be a goal in itself that produces great rewards.[5]

In discussions of learning to read a second language, fluency is often "a relatively undefined, informal concept,"[6] but William Grabe highlights four elements.[7] A person who reads fluently is able to process the signals in a text rapidly, accurately, and automatically, that is, without needing to stop and analyze the form, function, or meaning of a word or expression. Such fluency also includes the ability to recognize the rhythmical flow of the structural units of a passage.[8] Reading in this way, however, does not mean that there are no pauses, even for those reading their native language.

> Fluency does not describe a stage in which a reader is able to decode *all* words instantly; rather, we become fluent word by word. Studies in which the eye movements of readers are tracked have shown that a skilled reader pauses at between 50 and 80 percent of the words in a text. He needs to fixate on the words, essentially to scan them in, but does so very, very quickly because the words—their spelling patterns and pronunciations—are well known to him.[9]

Some discussions of reading a second language "separate *fluency* from *accuracy*; that is, fluency comes at the expense of accuracy, and accuracy comes at the expense of fluency."[10] In this case, fluent reading does not include attending to all the details, but rather getting the main ideas of the text and something of how they are developed.

Such rapid reading is a valuable exercise. C. S. Lewis describes the large sections of Homer his tutor assigned him to read each day and commented, "He appeared at this stage to value speed more than absolute accuracy. The great gain was that I very soon became able to understand a great deal without (even mentally) translating it; I was beginning to think in Greek."[11]

This rapid reading is one of the key practices for gaining fluency. But as you are learning a language, it is also important to practice reading with

---

5. Learning to read in a second language is a field of study in itself. See, e.g., William Grabe, *Reading in a Second Language: Moving from Theory to Practice*, Cambridge Applied Linguistics Series (Cambridge: Cambridge University Press, 2009).

6. Ibid., 292.

7. Ibid., 290–93.

8. Grabe refers to this ability as "recognition of prosodic phrasing" (ibid., 292).

9. Sally Shaywitz, *Overcoming Dyslexia: A New and Complete Science-Based Program for Reading Problems at Any Level* (New York: Vintage Books, 2003), 105.

10. Grabe, *Reading*, 292 (emphasis original).

11. C. S. Lewis, *Surprised by Joy: The Shape of My Early Life* (New York: Harcourt, Brace and World, 1955), 140–41.

attention to the details.[12] As Grabe notes, "Getting the language right, even if tentatively, should be the precursor of fluency development."[13] Commenting on a child learning their native language, Shaywitz says, "To acquire a new word for his vocabulary, a child must scrutinize the inner details of the word and not gloss over it."[14] So along with rapid reading there is this more careful reading.

The analogy with learning to play a musical instrument is often used. For many instruments, you need to learn some music theory and practice scales and work on various exercises in order to become accomplished and play smoothly and freely, even improvising. Common advice when practicing a scale or a piece is that you begin slowly enough to make few, if any, mistakes. The mantra is "practice does not make perfect; practice makes permanent." So you should begin slowly in order to lay a solid foundation. Then speed and interpretation come with familiarity with the basics. Once some competence is gained, it is good to include times of pushing yourself to play more quickly than is comfortable. Similarly, once the basics of Greek are in place, you should continue to read carefully but also practice reading fast. Such reading will probably include some mistakes and less clarity in understanding the passage, but it helps you learn to process the data more quickly and will highlight areas that need further work.

In chapter 5 I will discuss strategies and resources for practicing both rapid reading and careful reading. The more time you have for reading, the faster you will gain comfort and fluency in the language, of course. *But even if you have limited time you can make progress by focusing on one sentence at a time and one passage at a time.* Approaching Greek in this way means you are able to enjoy and benefit from amazing texts immediately, even as you build your knowledge and skill to become increasingly fluent in the language. *"How to become fluent one passage at a time" is a major focus in this book.*

Unfortunately, most students of Biblical Greek, in my experience, view even this limited sort of fluency as a goal far beyond their reach. Indeed, they often view this goal as not only impossible for them but also unnecessary since their focus will be on the exegesis of short passages. The multitude of excellent resources available for help with exegesis may seem to make the knowledge

12. See the helpful discussion in Constantine R. Campbell, *Keep Your Greek: Strategies for Busy People* (Grand Rapids: Zondervan, 2010), chap. 6. He emphasizes that such rapid reading should be done in conjunction with slow and careful reading, which he then discusses in chap. 7.

13. Grabe, *Reading*, 292. He says, "Guessing words from context represents an important independent word-learning strategy over time" (276), but it is not a good learning exercise, since "the outcomes of guessing to learn new words is far from accurate and consistent, particularly for readers with weak vocabulary knowledge who cannot use the lexical context to make a reasonable guess" (73).

14. Shaywitz, *Overcoming*, 106.

of Greek unnecessary, beyond perhaps knowing the alphabet and a few rudiments of the language needed for following the discussion in these resources.

Such a limited view of Greek's value may be part of the reason many students of Biblical Greek lose much of what they learn in Greek courses. One recent study of the use of Greek among a group of pastors found that the majority of them do not consult the Greek text directly for sermon preparation.[15] Rather, they draw upon their training in Greek to help with word studies and in the use of good reference material. Thus, instead of engaging the text in Greek themselves, they engage the English text and make use of resources to explore particular details in the Greek. Use of Greek on this level is helpful but misses much of what the language has to offer through more in-depth exegesis, as well as through meditation and fluency. Perhaps this group of pastors is unusual, but rumor has it that many people who learn basic Greek let their Greek go.[16]

The good news is that familiarity with particular bodies of literature is not beyond the reach of anyone who is able to learn basic Greek. It does not require an extraordinary investment of time, nor do you have to wait for years before enjoying the benefits of this more limited sort of fluency.

Note that such reading is not the same as translation. Reading is gathering the content of a passage straight from the Greek, without turning it into English. C. S. Lewis has an apt description of the difference:

> Those in whom the Greek word lives only while they are hunting for it in the lexicon, and who then substitute the English word for it, are not reading the Greek at all; they are only solving a puzzle. The very formula, "*Naus* [ναῦς] means a ship," is wrong. *Naus* and *ship* both mean a thing, they do not mean one another. Behind *Naus*, as behind *navis* or *naca*,[17] we want to have a picture of a dark, slender mass with sail or oars, climbing the ridges, with no officious English word intruding.[18]

Learning to read Greek in this way enables you to feel at home in the text and sets you free to explore a wide selection of passages, as well as return to well-known passages repeatedly to discover new insights. A. T. Robertson, in the preface to his 1,500-page Greek grammar, noted, "I have never gone to the Greek New Testament without receiving fresh illumination on some point. . . .

15. Richard G. Herbster, "Integrating Biblical Language Study and Homiletical Preparation" (DMin thesis, Trinity School for Ministry, 2013).

16. In 1930 A. T. Robertson could say, "It is a sad fact that many ministers, laymen, and women, who took courses in Greek at college, university, or seminary, have allowed the cares of the world and the deceitfulness of riches to choke off the Greek that they once knew" (*Word Pictures in the New Testament* [Nashville: Broadman, 1930], 1:viii).

17. Latin terms for a ship and a small boat.

18. Lewis, *Surprised*, 141.

Each student has the joy of discovery as the Greek opens its beauties to his mind and to his soul."[19] Elsewhere he says, "Three of the most gifted ministers of my acquaintance make it a rule to read the Greek Testament through once a year."[20] I remember Ockenga telling us of coming home from preaching one Sunday and relaxing by reading through Paul's Letter to Titus in Greek. I do not know how well Ockenga knew Greek, but there is joy and refreshment that come with familiarity, even if we are fluent in only a few texts.

Meditation

Along with reading portions of text you also can benefit greatly from engaging specific passages in depth through meditation. By meditation I mean repeating a passage over and over, listening to its sounds and reflecting on its details. This "sipping" exercise enables you to become intimately connected to the text so that, in a sense, you come to inhabit it and it becomes a living voice within you. Such reading of sacred texts is part of many religions, and, as we will see, professors of Classics sometimes recommend such an approach to passages from Greek and Latin authors. Meditation on God's word, referred to in the Old Testament (e.g., Deut. 6:4–7; Pss. 1:2; 119) and developed in later Judaism, has played a key role throughout the life of the church.

Within the Christian context, meditation is a prayerful engagement of the biblical text in order to hear the living word of God in the context of Christ.[21] In the Western church it is often referred to as *lectio divina*, and it is part of a larger picture of how the text communicates to us and how we should receive it. The relation of these ancient perspectives and practices to modern grammatical-historical exegesis can be understood in more than one way. In chapter 6 I will offer several approaches to such meditation. Engaging the text in this way enables it to have a transformative influence in our lives.

Four Key Features of Greek

In chapters 5 and 6 we will look at key practices for both fluency and meditation. Obviously both of these exercises require a knowledge of the basic features of the language. So in chapters 2–4 I will offer a discussion of the main elements of Greek. If you are currently studying Greek, some of this

19. A. T. Robertson, *A Grammar of the Greek New Testament in the Light of Historical Research* (Nashville: Broadman, 1934), xx.

20. A. T. Robertson, *The Minister and His Greek New Testament* (repr., Grand Rapids: Baker, 1977), 21.

21. The word *meditation* can refer either to some form of mental engagement or to practices that focus on silence. I will discuss both forms of meditation in chap. 6.

material may be a helpful supplement to what you are learning in your course. If you have been away from Greek for a while and are trying to get back to it, then these chapters will help you do so.

Building vocabulary and learning morphology, that is, knowledge of forms for parsing, are two of the key features of Greek covered by all basic Greek courses. The approaches to this material in chapters 2 and 3 can supplement most Greek courses, and, as just noted, be used for personal work after completing basic Greek.

A third key feature is grammar or syntax, that is, topics such as how the cases function, the use of the definite article, the participle, and the infinitive. Most basic courses and grammars introduce the key features, and there are several intermediate grammars to cover the further details.[22] I will not offer a review of this material, apart from mentioning a few of the most essential basics in chapter 5 and briefly introducing some of the current discussion of Greek verbs in appendix 5.

The fourth feature of Greek is not always taught very thoroughly in basic courses, namely, the ability to receive the message of a passage as it comes in Greek order. Too often Greek is approached more like a puzzle to be solved than a language to be read. If we only learn to approach a sentence by looking first for the verb and then the subject (or vice versa), we are unlikely to become comfortable in the language. Fortunately, basic courses introduce some of the elements of Greek structure necessary for fluency, and I will build on those elements in chapter 4. As you develop fluency, you will have to continue to puzzle for a while, but you can do it in such a way that you increasingly move beyond the need to do so.

Invitation

This book offers resources for you whether you are currently learning basic Greek or already know it—or even if you learned it years ago and would like to revive it. While my focus is primarily on the Greek New Testament, the material presented here applies to all ancient Greek literature. So whatever your interest in Greek and whichever texts in ancient Greek you want to focus on, I invite you to journey down this path to solidifying your knowledge of Greek and discovering its joys and benefits.[23]

22. See, e.g., Funk; Wallace; and Young.

23. I encourage you to share the journey with another person or a small group, since this provides motivation and encouragement as well as help with sorting out difficulties in passages you read together.

2

BUILDING VOCABULARY

Perhaps the biggest challenge to gaining fluency in Greek is learning vocabulary, that is, becoming familiar with the main meanings of words, or more precisely, lexemes.[1] To be sure, at the outset learning to recognize forms is a major hurdle. But the number of patterns to be learned in order to recognize the vast majority of words is very manageable, as we will see in the next chapter. With vocabulary, however, the task is larger and continues, to some degree, throughout your life in Greek. The total number of lexemes in the GNT is 5,393. Basic courses in Biblical Greek generally range between 350 and 600 words for students to learn and sometimes a total of a little more than a thousand over several courses, while one Classical Greek method has students learn approximately 2,250 words over several courses.[2] Learning vocabulary is certainly a challenge but very important.[3]

---

1. *Lexeme* refers to a particular unit of lexical meaning, usually a word, though some use the term to refer also to idioms or expressions. Most words in Greek can take a variety of forms, and *lexeme* refers to the word irrespective of form. By convention, most Greek grammars list nouns and adjectives by the nominative singular and verbs by the present indicative first person singular. This lexical form is called a *lemma*. For a more detailed description of what it means to know a word, see William Grabe, *Reading in a Second Language: Moving from Theory to Practice*, Cambridge Applied Linguistics Series (Cambridge: Cambridge University Press, 2009), 267–68.

2. Joint Association of Classical Teachers' Greek Course, *Greek Vocabulary* (Cambridge: Cambridge University Press, 1980). In comparison, those learning to read English need to aim at 10,000 words, while the average high school graduate has a vocabulary of about 40,000 words. American Heritage put together a list of 43,831 words that would provide 99 percent of the words found in most texts. For these figures, see Grabe, *Reading*, 269, 271.

3. Grabe (*Reading*, 196) notes that "vocabulary knowledge is perhaps the most important component skill and resource for reading. Major research studies in L.1 [first-language, i.e.,

Fortunately, resources now available enable us to read passages rapidly even before we have built up a large vocabulary. Books, software, and online resources provide vocabulary help for almost all of ancient Greek literature.[4] Nevertheless, learning the meanings of words is necessary for gaining fluency and benefitting the most from Greek. In this chapter we will look at resources and strategies for building your knowledge of Greek words. Not everyone finds the same strategy helpful, so I encourage you to try each of these to see what works best for you.

As you know, many words differ in meaning depending on their form or their grammatical or idiomatic construction. Most approaches to building vocabulary have you learn a few basic glosses (translations), and then you develop your familiarity with the nuances of words through reading. Fortunately, lexicons provide help in understanding the meaning of words in particular constructions and idioms. Here we will focus on ways to establish a foundation in the basic meanings of lexemes.

Basic Greek textbooks determine which words students should learn based on the body of literature students are preparing to read, whether Homeric Greek, Classical Attic Greek, or Koine Greek. In *Basics of Biblical Greek*, for example, William Mounce provides running statistics of how many words have been learned in each chapter and what percent of the total number of words in the GNT the student now knows. By the end of his book, the student has learned 320 words, which is 80.25 percent of the words on the pages of the GNT.[5]

This statistic is certainly more encouraging than saying that 320 words represents only 5.9 percent of the 5,423 different Greek lexemes found in the GNT.[6] With 320 words you will be able to recognize some lexemes in every verse (at least the definite article!), assuming you can recognize their inflected forms, but you will also need to look up a number of words in most verses. Indeed, there are 1,932 words used only one time in the GNT—that is over a third—and another 832 that are used only twice. This means that over half the words used in the GNT occur only one or two times.[7] So while it is important

---

one's native language] contexts have shown that vocabulary knowledge strongly predicts later reading abilities."

4. See chap. 5 for discussion of these resources.

5. William D. Mounce, *Basics of Biblical Greek: Grammar*, 3rd ed. (Grand Rapids: Zondervan, 2009), 338. Mounce cites the total number of words in the GNT as 138,162.

6. This is the number given by Mounce. You will find different figures for the number of lexemes used in the GNT, in part because some words may be counted in more than one way. For example, some lists include the aorist form εἶδον as a separate word, as it is listed in BDAG and *CGEL*. Other lists include it under ὁράω, since it serves as the aorist for that verb.

7. The different ways of counting words mentioned in the previous note and the particular edition used will produce slightly different totals, but the percentage of words used only once or

to begin by learning the most frequently occurring words, this approach must be supplemented by other ways of recognizing and learning words.

The good news is that many of the words used rarely in the GNT are related to words that are used more frequently. So you do not need to memorize a list with over five thousand words on it to read the GNT fluently. Instead, you can recognize many words if you are familiar with root words and have a little basic knowledge of how words are formed. So we will look first at root words and word formation and then consider several strategies for increasing vocabulary.

Root Words and Word Formation

Many Greek words are cognate to one another, meaning they are related by derivation from a common root word. New words can be formed by such methods as adding a preposition on the beginning of a word or adding a suffix on the end. You have probably already noticed this feature while learning basic vocabulary. Once you have learned that ἔρχομαι means "I come/go" and εἰς means "into," then the fact that εἰσέρχομαι means "I come/go into, I enter" is easy to remember. Similarly, if you know that the noun ending -της often is used for one doing an action (like "-er" in English), and if you already know βαπτίζω means "I baptize," you know that βαπτιστής may mean "baptizer." Thus, learning some of the suffixes and the meanings of prepositions when used in compound enables you to get some free vocabulary, or at least it helps you understand words and better remember what they mean.

Suffixes

Learning even a few suffixes can be a great help; the following are good ones to get you started.[8] Some of these suffixes can mean more than one

twice will be roughly the same. These word counts are from the vocabulary tool in BibleWorks 10, which lists the total vocabulary of the GNT at 5,393.

8. Similar lists are available in Bruce M. Metzger, *Lexical Aids for Students of New Testament Greek*, 3rd ed. (1969; repr., Grand Rapids: Baker 1998), 41–45; and Robert E. Van Voorst, *Building Your New Testament Greek Vocabulary*, 3rd ed. (Atlanta: Society of Biblical Literature, 2001), 4–7. More extensive lists are available in Mark Wilson with Jason Oden, *Mastering New Testament Greek Vocabulary through Semantic Domains* (Grand Rapids: Kregel, 2003), 14–16; Thomas A. Robinson, *Mastering New Testament Greek: Essential Tools for Students*, 3rd ed. (Peabody, MA: Hendrickson, 2007), 114–18; Warren C. Trenchard, *The Student's Complete Vocabulary Guide to the Greek New Testament: Complete Frequency Lists, Cognate Groupings & Principal Parts*, rev. ed. (Grand Rapids: Zondervan, 1998), 1–4; and Matthias Stehle, *Greek Word Building*, trans. F. Forrester Church and John S. Hanson (Missoula, MT: Scholars Press, 1976), 1–8. For Classical Greek, see the discussion in Herbert Weir Smyth, *Greek Grammar*, rev. Gordon M. Messing (Cambridge, MA: Harvard University Press, 1956), 225–54, available online (see bibliography). For an extensive discussion of word formation for the vocabulary of the New Testament, see Wilbert Francis Howard, *Accidence and Word-Formation with an*

thing, and sometimes these endings do not carry these nuances.[9] So learning suffixes is very helpful, but they are not always clear, and you will need to keep your lexicon near.

Noun Suffixes

-σις	an activity	κρίσις, judging, judgment[a]
-ια	an activity	ἀδικία, wrongdoing
-μος	an activity	βαπτισμός, washing, act of baptism (the action of which βάπτισμα is the result)
-της	agent of an action	βαπτιστής, baptizer
-τηρ	agent of an action	σωτήρ, savior
-μα	result of an action	βάπτισμα, baptism
-ια	quality/condition	ἀγνωσία, ignorance
-οτης	quality/condition	ἀγαθότης, goodness
-συνη	quality/condition	ἀγαθωσύνη, goodness
-τηριον	place	θυσιαστήριον, altar (place where sacrifice, θυσία, occurs)

a. The suffix -σις "often produces the abstract name of an action" (Metzger, *Lexical*, 42).

Adjective Suffixes

-ιος	related to, characteristic of	οὐράνιος, heavenly
-ικος	related to, characteristic of	πνευματικός, spiritual
-ης	quality or characteristic	ἀληθής, truthful
-ινος	material	λίθινος, (made of) stone

Verb Suffixes

-αω	action or state	ἀγαπάω, I love
-εω	action or state	τελέω, I bring to an end
-ευω	action or state	δουλεύω, I serve (as a slave)
-οω	causation	τελειόω, I complete, make perfect (τέλειος)
-αινω	causation	εὐφραίνω, I make glad/cheerful (εὔφρων)
-υνω	causation	μολύνω, I stain

Appendix on Semitisms in the New Testament, vol. 2 of *A Grammar of New Testament Greek*, by James Hope Moulton, Wilbert Francis Howard, and Nigel Turner (Edinburgh: T&T Clark, 1919, 1920, 1929), 268–410.

9. For example, I have included the example of the noun ending -ια, which can be used both of an activity and of a quality/condition. Sometimes, however, the ending seems to have little if any particular nuance, as in καρδία, heart.

Prepositional Compounds

When prepositions are added to the beginning of words, they can often have one of several nuances. Metzger,[10] Abbott-Smith,[11] and Harris[12] provide information about prepositions in composition. As a sample, here is what each says about ἐκ (formatted as in the original).

Metzger

ἐκ   (1) Root meaning *from out of*
             ἐκβάλλω, *I cast out*
             ἐξέρχομαι, *I go out*
    (2) *Perfective*
             ἐκπληρόω, *I fill completely*
             ἐξαπορέομαι, *I am utterly at a loss*[13]

Abbott-Smith

VI. In composition, ἐκ signifies, 1. procession, removal: ἐκβαίνω, ἐκβάλλω. 2. Opening out, unfolding: ἐκτείνω; metaph., ἐξαγγέλλω. 3. Origin: ἔκγονος. 4. Completeness: ἐξαπορέω . . . ἐκπληρόω, ἐκτελέω.[14]

Harris

F. Ἐκ in Compounds

There are 94 verbal compounds with ἐκ in the NT, and in more than half of them there is evidence of the sense "out" (for example, ἐκτείνω, stretch out) (MH 308–9).

1. Separation/emission: ἐκβάλλω, drive out, release; ἐκχέω, pour out
2. Thoroughness/completeness: ἐξαπατάω, utterly deceive; ἀπεκδύομαι, strip completely; ἐκζητέω, search diligently
3. Fulfillment (cf. BDF §318 [5]): ἐκκαθαίρω, clean out, make clean; ἐκνήφω, sober up, "of sobriety attained *out of* drunkenness" (MH 309); come to one's senses.[15]

Becoming familiar with the way prefixed prepositions affect the meaning of a word is an important part of understanding word formation and getting a good tailwind for increasing your stock of vocabulary.

---

10. Metzger, *Lexical*, 79–85.
11. Abbott-Smith is available in print but also free online (see bibliography).
12. Murray J. Harris, *Prepositions and Theology in the Greek New Testament* (Grand Rapids: Zondervan, 2012).
13. Metzger, *Lexical*, 82.
14. Abbott-Smith, 492.
15. Harris, *Prepositions*, 113. MH refers here to Howard's *Accidence*.

Cognates

There are several resources that can help you see cognate groups, that is, word families that share a common root.[16] Metzger, Van Voorst, and Robinson offer lists of the most frequent cognate groups for memorization, while Trenchard provides a complete list of cognates as well as a separate frequency list for all the words used in the New Testament, including those that have no cognates.[17] Each of these books has a variety of other helps as well, so you would need to compare them to see which offers the form of material that is most useful to you. Robinson contains the most help for memorizing lists of cognates, while Trenchard is the most helpful for looking up cognates of words you meet while reading.

Help with roots and cognate groups is also available in the revised version of Barclay Newman's *Concise Greek-English Dictionary of the New Testament*.[18] At the beginning of the article on ἀγγέλλω, for example, he provides a list of twenty cognates, and then at each cognate he refers back to ἀγγέλλω for the complete list. So, for example, ἐπαγγελία begins, "**ἐπ|αγγελία, ας**, f. (ἀγγέλλω) . . ."[19]

Semantic Domains

At the end of his dictionary Newman adds yet another way to build vocabulary, through semantic domains. He lists sixty-seven semantic domains and the main word groups within each. For example, his first semantic domain is "Accomplish, Finish, Complete." He gives the members of two word families associated with this concept.

> τέλος = *end, termination*; τελέω = *finish, complete*; τέλειος = *complete, perfect*; τελειόω = *make perfect/complete*
>
> πλήρης = *full, complete*; πληρόω = *complete, accomplish*; πλήρωμα = *fullness, completeness*; πληροφορέω = *accomplish*[20]

Note how these words provide further examples of the value of learning some of the suffixes. Here we see εω on a verb referring to an action or state,

---

16. The word "cognate" is used in many ways. I am following the usage found, e.g., in Robinson, *Mastering*, 1, 4–5; and Trenchard, *Complete*, 1.

17. Metzger, *Lexical*, 49–72; Van Voorst, *Building*, 12–67; Robinson, *Mastering*, 11–113. Trenchard, *Complete*, 5–126, 127–236. Each has a different way of choosing which groups and words to include, so the lists are not identical.

18. Barclay M. Newman, *A Concise Greek-English Dictionary of the New Testament*, rev. ed. (Stuttgart: Deutsche Bibelgesellschaft, 2010).

19. Bold original. Note Newman's use of a dividing line to show word formation.

20. Ibid., 207, bold and italics original.

οω on a verb for causation, and a noun with the μα ending referring to the result of an activity.

Rodney Decker provides definitions for vocabulary in his basic textbook.[21] You could build your vocabulary by working through his lists of vocabulary or by working through various semantic domains with the help of the list at the end of Newman's dictionary. For more thorough help see Mark Wilson, *Mastering New Testament Greek Vocabulary through Semantic Domains*, mentioned above. Wilson covers most of the vocabulary of the New Testament using, for the most part, the semantic domains in Louw and Nida's *Lexicon*.[22] For each Greek word he gives a meaning, its reference in Louw and Nida, and its frequency in the New Testament.

Just spending a few minutes now and then simply reading through a bit of this material could increase your vocabulary base significantly, assuming this is a strategy that works for you. In particular, the lists in either Newman or Wilson would familiarize you with vocabulary in the context of the domains, which would give you a sticking point for the word in your memory.

As you are reading through a passage, it can be helpful to see the semantic domains for a word in the passage. The lists in Newman and Wilson will not be of help since neither is comprehensive nor has an index. Louw and Nida's *Lexicon* or either of Danker's lexicons can provide the information you need.

Etymology

Etymology is the study of word derivations and thus includes attention to the role of roots, cognates, and the principles of word formation we have been discussing. It also includes study of words derived from other languages. Most manuals on exegesis warn strongly against etymology.[23] Etymology has certainly been overdone in the past, and it is very important to understand how to interpret the meanings of words in their context. But while etymology does not determine a word's meaning, in Greek it is often related to the meaning of the word in ways that can help you make connections between words and thereby help you retain vocabulary, which is our focus in this

---

21. Rodney J. Decker, *Reading Koine Greek: An Introduction and Integrated Workbook* (Grand Rapids: Baker Academic, 2014).

22. Johannes P. Louw and Eugene A. Nida, *Greek-English Lexicon of the New Testament Based on Semantic Domains*, rev. ed. (New York: United Bible Societies, 1988).

23. See, e.g., Gordon D. Fee, *New Testament Exegesis: A Handbook for Students and Pastors*, 3rd ed. (Louisville: Westminster/John Knox, 2002), 79–80; Moisés Silva, *Biblical Words and Their Meaning: An Introduction to Lexical Semantics*, rev. and exp. (Grand Rapids: Zondervan, 1995), 35–51; and D. A. Carson, *Exegetical Fallacies*, 2nd ed. (Grand Rapids: Baker, 1996), 28–33. Carson notes that at times a word's etymology does reflect its meaning and that etymology can be useful sometimes (32–33), as does Silva (41–44). Etymology can obviously be very valuable in the case of words for which we have only a single text.

chapter.[24] It is heartening to see inclusion of etymological data in *CGEL* and the revision of Newman's *Dictionary*. There are large etymological dictionaries for Greek,[25] but Abbott-Smith and *CGEL* offer plenty of help, supplemented at times by LS or LSJ. Unfortunately, Newman, *CGEL*, LS, and LSJ are in need of correction and updating, as John Lee has pointed out.[26] So their data at times can be conflicting, but nevertheless they can be very helpful for building vocabulary through associations if not always actual etymologies.[27]

For an example, consider the last word in the list of semantic domains just cited from Newman's *Dictionary*: πληροφορέω comes from two words, though the lexicons differ on the exact words. Newman gives "(πληρόω + φέρω),"[28] BDAG gives "(*πληροφόρος [πλήρης, φέρω via φορέω]),"[29] and *CGEL* gives "[πλήρης, φορέω 'bear constantly, wear,' cp. φορός 'bringing on one's way']."[30] So either the verb "I fill" or the adjective "full" combines with φέρω, which means "I bear, carry," and φορέω, which means "I bear constantly, wear." The idea of bearing something to the point of fullness, that is, "to reach a point at which nothing is lacking,"[31] might help you remember the meaning "I accomplish."

Etymology and other associations can sometimes help where cognates do not, either because there is no cognate or because the cognates are not very helpful by themselves. For example, ἐξουθενέω, "I despise," is listed by Trenchard in two of his cognate groups, εἰς and οὐ.[32] Newman also gives

24. We will consider other uses of etymology in chap. 6.
25. Pierre Chantraine, *Dictionnaire Étymologique de la Langue Grecque: Histoire des Mots*, new ed. (Paris: Klincksieck, 1999). BDAG (unlike *CGEL*) does not usually include information on etymology but does cite Chantraine (as DELG) at the end of articles for which DELG provides information. Robert Beekes with Lucien van Beek, *Etymological Dictionary of Greek*, 2 vols. (Leiden: Brill, 2010), is the most accurate and authoritative resource, but it is large, expensive, difficult to use, and beyond the needs of most of us, given the information in Abbott-Smith and *CGEL*.
26. John Lee, "Etymological Follies: Three Recent Lexicons of the New Testament," *Novum Testamentum* 55 (2013): 383–403. Available online (see bibliography). Of the resources I have mentioned, Lee considers Abbott-Smith the most reliable: "The information is sound, clearly presented, and carefully limited: questionable or obscure relationships are not entered into" (385). Lee's article will give you a good idea of the issues to watch for in these resources.
27. Indeed, *CGEL* seems to offer a mixture of etymologies, cognates, and associations. It suggests a direct connection when words are simply listed ("κατοικίζω [κατοικία]," 197) and provides a meaning for the word cited if it does not occur in *CGEL* otherwise ("κατοπτρίζω [κάτοπτρον "mirror"]," 197). But at times other connections are suggested. For example, for ὄξος *CGEL* says "[akin to ὀξύς]" (253); for γλῶσσα, "[cf. γλωχίς 'projecting point']" (80); for εἰλικρίνεια, "[association with εἴλη sun's heat is uncertain]" (110).
28. Newman, *Dictionary*, 147.
29. BDAG 827.
30. *CGEL* 287. Abbott-Smith does not provide such information for this word, perhaps because the etymology is unclear.
31. *CGEL* 287.
32. Trenchard, *Complete*, 36, 83.

these two words: "ἐξ|ου|θενέω (οὐ + εἷς)."[33] Reference to these two words is not as helpful for remembering this word as is Danker's note regarding its etymology/associations. Danker says that it is related to the word ἐξουδενέω,[34] which is from ἐξ and οὐδέν, "nothing" (neuter of οὐδείς).[35] So the word has the sense, "treat as of no account/as a nonentity."[36] In BDAG Danker adds, "Lit. 'to make an οὐδείς/οὐδέν of someone/someth.'"[37] This description certainly paints a picture that fits with the meaning "I despise." Seeing that the word is a compound of ἐκ/ἐξ and οὐδέν helps you understand the word and remember what it means. You can think of it as a verb ending added to οὐδέν and then compounded with ἐκ/ἐξ. If you look back over the possible nuances of ἐκ/ἐξ used in a compound cited above, it seems clear that in the case of ἐξουθενέω this preposition has a perfective force, that is, it adds a note of thoroughness/completeness.[38]

As you are reading you will often be able to work out the meaning of a word from its root and formation in combination with the way the word is used in its context. However, as already noted, the clues are not always entirely clear, so your lexicon remains vital.

Word Usage

Another way you can retain the meaning of a word is through a study of its breadth of meaning. If you familiarize yourself with the usage of a word throughout the GNT, and even in Classical and Jewish literature, you gain an understanding of the word and have a good chance of remembering at least some of its meanings through seeing them in a variety of contexts.[39] Even without doing a major word study, simple attention to the breadth of meanings given in lexicons can be useful in this way. One of the helpful features in Abbott-Smith and *CGEL* is their occasional inclusion of meanings and applications from the Classical period.[40] You need to be careful not to assume

---

33. Newman, *Dictionary*, 66.

34. Note the shift between the two dentals θ and δ. For details, see Howard, *Accidence*, 111. Such shifts between letters are common as a language develops.

35. BDAG 352.

36. *CGEL* 135.

37. BDAG 352.

38. Howard notes this function of ἐξ for ἐξουθενέω and adds that another reason ἐξ was probably appropriate was "to make the transitive clear—a function these prefixes often tend to achieve" (*Accidence*, 310).

39. For such study, a particularly accessible and valuable resource is *New International Dictionary of New Testament Theology and Exegesis*, ed. Moisés Silva, 2nd ed., 5 vols. (Grand Rapids: Zondervan, 2014).

40. Abbott-Smith also employs symbols to indicate when a word does not occur in (1) Classical Greek authors or (2) the Greek OT. He provides the Hebrew words translated by the Greek word in the LXX, and indicates by a symbol when a word occurs in a section of the Greek OT

that earlier meanings are still in use in the later period,[41] but sometimes seeing a basic meaning or use in *CGEL*, Abbott-Smith, or more extensively, in LS and LSJ can help you understand its meanings better.[42] For example, both Abbott-Smith and *CGEL* note "opinion" as the common meaning of δόξα in Classical Greek and suggest connections between this meaning and the senses found in Scripture.[43] Similarly, both of these resources give "custom" as the first meaning of δίκη, even though that meaning does not occur in the GNT. Danker goes on to explain: "[cp. δείκνυμι; 'custom, right,' then punishment for violation of custom]," which helps us see connections with the meanings "punishment" and "justice" found in the GNT.[44]

At times, Abbott-Smith and *CGEL* provide examples of particular contextual applications from outside the GNT. For example, *CGEL* gives very clear and helpful information for στοιχέω: "[στοῖχος 'series, row'] 'be in agreement,' in imagery of standing in a row with others, *be in line (with), hold to*."[45] Abbott-Smith adds some of the specific uses outside the GNT that help us picture the word: "*to be in rows* (of waves, plants, etc., as well as of men), *to walk in line* (esp. of marching in file to battle; Xen., *Cyr.*, vi, 3, 34, al.). Metaph., in late writers, *to walk by rule . . . to walk by* or *in* (as a rule of life)."[46] Abbott-Smith's additional details do not add to the basic meaning

---

that does not have a Hebrew original. A dagger (†) at the end of an article "signifies that all the instances of the word's occurrence in the NT have been cited" (xv). This means Abbott-Smith provides a comprehensive NT concordance for many words. Abbott-Smith's data must be updated with material in BDAG and *CGEL*, but it offers a number of features not found in other lexicons and presents the data in a very concise and clear fashion. *CGEL* and Abbott-Smith together are my favorite lexicons to consult regularly.

41. See Carson, *Fallacies*, 35–37.

42. Indeed, some linguists argue for "monosemy," the view that many words have one general meaning. They assert that the multiple meanings listed in dictionaries are often due in part to "a habit of overspecifying, of attributing to words meaning that in part is supplied by the context" (Charles Ruhl, *On Monosemy: A Study in Linguistic Semantics* [New York: SUNY Press, 1989], 1). Ruhl proposes that "a researcher's initial efforts are directed toward determining a unitary meaning for a lexical item, trying to attribute apparent variations in meaning to other factors. If such efforts fail, then the researcher tries to discover a means of relating the distinct meanings. If these efforts fail, then there are several words" (ibid., 4). Stanley Porter has drawn on research regarding monosemy as part of an assessment of strengths and shortcomings in Louw and Nida's *Lexicon*. Porter suggests monosemy as an important way forward, "if this type of lexicon is to be developed and expanded upon" (*Linguistic Analysis of the Greek New Testament: Studies in Tools, Methods, and Practice* [Grand Rapids: Baker Academic, 2015], 59).

43. Porter (*Linguistic Analysis*, 56–57) uses δόξα as one of his illustrations of shortcomings in the analysis in Louw and Nida and the contribution of monosemy.

44. *CGEL* 98.

45. *CGEL* 329.

46. Abbott-Smith, 418. The reference is to Xenophon, *Cyropaedia*, a text also cited in LSJ. Here is the first part of the entry in LSJ 1647: "A. *to be drawn up in a line* or *row*, οὐδ' ἐγκαταλείψω τὸν παραστάτην, ὅτῳ ἂν στοιχήσω *beside* whom *I stand* in battle,—from the oath of Athenian

of the word but may help you understand it and retain it. When Paul says πνεύματι καὶ στοιχῶμεν (Gal. 5:25), we could understand this as "Let us also live in alignment with the Spirit."

Strategies for Learning Vocabulary

Having seen the value of attention to word roots, formation, and usage, we can now consider ways you can work on increasing your knowledge of vocabulary. Basic to memorizing is repetition. Sometimes a word sticks after only five repetitions, and sometimes it takes fifty. If you see connections between a new word and words you already know, or through roots and formation, then usually you need fewer repetitions. The main way your knowledge of lexemes will develop is through reading, both rapid reading and careful reading.

> Fluency—reading a word accurately, quickly, smoothly, and with good expression—is acquired by practice, by reading a word over and over again. This is consistent with what we know about neural circuits that are reinforced and strengthened by repetition. A reader must have four or more successful encounters with a new word to be able to read it fluently.[47]

But along with reading, which we will discuss in chapter 5, there are also strategies specifically for working on vocabulary, somewhat like working on scales in music.[48]

Increasing Vocabulary as You Read

As you work through a passage, your main focus should be on learning what the words mean in the passage. But occasionally you might look over the range of meanings listed in a lexicon to see the semantic domains and various uses, note the suffixes that are used, and see whether the word is part of a family related to a root word. Such attention works well when you are studying a passage, but you might also pause at times while simply reading.

Trenchard and Newman are particularly valuable for building vocabulary in this way as you read. For example, if you are reading a text with the word ῥήγνυμι ("I break, burst") and wish to take a minute to see its word family, Newman gives "**ῥήγνυμι** and **ῥήσσω** (δια|ρρήγνυμι, περι|ρήγνυμι, προσ|ρήγνυμι,

---

citizens, ap. Stob. 4.1.48, cf. Poll. 8.105; *move in line*, X.Cyr. 6.3.34, *Eq.Mag.* 5.7; *to be in rows*, of leaves or joints, Thphr.*HP* 3.18.5, 3.5.3; κατὰ τὸ στοιχοῦν *in sequence*, Arist.*Int.* 19ᵇ24."

47. Sally Shaywitz, *Overcoming Dyslexia: A New and Complete Science-Based Program for Reading Problems at Any Level* (New York: Vintage Books, 2003), 105.

48. For further suggestions on learning vocabulary, see Constantine R. Campbell, *Keep Your Greek: Strategies for Busy People* (Grand Rapids: Zondervan, 2010), chap. 4.

ῥῆγμα),"[49] and Trenchard lets you see the meanings and frequency of each word in the family.

ῥήγνυμι

ῥήγνυμι	(7)	I tear, burst, tear loose, break out, throw out
διαρήγνυμι	(5)	I tear, break
περιρήγνυμι	(1)	I tear off
προσρήγνυμι	(2)	I burst upon
ῥῆγμα, ατος, τό	(1)	wreck, ruin, collapse[a]

a. Trenchard, *Complete*, 97.

You do not need to try to memorize this list. Simply reading over such a list and noticing the meanings in connection with the root and formation can be of benefit. A survey of the words in the family increases your familiarity with a larger collection of words and with how words are formed. Attending to words in the context both of the passage you are reading and of their cognate groups adds more sticking points for your memory.

Word Frequency Lists

While it seems best to work on vocabulary as you are reading texts, you may also want to do concentrated work on just vocabulary. I have already mentioned the options of memorizing vocabulary according to cognate groups or semantic domains. The more common approach, as you know, is to memorize vocabulary by frequency. I will focus on resources for the GNT, but there are frequency lists available for other bodies of literature as well, such as the LXX and Plato.[50]

In chapter 5 we will look at two reader's editions of the GNT that each assume you know the words used 30 times or more in the GNT, so this is a good first goal. You will find a list of these 470 words on the website for this book. Your next goal might be the words occurring ten times or more in the GNT. For decades the main help in learning New Testament vocabulary was Bruce Metzger's *Lexical Aids* with its list of 1,066 words arranged by frequency down to those used ten times. There is nothing magical about this

49. Newman, *Dictionary*, 161, bold original. For the switch between single and double rho (ρ), see Howard, *Accidence*, 101–2.

50. E.g., Rodney J. Decker has produced a list of words occurring 100 times or more in the LXX: "LXX Vocabulary," available online (see bibliography). Some texts provide frequency lists, e.g., Geoffrey Steadman's *Plato's Symposium: Greek Text with Facing Vocabulary and Commentary* (self-published, 2011) includes a list of words occurring seven times or more in Plato's *Symposium*.

number, but it is a very manageable goal. The majority of the words used fewer than ten times are related to words in this list, so you have a chance of recognizing them if you pay attention to roots and formation.

There are websites that generate vocabulary flash cards for the GNT, and the major Bible software packages (BibleWorks, Accordance, and Logos) have powerful tools that enable you to generate a vocabulary list for specific books or passages, arranged by frequency. So, for example, if you have decided to become familiar with the Sermon on the Mount or Paul's Letter to the Galatians, you can have a list of the most frequent words to focus on memorizing while reading.

When working with word lists, you can create links through the sound of a particular word you are memorizing.[51] In this approach you link the sound of the Greek word to a picture, link the meaning of the word to another picture, and then link the two in a way that is memorable, usually by being ridiculous. For example, if you are learning that ἐγείρω means, "I raise," you might think ἐγείρω sounds like "egg arrow." So you could picture a guy in a Robin Hood outfit raising up an arrow that has an egg for its tip. As you picture this scene in action, say "I raise up an egg arrow." The sound of the word triggers this picture and these associations, which bring the meaning to mind.

I have taken this example from *Greek to Me*, a basic Greek method by Lyle and Cullen Story that uses such pictures to help students learn not only vocabulary but also the basic Greek paradigms.[52] Over 600 vocabulary words are assigned, and there is a set of vocabulary cards with a picture for each one.[53] So you could use their cards, or simply make up your own pictures for the words you wish to learn.

It is important to pronounce the words as you are memorizing them. If you use flash cards, I suggest working with seven new words at a time, going forward and backward through the deck, pronouncing the Greek word and then giving yourself only a second or two to come up with the meaning(s). This repetition with pronunciation and attention is key. Once you have learned a word, put it in another pile for review. A third pile can be used for words you are very confident you know. Along with such work with vocabulary cards, you might also record your words and their meanings to listen to while driving or at other times. Jonathan Pennington has published an audio CD you

51. See Harry Lorayne and Jerry Lucas, *The Memory Book: The Classic Guide to Improving Your Memory at Work, at School, and at Play* (New York: Ballantine, 1974).

52. J. Lyle Story and Cullen I. K. Story, illus. Peter Allen Miller, *Greek to Me: Learning New Testament Greek through Memory Visualization* (Fairfax, VA: Xulon, 2002). This is a more comprehensive textbook than many first-year books, despite one's initial impression from the pictures.

53. For the flash cards, see J. Lyle Story, "Curriculum Resources." Available online (see bibliography).

could use in this way.[54] The flashcard programs on BibleWorks, Accordance, and Logos also provide audio files.

For a word that you find especially difficult to remember, you can try learning it in connection with a verse of the GNT in which it occurs. If the verse is already familiar to you in your native language, then this provides a sticking point for the Greek word. In effect, this is how you build your vocabulary—by becoming fluent passage by passage, so you can apply the approach to particular words when working on vocabulary in general.

Concluding Encouragement

The number of resources available and the variety of useful ways to study this material could be overwhelming. Don't panic. Make it a priority to read in the Greek. As you use lexicons, it is not difficult to pay attention to roots and formation. Beyond that, as you have time, you can work on building your vocabulary through one or more of the approaches in this chapter. The main thing is to keep reading and become fluent sentence by sentence, passage by passage. Indeed, "we become fluent word by word."[55]

54. Jonathan T. Pennington, *New Testament Greek Vocabulary* (Grand Rapids: Zondervan, 2001).

55. Shaywitz, *Overcoming*, 105.

3

ESSENTIAL PARSING

W hile you are learning basic Greek, it seems there is no end to the end-ings and the other morphological changes you need to learn. But, in fact, the basic patterns are finite. Indeed, the amount of material you need to learn, through rote memory or otherwise, can fit on one sheet of paper (8.5 x 11 in.)—without microscopic print. This is encouraging![1]

Computer software, such as BibleWorks, Accordance, and Logos, and websites like *Perseus*[2] enable you to get parsings very quickly and easily.[3] But if you need to look up most of the words you encounter in a text, you will be very limited in your use and enjoyment of Greek. It is worth the effort to get the basics down thoroughly and then use these wonderful resources for the bits you still do not know and things that are simply irregular. Once you are able to read with a little fluency, your ability to do so will increase through the reading itself, filling in your knowledge of forms through encountering new items in your reading and reviewing the old ones as you use them.

In this chapter I want to help you answer two questions for words you come across in a text: "What is the parsing of this form?" and "What is its

1. The core patterns are gathered together in app. 4. A one-page summary is available on the website for this book.
2. See bibliography for the URL.
3. These resources are discussed in chap. 5.

lemma, that is, its lexical form?" The parsing gives you the information you need for understanding how the word is functioning in the sentence, and the lemma helps you find it in a lexicon. When you are using software, you are given the lemma, but knowing how to find it yourself enables you to look up words when not working on an electronic device and generally deepens your familiarity with the language.

This chapter is a review of the most important data covered in basic textbooks, arranged around the least amount of rote memorizing possible and with a number of shortcuts. For example, the approach to nominal endings will enable you to identify the case and number but not the gender of some nouns. A nominal's gender is usually not necessary for accurate reading, and, in any case, it can often be determined by the presence of an article. So this approach cuts some corners on details that are not usually necessary for reading.

If you have been away from Greek for a while, you may find you need to review most or all of the material in this chapter. If you have learned Greek recently or have maintained your knowledge, then you can skim the chapter to see which parts you already know well and which, if any, you should work on further.

While the core patterns provide the key data you should be familiar with, just memorizing this material is not enough. Careful study of the actual paradigms is essential, as well as learning some further details to see how this core material is applied. In this chapter I will walk through the core patterns and the major paradigms, indicating how the data to be learned relates to the key ingredients needed to master this material for the purposes of reading.[4]

The point is to become familiar with the data and its significance, not simply to memorize paradigms. Robert Funk comments,

> Although in almost daily touch with some Greek text for twenty-five years, I find that each time I teach beginning Greek from a traditional grammar, it is necessary for me to recommit portions of that grammar to memory. There seems to be little correlation between my ability to read and understand a Greek text and the ability, say, to reproduce nominal and verbal paradigms by heart.[5]

---

4. The paradigms provided in this chapter are similar to those found in most basic Greek textbooks. For more extensive sets of paradigms, see Dale Russell Bowne, *Paradigms and Principal Parts for the Greek New Testament* (Lanham, MD: University Press of America, 1987); Erikk Geannikis, Andrew Romiti, and P. T. Wilford, *Greek Paradigm Handbook* (Newburyport, MA: Focus/Pullins, 2008); and Herbert Weir Smyth, *Greek Grammar*, rev. Gordon M. Messing (Cambridge, MA: Harvard University Press, 1920, 1956), §§189–821. Smyth is in print but also available online (see bibliography).

5. Funk, xv.

So familiarity is the goal, not rote memorization. Many, however, find rote memorization to be the most efficient means to begin learning the morphological signals. Then, through actual usage as you read and study texts, you eventually no longer need the patterns. This chapter presents the basic data needed for parsing most forms you will encounter in Greek texts, in whatever way you may find it helpful to learn it.

If you want to practice applying the approach I describe in this chapter, the website for this book has parsing exercises with answers. Doing these exercises can help you find which topics you need further work on.

Once you have worked through this chapter, there are two excellent resources for filling in the gaps and explaining why certain morphological changes take place. Robert W. Funk's *Beginning-Intermediate Grammar of Hellenistic Greek* is both a reference grammar and a textbook.[6] This means it is written so you can work your way through it, building a very solid foundation that goes beyond what is covered in basic textbooks, as the title indicates.[7] The other resource I recommend when you want to sort out morphological details is William D. Mounce, *The Morphology of Biblical Greek*.[8] This reference book is valuable for looking up particular words, patterns, and morphological concepts. What I offer here is along the lines of the material in Funk and Mounce but with a focus on the most essential parts of morphology and a somewhat different approach to some of the material meant to aid in memorization and recognition.

Memorizing Paradigms

When memorizing, you should use as many of your five senses as you can—make use of all the pathways into your brain to help it notice the material

---

6. Funk, 64–266. Funk's method has been formative in my approach to Greek. I taught basic Greek using his first edition in the 1970s and had the privilege of contributing feedback for the second edition (see Funk, xxi), which I also used. It is not an easy method to teach with, and I have used several other methods over the years, each with its own strengths. But Funk's description of the language, especially the morphology and sentence structures, remains the best overall analysis I have found for laying an excellent foundation.

7. The textbook by Rodney J. Decker also includes material often left for intermediate books. See *Reading Koine Greek: An Introduction and Integrated Workbook* (Grand Rapids: Baker Academic, 2014).

8. William D. Mounce, *The Morphology of Biblical Greek* (Grand Rapids: Zondervan, 1994). Wilbert Francis Howard, *Accidence and Word-Formation with an Appendix on Semitisms in the New Testament* (vol. 2 of *A Grammar of New Testament Greek*, by James Hope Moulton, Wilbert Francis Howard, and Nigel Turner [Edinburgh: T&T Clark, 1919, 1920, 1929]) provides very detailed discussion. Smyth's *Grammar* is another very helpful resource for morphology and covers more than the Greek of the New Testament.

and retain it. When memorizing patterns, many people find it is best to write out the pattern repeatedly, saying the sounds out loud as they do so. For some of the patterns you could develop linking devices as described in chapter 2. You might also find it helpful to sing the patterns.[9] Once you establish a beachhead in your brain, the material will be reinforced as you read Greek texts, so that eventually you will just recognize the forms as they come.

Video Resources for this Chapter

I have tried to present the material in this chapter clearly, but nevertheless it is dense. You must go through it slowly. In class students find an oral presentation easier to follow, so I have prepared a series of videos to introduce the main points in this chapter. See the website for this book.

The Nominal System

The definite article provides the core pattern for the first and second declension nouns and adjectives. You could learn this core pattern in the following form, which includes several items added in brackets, or just focus on the endings.

	Definite Article			Endings		
Sg.	Masc.	Fem.	Neut.	Masc.	Fem.	Neut.
Nom.	ὁ [ος]	ἡ [α]	τό [ον]	ος	η/α	ον
Gen.	τοῦ	τῆς	τοῦ	ου	ης/ας	ου
Dat.	τῷ	τῇ	τῷ	ῳ	η/ᾳ	ῳ
Acc.	τόν	τήν	τό [ον]	ον	ην/αν	ον
Voc.	[ε]			ε		
Pl.						
Nom.	οἱ	αἱ	τά	οι	αι	α
Gen.	τῶν	τῶν	τῶν	ων	ων	ων
Dat.	τοῖς	ταῖς	τοῖς	οις	αις	οις
Acc.	τούς	τάς	τά	ους	ας	α

9. See Kenneth Berding, *Sing and Learn New Testament Greek: The Easiest Way to Learn Greek Grammar* (Grand Rapids: Zondervan, 2008).

First Declension Nouns

The definite article provides the basic endings for the first declension. The main variations in this paradigm occur in the singular forms:

	Fem.			Masc.	
Nom.	η	α	α	ας	ης
Gen.	ης	ας	ης	ου	ου
Dat.	ῃ	ᾳ	ῃ	ᾳ	ῃ
Acc.	ην	αν	αν	αν	ην

- The first three columns are feminines and the last two columns are masculines.
- The first pattern is closest to the feminine definite article since it has η throughout.
- The α in brackets in the pattern for the definite article signals the α/η options in different patterns of the first declension.
- The use of α in the gen. sg. and dat. sg. (second column above) normally occurs only when the stem ends in ε, ι, or ρ. So if you see ας on a first declension feminine noun, it should be the acc. pl. form, unless the stem ends in ε, ι, or ρ, in which case the ας could be either acc. pl. or gen. sg. In the GNT there are very few places where ας lacks an article or other clarifying signal when this ending is gen. sg.
- The middle pattern above does not add any new signals for parsing, but it can cause problems for recognizing the lexical form. For example, if a noun ends in η, then it will be a dat. sg., but you will not know from the pattern memorized whether the lexical form ends with η or α. This is usually not a big deal if you remember to look for both options in the lexicon. If one of these nouns ends in η and has a masculine article with it (for example, τῷ τελώνῃ), then you expect the lexical form to end in ης. You also do not know for sure from the ending whether it is feminine or masculine, but this ambiguity does not affect your understanding most of the time.
- The gender is important primarily when there is an adjective modifying the noun and thus there must be agreement in gender as well as in number and case.
- The case and number are clear except for the nom. sg. endings in the two masculine patterns. The fact that you have memorized some of these masculine first declension words for your basic vocabulary, such as

μαθητής and προφήτης, should help you remember that ης can be a nom. sg. ending, even though most often it is a gen. sg. (or a verb ending!).

- The ου is easily recognized as a gen. sg. since it is also found in the second declension. If you see τελώνου in a passage and go to the lexicon, you expect to find a word ending in ος or ον. When you discover it does not exist, then you have to look around, usually on the same part of the page, to see what else is there, and then you find the word with a nominative ης ending.

- The same pattern is used for the plural of all of these types of first declension words: αι, ων, αις, ας.

The following paradigms illustrate these first declension patterns.

Sg.	Fem.			Masc.	
Nom.	φωνή	ἡμέρα	δόξα	μεσσίας	προφήτης
Gen.	φωνῆς	ἡμέρας	δόξης	μεσσίου	προφήτου
Dat.	φωνῇ	ἡμέρᾳ	δόξῃ	μεσσίᾳ	προφήτῃ
Acc.	φωνήν	ἡμέραν	δόξαν	μεσσίαν	προφήτην
Pl.					
Nom.	φωναί	ἡμέραι	δόξαι	μεσσίαι	προφῆται
Gen.	φωνῶν	ἡμερῶν	δοξῶν	μεσσιῶν	προφητῶν
Dat.	φωναῖς	ἡμέραις	δόξαις	μεσσίαις	προφήταις
Acc.	φωνάς	ἡμέρας	δόξας	μεσσίας	προφήτας

Second Declension Nouns

The definite article also provides the basic endings for the second declension.

Sg.	Masc.	Neut.
Nom.	θεός	ἔργον
Gen.	θεοῦ	ἔργου
Dat.	θεῷ	ἔργῳ
Acc.	θεόν	ἔργον
Voc.	θεέ	
Pl.		
Nom.	θεοί	ἔργα
Gen.	θεῶν	ἔργων
Dat.	θεοῖς	ἔργοις
Acc.	θεούς	ἔργα

- Three forms in brackets in the core pattern provide the noun and adjective endings where they differ from the article ending, namely, the masc. nom. sg., neut. nom. sg., and neut. acc. sg.

- The core pattern does not contain most of the vocatives. Vocative plurals are identical with the nominative form of the pattern. Vocative singulars are usually identical with the nominative form of the pattern. The most common exception is masc. voc. sg. in the second declension: ε, for example, θεέ, δοῦλε. This ε is included in brackets in the definite article paradigm.[10]

- Some nouns follow the same pattern as ὁ θεός but are feminine, for example, ἡ βίβλος.

Third Declension Nouns

- While some basic Greek methods teach the third declension as several different patterns (usually around seven patterns), there is actually one basic pattern of endings, and it can be learned with the help of τις, τι, the indefinite pronoun.

- The problem is not that there are a lot of endings, but rather the ways in which this one set of endings changes when it comes in contact with the various stem endings of nominals.

- Some of the changes are caused when a stem ending with a consonant comes into contact with an ending that is also a consonant. These changes are summarized below in the "square of stops,"[11] which is a core pattern to be familiar with.

- The other main set of changes occurs when a stem ending in a vowel comes in contact with an ending that is also a vowel. The vowels contract, as summarized in the "vowel contraction" chart below, a core pattern to be familiar with when we come to pattern 5.

- To add to the excitement, some third declension forms in pattern 5 shift their stem endings!

So one way to master the third declension is by memorizing thoroughly either the pattern of τις, τι as given here, with the items added in brackets, or the associated set of endings.

---

10. For other vocatives that are not identical with the nominative form, see Funk, §205.3.
11. This is Funk's term (§904.1), which is also used by Mounce.

	Indefinite Pronoun		Endings	
Sg.	Masc./Fem.	Neut.	Masc./Fem.	Neut.
Nom.	τις [–]	τι [–]	ς, –	–
Gen.	τινος	τινος	ος	ος
Dat.	τινι	τινι	ι	ι
Acc.	τινα [ν]	τι [–]	α, ν	–
Pl.				
Nom.	τινες	τινα	ες	α
Gen.	τινων	τινων	ων	ων
Dat.	τισι(ν)	τισι(ν)	σι(ν)	σι(ν)
Acc.	τινας [ες]	τινα	ας, ες	α

Examine carefully the set of endings abstracted from the paradigm of τις, τι.

- In three places, two endings are given, because some types of third declensions will take one ending and some the other ending. Thus, for the masc./fem. nom. sg. some words will have a ς ending and some will have a blank ending (represented above by a dash, also called a "zero form"), that is, there is no ending as such.

- This zero form itself can cause changes because there are some letters that cannot end a word. So if the stem ending is such a letter, for example, τ, then adding a zero form will cause the τ to drop out. All of this will be explained further below.

Because the third declension has only one set of endings, which undergoes some changes depending on stem endings, the various patterns of the third declension can be organized by the stem endings.

In preparation for tackling the first pattern of the third declension, become familiar with the square of stops.[12]

Square of Stops

- labials   π, β, φ $+ \sigma = \psi$
- velars   κ, γ, χ $+ \sigma = \xi$
- dentals   τ, δ, θ, ζ $+ \sigma = \varsigma$

---

12. The letters are listed not in alphabetical order, but "according to the degree of force in the expiratory effort" (Smyth, *Grammar*, §16). ζ is not usually included, but it will show up in the verbal system with similar behavior since it has a hidden δ (Funk, §9030.3). So it is worth learning now as part of the square of stops.

Pattern 1: Stems ending in one of the square of stops. The first set of third declension patterns is associated with the square of stops, that is, words whose stems end in a labial (π, β, φ), a velar (κ, γ, χ; also called palatal or guttural), or a dental (τ, δ, θ, ζ). The names relate to how the letters are sounded: the labials with the lips, the velars (palatals/gutturals) with the back of the tongue and the throat, and the dentals with the teeth. Here are paradigms representing these three types within this pattern. Note that these words are normally masculine or feminine.

Pattern 1. Masculine/Feminine

Sg.	Fem.	Fem.	Masc.
Nom.	σάρξ	χάρις	κώνωψ
Gen.	σαρκός	χάριτος	κώνωπος
Dat.	σαρκί	χάριτι	κώνωπι
Acc.	σάρκα	χάριτα (χάριν)	κώνωπα
Pl.			
Nom.	σάρκες	χάριτες	κώνωπες
Gen.	σαρκῶν	χαρίτων	κωνώπων
Dat.	σαρξί(ν)	χάρισι(ν)	κώνωψι(ν)
Acc.	σάρκας	χάριτας	κώνωπας

As we walk through the paradigm of σάρξ keep in mind the basic set of endings, the rules of the square of stops, and the fact that the stem of this word ends in κ throughout the paradigm.

Sg.	Fem.	
Nom.	σάρξ	(σαρκ - ς)
Gen.	σαρκός	(σαρκ - ος)
Dat.	σαρκί	(σαρκ - ι)
Acc.	σάρκα	(σαρκ - α)
Pl.		
Nom.	σάρκες	(σαρκ - ες)
Gen.	σαρκῶν	(σαρκ - ων)
Dat.	σαρξί(ν)	(σαρκ - σι[ν])
Acc.	σάρκας	(σαρκ - ας)

- In most of the forms of this word, the κ stem ending is clear and the endings in the core pattern from τις, τι fit neatly, with no problem.

- In the case of the nom. sg. and dat. pl. the stem also ends in κ, but it has come up against the σ of the endings (ς in the nom. sg. and σι[ν] in the dat. pl.). The square of stops indicates that when κ and σ meet, they form ξ (which makes sense intuitively since the sound of κ + σ is ξ). So the nom. sg. and dat. pl. are σαρκ-ς and σαρκ-σιν, but they come out σάρξ and σαρξίν. This means that when you see a word that ends in ξ, you should recognize that there is a good chance it has the nom. sg. ending ς hidden in it, while a word ending in ξιν may well contain the dat. pl. ending σιν.

- If you come across σαρκός and you are not familiar with this word, then you would expect it to be a nom. sg. second declension. However, clues in the text might steer you away from this analysis. For example, if you saw τῆς σαρκός, then the article would lead you to expect this to be a third declension genitive. Or perhaps the structure of the sentence might lead you to expect a genitive at this point instead of a nominative. But if there are no such clues, then when you look for the word in a lexicon, you would discover that the form σαρκός is not listed. Because you are thoroughly familiar with the core patterns, you would know that ος is also a common gen. sg. ending in the third declension. But then arises the problem of determining the lexical form, that is, the nom. sg. Since you know that you are probably dealing with a third declension form, you can expect the lexical form will end in ς or –. So, if you add these endings according to the rules of the square of stops, you will come up with σάρξ.

The third declension words that have a stem with a velar (κ, γ, χ) or a labial (π, β, φ) make changes in the nom. sg. and dat. pl. similar to those we have seen in the case of σάρξ.

The other pattern in the square of stops, the dentals (τ, δ, θ, ζ), has a feature that makes it look a little different. Consider the paradigm of the common word χάρις.

Sg.	Fem.	
Nom.	χάρις	ς, –
Gen.	χάριτος	ος
Dat.	χάριτι	ι
Acc.	χάριτα (χάριν)	α, ν
Pl.		
Nom.	χάριτες	ες
Gen.	χαρίτων	ων
Dat.	χάρισι(ν)	σι(ν)
Acc.	χάριτας	ας, ες

Here the endings are clear in all the same places as in σάρξ. But now the endings are also clear in the nom. sg. and dat. pl., because when a σ comes up against a dental, the dental drops out. Notice also that for this particular word both of the options listed in the core pattern for the acc. sg. ending (α and ν) are employed. Some words use more than one formation at times.

Work through the paradigms above for σάρξ, χάρις, and κώνωψ to see how the endings in the core pattern are present in each of these words and can be recognized. This exercise is the basic task for all our work in the third declension.

Also learn how to get back to the lexical form. Attention to the stem endings is key for each of the third declension patterns. For our first pattern you can learn the following rule for getting back to the lexical form; it is simply an application of the square of stops:

π, β, φ	$+ \sigma = \psi$	The nom. sg. ending for these labials,
κ, γ, χ	$+ \sigma = \xi$	velars, and dentals is ς. Adding σ to the
τ, δ, θ, ζ	$+ \sigma = \varsigma$	stem produces ψ, ξ, or ς

In other words, think:

If the stem ends in π, β, φ, add ς to get ψ.

If the stem ends in κ, γ, χ, add ς to get ξ.

If the stem ends in τ, δ, θ, ζ, drop the dental and add ς.

For example, if you come across λαίλαπος in 2 Pet. 2:17, you can see the gen. sg. ending of the third declension (ος), which gives you the basic parsing. You are not sure of the gender, though you can expect it to be either masculine or feminine since the stem ends π and thus is a pattern 1 third declension form. Applying the rule I have just given, you expect the lexical form to be λαῖλαψ, and this is correct.

When you read Heb. 12:10 and come across ἁγιότητος, you might think it is a second declension masculine form, but you know it is a third declension genitive because it has τῆς before it. Taking off the ending (ος), you see the stem ends in τ (ἁγιοτητ-); so you drop the dental (τ), add ς, and expect the lexical form to be ἁγιότης, which is correct.

Pattern 2: Stems ending in μστ. The second pattern is a development of the dentals of the first pattern. This is a pattern for the neuters with μα in the stem.

Pattern 2. Neuter

Sg.		
Nom.	ὄνομα	–
Gen.	ὀνόματος	ος
Dat.	ὀνόματι	ι
Acc.	ὄνομα	–
Pl.		
Nom.	ὀνόματα	α
Gen.	ὀνομάτων	ων
Dat.	ὀνόμασι(ν)	σι(ν)
Acc.	ὀνόματα	α

- Notice how the endings fit neatly on the stem in most places, once you realize that the stem ending is really τ, as in ὀνοματ-, not just μα.
- There are two places the τ drops out. The first is in the dat. pl. when the ending σι(ν) is added, which follows the rule in pattern 1, where σ causes a dental to drop.
- The other place the τ drops is in the nom. sg. and acc. sg., when the zero form is added. It drops here because τ cannot end a word. Once you know this extra fact about τ, then the pattern makes perfect sense.

The little rule for getting back to the lexical form for pattern 2 is as follows:

If the stem ends in τ, drop the τ and leave it (that is, when the ending is –) or add ς.

The possibility of adding ς makes the rule take into account not only the words from patterns 1 and 2 that end in τ but also a few other irregular words.[13] If there is a μα before the τ, then the word is almost always a neuter of this second pattern and uses the zero form.

Pattern 3: Stems ending in ρ and ν. In the next pattern we are back to masculine/feminine words. Once again, go through the following patterns of actual words to see how the abstract set of endings enables you to identify the case and number of these forms. Note that the nom. sg. uses the zero form.

---

13. For example, ἅλας, ἅλατος, τό. See Funk, §§170–173.4; Mounce, *Morphology*, 195–98.

Pattern 3. Masculine/Feminine

Sg.	Masc.	Fem.	
Nom.	πατήρ	εἰκών	ς, –
Gen.	πατρός	εἰκόνος	ος
Dat.	πατρί	εἰκόνι	ι
Acc.	πατέρα	εἰκόνα	α, ν
Pl.			
Nom.	πατέρες	εἰκόνες	ες
Gen.	πατέρων	εἰκόνων	ων
Dat.	πατράσι(ν)	εἰκόσι(ν)	σι(ν)
Acc.	πατέρας	εἰκόνας	ας, ες

- There are two points that call for special attention in this pattern. The first concerns the dat. pl. In both words the σι(ν) ending is nice and clear so you know it is a dat. pl., but in πατράσι(ν) there is an added α, and in εἰκόσι(ν) the ν has dropped out. These features are problems only for finding the lexical form, with the lack of the ν being the more troublesome, since the stem ending itself is missing.
- The other peculiarity of these patterns is how the vowel in the middle of the words near their stems shifts from long to short to disappearing altogether, for example, πατήρ—πατέρα—πατρός. If you were writing or speaking the language, you would need to remember all of this, but for just reading texts, this feature does not affect the recognition of case and number, as long as you know such things happen.

This vowel gradation could confuse you, however, when you look up the meaning of the word in a lexicon. The following rule takes care of this problem:

If the stem ends in ρ, the final syllable is ηρ or ωρ.
If the stem ends in ν, the final syllable is ην or ων.

If you see a word like πατέρα in a text, your first thought, unless the context helps you out, is that this is either a fem. nom. sg. of the first declension or a neut. nom./acc. pl. of the second declension. When you do not find πατερα or πατερον in the lexicon, then you realize it is a third declension form with a ρ stem ending. The fact that it is in this particular pattern means the α ending will be acc. sg., since this pattern is masculine/feminine (that is, this α is not the *neut.* pl. α). It also means you expect the lexical form to end in ηρ since the vowel before the ρ in πατέρα is ε, which lengthens to η.

But if you see a word like πατρός and you know you are dealing with a third declension, then you cannot know whether the final syllable is ηρ or ωρ (since there is no visible vowel to lengthen). In such a case you simply look in the lexicon for both possibilities according to rule number 3, that is, πατήρ and πατώρ, and discover that the first one is correct.

Pattern 4: Stems ending in ντ. The fourth pattern combines elements of the previous patterns.

Pattern 4. Masculine

Sg.		
Nom.	ἄρχων	ς, –
Gen.	ἄρχοντος	ος
Dat.	ἄρχοντι	ι
Acc.	ἄρχοντα	α, ν
Pl.		
Nom.	ἄρχοντες	ες
Gen.	ἀρχόντων	ων
Dat.	ἄρχουσι(ν)	σι(ν)
Acc.	ἄρχοντας	ας, ες

Here the endings are all clear (noting the zero form in the nom. sg.). There is a τ ending, which drops in the nom. sg. and dat. pl. as in pattern 1 and pattern 2. When this τ drops out in the nom. sg., the vowel before the ν lengthens, as in pattern 3. The problem point in this pattern is the dat. pl. When the ending σι(ν) is added, it causes both the ν and the τ to drop, and the vowel lengthens to compensate. This form needs special attention since it is identical to common verb forms: 3 pl. act. Pres. ind.[14] and dat. pl. masc./neut. act. Pres. ptc.! Fortunately, context usually makes it clear which sort of word you are working with. The hard part is simply remembering the options.

Pattern 5: Stems ending in ε. In pattern 5 we do not have the problems caused by consonants coming up against one another. Now the problem is vowels coming into contact with other vowels. When certain vowels come in contact with each other, they contract. So in preparation for pattern 5, you need to be familiar with the following set of vowel contractions.

---

14. I capitalize the tense-form in each case to highlight it, partly to break up the string of information visually and partly because I find the tense-form of particular interest.

This set of contractions gives the most common combinations, and they are arranged in the way you meet them when reading.[15] That is, when you see a word in a text with an α that may be a contraction, you need to know it probably comes from α + ε.

Vowel Contraction

- α < α + ε
- ει < ε + ε
- η < ε + α
- οι < ο + ει
- ου < ε + ο, ο + ε, or ο + ο
- ω < any vowel + ο or ω (except as above)

Furthermore, things really get interesting because many of the specific patterns within pattern 5 include a shift of the stem ending in some of their forms. Pattern 5 of the third declension contains some of the more troublesome elements of Greek morphology, in my opinion. But there is a pattern to it, and it does continue to use the same set of basic endings we have been working with.

There are three specific paradigms within pattern 5. We will look at them one at a time.

Pattern 5a. Stems Ending in ος/ε —Neuter

Sg.		
Nom.	ἔθνος	(ἔθνος - -)
Gen.	ἔθνους	(ἔθνε - ος)
Dat.	ἔθνει	(ἔθνε - ι)
Acc.	ἔθνος	(ἔθνος - -)
Pl.		
Nom.	ἔθνη	(ἔθνε - α)
Gen.	ἐθνῶν	(ἔθνε - ων)
Dat.	ἔθνεσι(ν)	(ἔθνε - σι[ν])
Acc.	ἔθνη	(ἔθνε - α)

- This is a neuter pattern, so it uses the neuter endings from the main set, following τις, τι.

15. For more extensive lists and discussion, see Funk, §§916–917.10; Mounce, *Morphology*, 2–7; Smyth, *Grammar*, §§48–59.

- The endings have been separated so that you can see how these basic endings are present, though usually contracted.
- This pattern has a stem ending in ος in the nom. sg. and acc. sg., and a stem ending in ε everywhere else. So the form ἔθνος is really the stem plus a zero form.
- In the gen. sg. the stem is ἐθνε-. When the gen. sg. ending ος is added, the ε of the stem ending and the o in ος contract to form ου; hence the form ἔθνους.
- In the dat. sg. and dat. pl. the endings are clear.
- In the nom. pl. and acc. pl. the ε contracts with the α ending to produce η. In the gen. pl. the ε and ω contract to form ω with a circumflex accent.

The ability to see how the forms in this pattern continue the basic pattern for neuter third declension forms is helpful for learning to recognize these forms, but they remain difficult, since most of the forms in this pattern can be confused with forms in other patterns, even at some points with verbs! Fortunately, the definite article is often present to help you identify what you are looking at.

Finding the lexical form is another difficulty in this pattern because of the stem shift between ος and ε. I have a rough-and-ready rule for dealing with this chaos, but first we need to see the other paradigms within pattern 5.

Pattern 5b. Stems Ending in ι/ε —Feminine

Sg.		
Nom.	πόλις	(πολι - ς)
Gen.	πόλεως	(πολε - ος)
Dat.	πόλει	(πολε - ι)
Acc.	πόλιν	(πολι - ν)
Pl.		
Nom.	πόλεις	(πολε - ες)
Gen.	πόλεων	(πολε - ων)
Dat.	πόλεσι(ν)	(πολε - σι[ν])
Acc.	πόλεις	(πολε - ες)

- This pattern uses the masculine/feminine set of endings since all the words that follow this pattern are in the feminine. The stem shifts between ending in ι and ε.
- Several of the forms show the ε stem and the ending clearly.
- Likewise, the ι stem in the nom. sg. and acc. sg. in these two forms is clear, as are the endings (note the use of the ν ending instead of α for the acc. sg. in this pattern).

- There are two points that call for more careful attention. In the gen. sg. the ending ος has lengthened to ως through a series of stages in the history of the language.[16] It is probably easiest just to learn εως as another form for the third declension gen. sg. in some patterns that have a stem shift. Recognizing the connection with the normal gen. sg. third declension ending ος should help you remember this form.

- In the nom. pl. and the acc. pl. the stem ends in ε, and the ending in both cases is ες. That is, in the acc. pl., instead of the ending ας (as in most third declension masc. or fem. patterns), the alternative ending in the core pattern is used. The combination of ε + ε produces the diphthong ει. While all of this follows the basic pattern and the rules of vowel contraction, what results is quite confusing because it looks like a verb (2 sg. act. Pres. ind., e.g., λύεις), and the alternative ending for the acc. pl. (ες instead of ας) looks like the more common nom. pl. ending. Fortunately, the definite article is often present to help (αἱ πόλεις, τὰς πόλεις), but this one still takes some getting used to. It is a good example of why you cannot simply memorize the core patterns and not pay attention to the actual paradigms.

Pattern 5c. Stems Ending in ευ/ε —Masculine

Sg.		
Nom.	βασιλεύς	(βασιλευ - ς)
Gen.	βασιλέως	(βασιλε - ος)
Dat.	βασιλεῖ	(βασιλε - ι)
Acc.	βασιλέα	(βασιλε - α)
Pl.		
Nom.	βασιλεῖς	(βασιλε - ες)
Gen.	βασιλέων	(βασιλε - ων)
Dat.	βασιλεῦσι(ν)	(βασιλευ - σι[ν])
Acc.	βασιλεῖς	(βασιλε - ες)

- The final pattern among the third declension forms of pattern 5 has a stem that shifts between ending in ευ in the nom. sg. and dat. pl. and in ε elsewhere.

- Several issues we looked at in the gen. sg., nom. pl., and acc. pl. in the 5b pattern recur here.

---

16. For the details, see Funk, §2001.3; Mounce, *Morphology*, 16; Smyth, *Grammar*, §34.

- The α of the acc. sg. does not contract with the ε stem ending, making this ending easier to recognize.
- Whereas 5b words are feminine, 5c words are masculine.

I have not found any easy way to get to the lexical form of pattern 5 words with precision. So my rough-and-ready rule is as follows:

If the stem ends in ε (usually in a contracted form), the nominative form is usually ος, υς, ις, ευς, or ης.

In other words, if you see a form that you suspect is a third declension with an ε stem, then go to the lexicon and look for a word with the stem plus one of these five endings. I have included υς and ης at this point because they will come up in third declension adjectives.

So, for example, if you are reading Acts 10:32 and see βυρσέως, you can recognize the word as a gen. sg. from an ε stem third declension. In the lexicon you would look it up under βυρσ- and then start adding these five endings, that is, the forms βυρσος, βυρσυς, βυρσις, βυρσευς, and βυρσης. This is easy to do since any of these forms will be on the same page of the lexicon—just look to see which one actually occurs. If you know the paradigms of these types of words well, then there are only two of these endings that are real possibilities, since εως normally occurs only in the ις and ευς patterns. But until you have mastered the details of the patterns, my rough rule should work quite well for finding the lexical form of most of the words that follow the third declension pattern 5. Remember, however, that there are irregular words out there as well, for which, as I have said, see Funk or Mounce.

Pattern 6: Stems ending in υ.

Pattern 6. Masculine/Feminine

Sg.		
Nom.	ἰχθύς	(ἰχθυ - ς)
Gen.	ἰχθύος	(ἰχθυ - ος)
Dat.	ἰχθύϊ	(ἰχθυ - ι)
Acc.	ἰχθύν	(ἰχθυ - ν)
Pl.		
Nom.	ἰχθύες	(ἰχθυ - ες)
Gen.	ἰχθύων	(ἰχθυ - ων)
Dat.	ἰχθύσι(ν)	(ἰχθυ - σι[ν])
Acc.	ἰχθύας	(ἰχθυ - ας)

After the complexity of pattern 5, this sixth pattern is a relief. The stem, υ, does not change, and the endings are all clear. Recall that the diaeresis in the dat. sg. (ϊ) means two letters that normally form a diphthong are here functioning as separate vowels and are pronounced separately.

Adjectives

2-1-2 Pattern Adjectives

Two common patterns for adjectives use the basic endings of the first and second declensions (hence the label 2-1-2).

Sg.	Masc.	Fem.	Neut.
Nom.	ἀγαθός	ἀγαθή	ἀγαθόν
Gen.	ἀγαθοῦ	ἀγαθῆς	ἀγαθοῦ
Dat.	ἀγαθῷ	ἀγαθῇ	ἀγαθῷ
Acc.	ἀγαθόν	ἀγαθήν	ἀγαθόν
Pl.			
Nom.	ἀγαθοί	ἀγαθαί	ἀγαθά
Gen.	ἀγαθῶν	ἀγαθῶν	ἀγαθῶν
Dat.	ἀγαθοῖς	ἀγαθαῖς	ἀγαθοῖς
Acc.	ἀγαθούς	ἀγαθάς	ἀγαθά

Sg.	Masc.	Fem.	Neut.
Nom.	ἄξιος	ἀξία	ἄξιον
Gen.	ἀξίου	ἀξίας	ἀξίου
Dat.	ἀξίῳ	ἀξίᾳ	ἀξίῳ
Acc.	ἄξιον	ἀξίαν	ἄξιον
Pl.			
Nom.	ἄξιοι	ἄξιαι	ἄξια
Gen.	ἀξίων	ἀξίων	ἀξίων
Dat.	ἀξίοις	ἀξίαις	ἀξίοις
Acc.	ἀξίους	ἀξίας	ἄξια

Two-Termination Adjectives in First and Second Declensions

Another common pattern contains adjectives that are called "two-termination adjectives" because they have only two sets of endings, rather than three. One form serves for both masculine and feminine. The two-termination adjectives do not have any new endings, but they can be confusing when modifying feminine nouns. For example, ἡ αἰώνιος ζωή looks weird if you do not remember that two-termination adjectives use the same form for both masculine and feminine.

Sg.	Masc./Fem.	Neut.
Nom.	αἰώνιος	αἰώνιον
Gen.	αἰωνίου	αἰωνίου
Dat.	αἰωνίῳ	αἰωνίῳ
Acc.	αἰώνιον	αἰώνιον
Pl.		
Nom.	αἰώνιοι	αἰώνια
Gen.	αἰωνίων	αἰωνίων
Dat.	αἰωνίοις	αἰωνίοις
Acc.	αἰωνίους	αἰώνια

3-1-3 Pattern Adjectives

Some adjectives use third declension endings for the masculine and neuter forms and first declension endings for the feminine (hence the label 3-1-3). The basic pattern for these adjectives is πᾶς, πᾶσα, πᾶν, which is one of the core patterns to learn.

πᾶς, πᾶσα, πᾶν

Sg.	Masc.	Fem.	Neut.
Nom.	πᾶς	πᾶσα	πᾶν
Gen.	παντός	πάσης	παντός
Dat.	παντί	πάσῃ	παντί
Acc.	πάντα	πᾶσαν	πᾶν
Pl.			
Nom.	πάντες	πᾶσαι	πάντα
Gen.	πάντων	πασῶν	πάντων
Dat.	πᾶσι(ν)	πάσαις	πᾶσι(ν)
Acc.	πάντας	πάσας	πάντα

Since the masculine and neuter forms follow the third declension, work through this pattern with the notes above on pattern 4 third declension words.

- There are two main differences from that pattern. The first is the use of ς in the masc. nom. sg. (which, as usual, makes the ντ drop out and the vowel lengthen, here evident in the accent on the α; the same thing happens in the dat. pl.).

- The other important feature to note is the inclusion of σ in the feminine forms.[17] Because σ is added, the ντ drops out, the vowel is then lengthened, and the accent changes. This pattern occurs also in the participles, discussed below.

Another 3-1-3 adjective pattern has a stem shift between υ and ε.

Sg.	Masc.		Fem.	Neut.	
Nom.	εὐθύς	(εὐθυ - ς)	εὐθεῖα	εὐθύ	(εὐθυ - –)
Gen.	εὐθέως	(εὐθε - ος)	εὐθείας	εὐθέως	(εὐθε - ος)
Dat.	εὐθεῖ	(εὐθε - ι)	εὐθείᾳ	εὐθεῖ	(εὐθε - ι)
Acc.	εὐθύν	(εὐθυ - ν)	εὐθεῖαν	εὐθύ	(εὐθυ - –)
Pl.					
Nom.	εὐθεῖς	(εὐθε - ες)	εὐθεῖαι	εὐθέα	(εὐθε - α)
Gen.	εὐθέων	(εὐθε - ων)	εὐθειῶν	εὐθέων	(εὐθε - ων)
Dat.	εὐθέσι(ν)	(εὐθε - σι[ν])	εὐθείαις	εὐθέσι(ν)	(εὐθε - σι[ν])
Acc.	εὐθεῖς	(εὐθε - ες)	εὐθείας	εὐθέα	(εὐθε - α)

- The masc. follows the same pattern as 5b of the third declension (πόλις), except that υ is used in the stem instead of ι.
- The gen. sg. and dat. sg. have the same changes in both masculine and neuter.
- The endings in the feminine are simple first declension endings. The stem change to εὐθει- is the thing to watch.[18]
- The neut. nom. sg. and neut. acc. sg. look a little weird, but they use the normal zero form ending.
- If you memorize all three nom. sg. forms for words in this pattern, you will have in your memory examples of the masculine and neuter nominative endings and the augmented stem in the feminine. So do not memorize εὐθύς, but εὐθύς, εὐθεῖα, εὐθύ.

Two-Termination Adjectives in Third Declension

There are also quite a few two-termination adjectives that use third declension endings.

---

17. For details on this σ, see Funk, §§2300–2300.1; Mounce, *Morphology*, 228n2; Smyth, *Grammar*, §299b.
18. For an explanation of this fem. stem, see Funk, §2003.2; Mounce, *Morphology*, 230; or Smyth, *Grammar*, §§296–97.

Sg.	Masc./Fem.	Neut.	Masc./Fem.	Neut.
Nom.	ἀληθής	ἀληθές	ἄφρων	ἄφρον
Gen.	ἀληθοῦς	ἀληθοῦς	ἄφρονος	ἄφρονος
Dat.	ἀληθεῖ	ἀληθεῖ	ἄφρονι	ἄφρονι
Acc.	ἀληθῆ	ἀληθές	ἄφρονα	ἄφρον
Pl.				
Nom.	ἀληθεῖς	ἀληθῆ	ἄφρονες	ἄφρονα
Gen.	ἀληθῶν	ἀληθῶν	ἀφρόνων	ἀφρόνων
Dat.	ἀληθέσι(ν)	ἀληθέσι(ν)	ἄφροσι(ν)	ἄφροσι(ν)
Acc.	ἀληθεῖς	ἀληθῆ	ἄφρονας	ἄφρονα

- The key to the paradigm for ἀληθής is that the stem ends in ες throughout. This stem is clearly seen in the neut. nom. sg. and neut. acc. sg., since they use the zero form ending.
- The masc. nom. sg. also uses the zero form option for its ending, and the ε is lengthened, which enables it to be distinguished from the two neuter forms.
- For all of the other forms, the σ of the stem ending drops out when the endings are added, which means the ε is left to contract with the endings in ways we have seen in pattern 5 third declension forms, except in the dat. pl., where there is no contraction.
- Ἄφρων is similar to pattern 3 of the third declension.

Mixed Patterns

A couple of important words have a mixed pattern, for example, πολύς, πολλή, πολύ and μέγας, μεγάλη, μέγα.

Sg.	Masc.	Fem.	Neut.	Masc.	Fem.	Neut.
Nom.	πολύς	πολλή	πολύ	μέγας	μεγάλη	μέγα
Gen.	πολλοῦ	πολλῆς	πολλοῦ	μεγάλου	μεγάλης	μεγάλου
Dat.	πολλῷ	πολλῇ	πολλῷ	μεγάλῳ	μεγάλη	μεγάλῳ
Acc.	πολύν	πολλήν	πολύ	μέγαν	μεγάλην	μέγα
Pl.						
Nom.	πολλοί	πολλαί	πολλά	μεγάλοι	μεγάλαι	μεγάλα
Gen.	πολλῶν	πολλῶν	πολλῶν	μεγάλων	μεγάλων	μεγάλων
Dat.	πολλοῖς	πολλαῖς	πολλοῖς	μεγάλοις	μεγάλαις	μεγάλοις
Acc.	πολλούς	πολλάς	πολλά	μεγάλους	μεγάλας	μεγάλα

In these patterns only the masculine/neuter nom. sg. and masculine/neuter acc. sg. follow the third declension; the rest of the pattern is regular 2-1-2. If you learn such words with all three nom. sg. forms, then you will have most of the irregularities. That is, for vocabulary, memorize πολύς, πολλή, πολύ, not just πολύς. Knowledge of third declension endings should enable you to recognize the masc. acc. sg. form.

Pronouns

First and Second Person Pronouns

The forms of first and second person pronouns have endings that are similar at many points to the nominal endings. There are also some distinctives, so they form one of the core patterns that have to be learned.

Personal Pronouns

	First Person		Second Person	
	Sg.	Pl.	Sg.	Pl.
Nom.	ἐγώ	ἡμεῖς	σύ	ὑμεῖς
Gen.	ἐμοῦ, μου	ἡμῶν	σοῦ, σου	ὑμῶν
Dat.	ἐμοί, μοι	ἡμῖν	σοί, σοι	ὑμῖν
Acc.	ἐμέ, με	ἡμᾶς	σέ, σε	ὑμᾶς

Third Person Pronouns

The third person pronoun is αὐτός, ή, ό, which follows the regular 2-1-2 pattern, though the neuter singular lacks a ν, as in the definite article (τό). Learning all three forms of the nom. sg. will lock this irregularity into your data bank.

Sg.	Masc.	Fem.	Neut.
Nom.	αὐτός	αὐτή	αὐτό
Gen.	αὐτοῦ	αὐτῆς	αὐτοῦ
Dat.	αὐτῷ	αὐτῇ	αὐτῷ
Acc.	αὐτόν	αὐτήν	αὐτό
Pl.			
Nom.	αὐτοί	αὐταί	αὐτά
Gen.	αὐτῶν	αὐτῶν	αὐτῶν
Dat.	αὐτοῖς	αὐταῖς	αὐτοῖς
Acc.	αὐτούς	αὐτάς	αὐτά

Verbal System

Augment, Reduplication, Tense-Form Signs,[19] and Personal Endings

Verbs can have an augment either by adding an ε to the front of the stem or by lengthening a vowel if the verb begins with a vowel. Verbs may be reduplicated either by doubling the initial consonant or with a simple augment. Both augmentation and reduplication are illustrated in the paradigms that follow.[20] The functions of the square of stops and vowel contraction that are seen in the third declension also occur in some verb patterns. As you work through the discussion that follows, you should carefully study the actual paradigms, noting which endings are applied in each paradigm and whether they are affected by vowel contraction or the square of stops.

The following chart provides a map as you work through the verb system presented here. It lists the six principal parts and the components found in various verb forms. You should either memorize the chart by rote or learn the signs by working with each of the components as you work through the verb system. The column for the stem is oversimplified. We will see that there are often minor stem changes in addition to those noted in the chart. Under the chart there are several general details to keep in mind as you work on recognizing verb forms.

Principal Part	Tense-Form	Augment or Reduplication	Stem	Tense-Form Sign	Variable Vowel	Endings
1st	Pres. A/M/P		λυ		ο ε	Primary
	Impf. A/M/P	ε	λυ		ο ε	Secondary
2nd	Fut. A/M		λυ	σ	ο ε	Primary
	Liq. Fut. A/M		λ/μ/ν/ρ	ε(σ)	ο ε	Primary
3rd	1 Aor. A/M	ε	λυ	σα/ε		Secondary
	2 Aor. A/M	ε	?		ο ε	Secondary
	Liq. Aor. A/M	ε	λ/μ/ν/ρ	α/ε		Secondary
	κ Aor. A/M	ε	stem	κα/ε		Secondary
4th	1 Pf. Act.	λε	λυ	κα/ε		Primary
	2 Pf. Act.	λε	λυ	α/ε		Primary
	Plpf. Act.	(ε)λε	λυ	κει		Secondary

---

19. For the use of "tense-form" instead of "tense," see app. 5.

20. If your knowledge of these features is rusty, then you should review this information from your first-year book or see Funk, §§0335–3450.3; or Mounce, *Morphology*, 65–73.

Principal Part	Tense-Form	Augment or Reduplication	Stem	Tense-Form Sign	Variable Vowel	Endings
5th	Pf. M/P	λε	λυ			Primary
	Plpf. M/P	(ε)λε	λυ			Secondary
	Fut. Pf. M/P	λε	λυ	σ	ο ε	Primary
6th	Aor. Pass.	ε	λυ	θη		Secondary
	2 Aor. Pass.	ε	λυ	η		Secondary
	Fut. Pass.		λυ	θησ	ο ε	Primary
	2 Fut. Pass.		λυ	ησ	ο ε	Primary

- A variable vowel is ο before endings beginning with μ or ν (e.g., ομεν and ομεθα), and ε elsewhere (though in the present and future indicative the ε variable vowel is ει in the singular).

- When a form has a zero ending and you see an α, it is a 1 sg. If you see an ε, then it is either a 3 sg. indicative or a 2 sg. imperative.

- Moveable ν occurs only after ε and ι. So ον is always an ending; its ν is not moveable.

Indicative Mood: Primary Tense-Forms (Present, Future, Perfect)

Learn the personal endings for the primary tense-forms.

Primary Personal Endings

	Act.	Mid./Pass.
1 Sg.	ω, μι, –	μαι
2 Sg.	ς	σαι (= ῃ)
3 Sg.	–(ν), σι(ν)	ται
1 Pl.	μεν	μεθα
2 Pl.	τε	σθε
3 Pl.	ουσι(ν), ασι(ν)	νται

Present Active and Middle/Passive

Act.	λύω	ἀγαπάω	ποιέω	πληρόω
1 Sg.	λύω	ἀγαπῶ	ποιῶ	πληρῶ
2 Sg.	λύεις	ἀγαπᾷς	ποιεῖς	πληροῖς
3 Sg.	λύει	ἀγαπᾷ	ποιεῖ	πληροῖ
1 Pl.	λύομεν	ἀγαπῶμεν	ποιοῦμεν	πληροῦμεν
2 Pl.	λύετε	ἀγαπᾶτε	ποιεῖτε	πληροῦτε
3 Pl.	λύουσι(ν)	ἀγαπῶσι(ν)	ποιοῦσι(ν)	πληροῦσι(ν)
Mid./Pass.				
1 Sg.	λύομαι	ἀγαπῶμαι	ποιοῦμαι	πληροῦμαι
2 Sg.	λύῃ	ἀγαπᾷ	ποιῇ	πληροῖ
3 Sg.	λύεται	ἀγαπᾶται	ποιεῖται	πληροῦται
1 Pl.	λυόμεθα	ἀγαπώμεθα	ποιούμεθα	πληρούμεθα
2 Pl.	λύεσθε	ἀγαπᾶσθε	ποιεῖσθε	πληροῦσθε
3 Pl.	λύονται	ἀγαπῶνται	ποιοῦνται	πληροῦνται

Act.	τίθημι	ἵστημι	δίδωμι	δείκνυμι
1 Sg.	τίθημι	ἵστημι	δίδωμι	δείκνυμι
2 Sg.	τίθης	ἵστης	δίδως	δείκνυς
3 Sg.	τίθησι(ν)	ἵστησι(ν)	δίδωσι(ν)	δείκνυσι(ν)
1 Pl.	τίθεμεν	ἵσταμεν	δίδομεν	δείκνυμεν
2 Pl.	τίθετε	ἵστατε	δίδοτε	δείκνυτε
3 Pl.	τιθέασι(ν)	ἱστᾶσι(ν)	διδόασι(ν)	δεικνύασι(ν)
Mid./Pass.				
1 Sg.	τίθεμαι	ἵσταμαι	δίδομαι	δείκνυμαι
2 Sg.	τίθεσαι	ἵστασαι	δίδοσαι	δείκνυσαι
3 Sg.	τίθεται	ἵσταται	δίδοται	δείκνυται
1 Pl.	τιθέμεθα	ἱστάμεθα	διδόμεθα	δεικνύμεθα
2 Pl.	τίθεσθε	ἵστασθε	δίδοσθε	δείκνυσθε
3 Pl.	τίθενται	ἵστανται	δίδονται	δείκνυνται

- The use of ει in 2 and 3 sg. is difficult to explain.[21] Its existence is noted under the verb chart given above.
- The alternatives given for 3 sg. and 3 pl. on the primary personal endings chart (σι[ν] and ασι[ν]) are used for μι verbs.

21. Mounce offers an explanation (*Morphology*, 80n3), while Funk says it is "inexplicable" (§3670.2).

- The σαι ending in 2 sg. mid./pass. occurs in μι verbs, and in ω verbs the σ drops out, the variable vowel contracts with α, and the ι is subscripted to produce ῃ.
- Note carefully how the personal endings in the core patterns are affected by the rules of contraction in the contract verbs.
- The μι verb endings are clear enough from the personal endings in the core pattern, but note the shift from long to short vowels in the stems of some of the words. Both the 3 sg. and 3 pl. use the same ending, so this shift is what distinguishes them. For reading purposes these shifts are not a problem, since they do not obscure the personal endings and you can usually figure out the tense-form and mood, especially if you learn the principal parts for these words.

The present indicative pattern for εἰμί has irregularities, so it is a core pattern to become familiar with.

Present Indicative of εἰμί

	Sg.	Pl.
1	εἰμί	ἐσμέν
2	εἶ	ἐστέ
3	ἐστίν	εἰσί(ν)

Future Active and Middle

Act.	λύω	πέμπω	μένω
1 Sg.	λύσω	πέμψω	μενῶ
2 Sg.	λύσεις	πέμψεις	μενεῖς
3 Sg.	λύσει	πέμψει	μενεῖ
1 Pl.	λύσομεν	πέμψομεν	μενοῦμεν
2 Pl.	λύσετε	πέμψετε	μενεῖτε
3 Pl.	λύσουσι(ν)	πέμψουσι(ν)	μενοῦσι(ν)
Mid.			
1 Sg.	λύσομαι	πέμψομαι	μενοῦμαι
2 Sg.	λύσῃ	πέμψῃ	μενῇ
3 Sg.	λύσεται	πέμψεται	μενεῖται
1 Pl.	λυσόμεθα	πεμψόμεθα	μενούμεθα
2 Pl.	λύσεσθε	πέμψεσθε	μενεῖσθε
3 Pl.	λύσονται	πέμψονται	μενοῦνται

The σ futures are no problem except when the stem ends in a consonant, for which you need the square of stops. Liquid futures have a stem ending in λ, μ, ν, or ρ.[22] Their pattern looks like the present tense-form ε contract paradigm. Contract verbs lengthen their stem endings (e.g., ἀγαπήσω).

Note the future indicative pattern for εἰμί, another of the core patterns to know well.

Future Indicative of εἰμί

	Sg.	Pl.
1	ἔσομαι	ἐσόμεθα
2	ἔσῃ	ἔσεσθε
3	ἔσται	ἔσονται

Future Passive

	λύω	γράφω
1 Sg.	λυθήσομαι	γραφήσομαι
2 Sg.	λυθήσῃ	γραφήσῃ
3 Sg.	λυθήσεται	γραφήσεται
1 Pl.	λυθησόμεθα	γραφησόμεθα
2 Pl.	λυθήσεσθε	γραφήσεσθε
3 Pl.	λυθήσονται	γραφήσονται

- The distinctive tense-form sign θησ usually identifies this one. It uses middle endings, but the person and number are clear.
- There is also a second future passive that lacks the θ, as you see for γραφω.

Perfect Active

	λύω	ἀγαπάω	τηρέω	πληρόω	γίνομαι
1 Sg.	λέλυκα	ἠγάπηκα	τετήρηκα	πεπλήρωκα	γέγονα
2 Sg.	λέλυκας	ἠγάπηκας	τετήρηκας	πεπλήρωκας	γέγονας
3 Sg.	λέλυκε(ν)	ἠγάπηκε(ν)	τετήρηκε	πεπλήρωκε(ν)	γέγονε(ν)
1 Pl.	λελύκαμεν	ἠγαπήκαμεν	τετηρήκαμεν	πεπληρώκαμεν	γεγόναμεν
2 Pl.	λυλύκατε	ἠγαπήκατε	τετηρήκατε	πεπληρώκατε	γεγόνατε
3 Pl.	λελύκασι(ν)	ἠγαπήκασι(ν)	τετηρήκασι(ν)	πεπληρώκασι(ν)	γεγόνασι(ν)

22. M and ν are nasals, but usually this pattern is simply referred to as the liquid future.

- The stem is reduplicated by doubling the initial consonant or lengthening the initial vowel.
- The 1 sg. and 3 sg. endings are zero forms.
- The tense-form sign changes to κε in the 3 sg., which distinguishes it from the 1 sg.
- The 3 pl. takes the second alternative, ασι(ν).
- Contract verbs lengthen the vowel on their stem ending (α and ε become η, ο becomes ω).
- The 2 perfect is the same pattern, but without the distinctive κ in the tense-form sign and usually with a modified stem.

Perfect Middle/Passive

	λύω	γράφω	δέχομαι	πείθω
1 Sg.	λέλυμαι	γέγραμμαι	δέδεγμαι	πέπεισμαι
2 Sg.	λέλυσαι	γέγραψαι	δέδεξαι	πέπεισαι
3 Sg.	λέλυται	γέγραπται	δέδεκται	πέπεισται
1 Pl.	λελύμεθα	γεγράμμεθα	δεδέγμεθα	πεπείσμεθα
2 Pl.	λέλυσθε	γέγραφθε	δέδεχθε	πέπεισθε
3 Pl.	λέλυνται	γεγραμμένοι εἰσί(ν)	δεδεγμένοι εἰσί(ν)	πεπεισμένοι εἰσί(ν)

- The key sign is the lack of a tense-form sign or a variable vowel.
- Contract verbs lengthen their stem endings (e.g., ἠγάπημαι).
- The lack of a tense-form sign or a variable vowel means that a stem that ends in a consonant will come up against a consonant in the ending and undergo changes.

Before the σαι ending (2 sg.), the final consonant of the stem will change according to the square of stops:

- π, β, φ   + σ >   ψ   γεγραφ + σαι > γέγραψαι
- κ, γ, χ   + σ >   ξ   δεδεχ + σαι > δέδεξαι
- τ, δ, θ, ζ   + σ >   σ   πεπειθ + σαι > πέπεισαι

Before μαι and μεθα, the final consonant of the stem will change as follows:

- π, β, φ   + μ >   μ   γεγραφ + μαι > γέγραμμαι
- κ, γ, χ   + μ >   γ   δεδεχ + μαι > δέδεγμαι
- τ, δ, θ, ζ   + μ >   σ   πεπειθ + μαι > πέπεισμαι

Before ται and θε (that is, σθε with the σ dropped out), the final consonant of the stem will change as follows:

- π, β, φ   + τ >   π   γεγραφ   + ται > γέγραπται
- κ, γ, χ   + τ >   κ   δεδεχ   + ται > δέδεκται
- τ, δ, θ, ζ   + τ >   σ   πεπειθ   + ται > πέπεισται

- π, β, φ   + τ >   φ   γεγραφ   + (σ)θε > γέγραφθε
- κ, γ, χ   + τ >   χ   δεδεχ   + (σ)θε > δέδεχθε
- τ, δ, θ, ζ   + τ >   σ   πεπειθ   + (σ)θε > πέπεισθε

As you can see from the paradigms, once you understand the kind of changes to expect, most of these forms can be identified well enough for reading without learning the details of these changes. The third plural of verbs whose stem ends in a consonant is usually expressed using a periphrastic participle.

Indicative Mood: Secondary Tense-Forms (Imperfect, Aorist, Pluperfect)

You should be familiar with the personal endings for the secondary tense-forms.

Secondary Personal Endings

	Act.	Mid./Pass.
1 Sg.	ν, –	μην
2 Sg.	ς	σο (= ου)
3 Sg.	–(ν)	το
1 Pl.	μεν	μεθα
2 Pl.	τε	σθε
3 Pl.	ν, σαν	ντο

Imperfect

Act.	λύω	γεννάω	ποιέω	φανερόω
1 Sg.	ἔλυον	ἐγέννων	ἐποίουν	ἐφανέρουν
2 Sg.	ἔλυες	ἐγέννας	ἐποίεις	ἐφανέρους
3 Sg.	ἔλυε(ν)	ἐγέννα	ἐποίει	ἐφανέρου
1 Pl.	ἐλύομεν	ἐγεννῶμεν	ἐποιοῦμεν	ἐφανεροῦμεν
2 Pl.	ἐλύετε	ἐγεννᾶτε	ἐποιεῖτε	ἐφανεροῦτε
3 Pl.	ἔλυον	ἐγέννων	ἐποίουν	ἐφανέρουν

Mid./Pass.				
1 Sg.	ἐλυόμην	ἐγεννώμην	ἐποιούμην	ἐφανερούμην
2 Sg.	ἐλύου	ἐγεννῶ	ἐποιοῦ	ἐφανεροῦ
3 Sg.	ἐλύετο	ἐγεννᾶτο	ἐποιεῖτο	ἐφανεροῦτο
1 Pl.	ἐλυόμεθα	ἐγεννώμεθα	ἐποιούμεθα	ἐφανερούμεθα
2 Pl.	ἐλύεσθε	ἐγεννᾶσθε	ἐποιεῖσθε	ἐφανεροῦσθε
3 Pl.	ἐλύοντο	ἐγεννῶντο	ἐποιοῦντο	ἐφανεροῦντο

Act.	τίθημι	ἵστημι	δίδωμι	δείκνυμι
1 Sg.	ἐτίθην	ἵστην	ἐδίδουν	ἐδείκνυν
2 Sg.	ἐτίθεις	ἵστης	ἐδίδους	ἐδείκνυς
3 Sg.	ἐτίθει	ἵστη	ἐδίδου	ἐδείκνυ
1 Pl.	ἐτίθεμεν	ἵσταμεν	ἐδίδομεν	ἐδείκνυμεν
2 Pl.	ἐτίθετε	ἵστατε	ἐδίδοτε	ἐδείκνυτε
3 Pl.	ἐτίθεσαν	ἵστασαν	ἐδίδοσαν	ἐδείκνυσαν
Mid./Pass.				
1 Sg.	ἐτιθέμην	ἱστάμην	ἐδιδόμην	ἐδεικνύμην
2 Sg.	ἐτίθεσο	ἵστασο	ἐδίδοσο	ἐδείκνυσο
3 Sg.	ἐτίθετο	ἵστατο	ἐδίδοτο	ἐδείκνυτο
1 Pl.	ἐτιθέμεθα	ἱστάμεθα	ἐδιδόμεθα	ἐδεικνύμεθα
2 Pl.	ἐτίθεσθε	ἵστασθε	ἐδίδοσθε	ἐδείκνυσθε
3 Pl.	ἐτίθεντο	ἵσταντο	ἐδίδοντο	ἐδείκνυντο

- The uncontracted forms in the first column are straightforward.
- The contracted forms use the same personal endings, but carefully study the effects of the rules of contraction.
- The endings of μι verbs follow the regular personal endings in the core pattern but use some of the alternate endings.

The imperfect indicative pattern for εἰμί has irregularities, so it is a core pattern to learn.

Imperfect Indicative of εἰμί

	Sg.	Pl.
1	ἤμην	ἦμεν, ἤμεθα
2	ἦς, ἦσθα	ἦτε
3	ἦν	ἦσαν

1 Aorist Active and Middle of λύω

	Act.	Mid.
1 Sg.	ἔλυσα	ἐλυσάμην
2 Sg.	ἔλυσας	ἐλύσω
3 Sg.	ἔλυσε(ν)	ἐλύσατο
1 Pl.	ἐλύσαμεν	ἐλυσάμεθα
2 Pl.	ἐλύσατε	ἐλύσασθε
3 Pl.	ἔλυσαν	ἐλύσαντο

- The first aorist uses the zero form in both 1 sg. and 3 sg.
- The tense-form sign changes to σε in the 3 sg. to distinguish it from the 1 sg.
- Because the tense-form sign has a σ, the square of stops is needed.
- The 2 sg. mid. elides the σ of σο, and then the vowels α and ο contract to produce ω, for example, ἐ-πιστευ-σα̱-σο̱ > ἐπιστεύσω. The augment distinguishes this form from a future.
- Contract verbs lengthen their stem endings (e.g., ἠγάπησα).

2 Aorist Active and Middle of λαμβάνω

	Act.	Mid.
1 Sg.	ἔλαβον	ἐλαβόμην
2 Sg.	ἔλαβες	ἐλάβου
3 Sg.	ἔλαβε(ν)	ἐλάβετο
1 Pl.	ἐλάβομεν	ἐλαβόμεθα
2 Pl.	ἐλάβετε	ἐλάβεσθε
3 Pl.	ἔλαβον	ἐλάβοντο

This paradigm has exactly the same signs as the imperfect, but the stem is not the same as the present. The imperfect uses the present stem, so the 2 aorist is distinguished by its stem.

Liquid Aorist Active and Middle of μένω

	Act.	Mid.
1 Sg.	ἔμεινα	ἐμεινάμην
2 Sg.	ἔμεινας	ἐμείνω
3 Sg.	ἔμεινε(ν)	ἐμείνατο
1 Pl.	ἐμείναμεν	ἐμεινάμεθα
2 Pl.	ἐμείνατε	ἐμείνασθε
3 Pl.	ἔμειναν	ἐμείναντο

Technically, μ and ν are nasals, but usually the forms in this pattern are simply referred to as liquid aorists. The stem ending (λ, μ, ν, or ρ) causes the σ to drop, but the endings are not modified. The stem is usually lengthened.

Root Aorist Active

	ἵστημι	ἀναβαίνω	γίνωσκω
1 Sg.	ἔστην	ἀνέβην	ἔγνων
2 Sg.	ἔστης	ἀνέβης	ἔγνως
3 Sg.	ἔστη	ἀνέβη	ἔγνω
1 Pl.	ἔστημεν	ἀνέβημεν	ἔγνωμεν
2 Pl.	ἔστητε	ἀνέβητε	ἔγνωτε
3 Pl.	ἔστησαν	ἀνέβησαν	ἔγνωσαν

The personal endings are added directly to the root, that is, the stem. There are not many root aorists, but some of them are common.[23]

K Aorist Active and Middle

Act.	τίθημι	δίδωμι	ἀφίημι
1 Sg.	ἔθηκα	ἔδωκα	ἀφῆκα
2 Sg.	ἔθηκας	ἔδωκας	ἀφῆκας
3 Sg.	ἔθηκε(ν)	ἔδωκε(ν)	ἀφῆκε(ν)
1 Pl.	ἐθήκαμεν	ἐδώκαμεν	ἀφήκαμεν
2 Pl.	ἐθήκατε	ἐδώκατε	ἀφήκατε
3 Pl.	ἔθηκαν	ἔδωκαν	ἀφῆκαν
Mid.			
1 Sg.	ἐθέμην	ἐδόμην	
2 Sg.	ἔθου	ἔδου	
3 Sg.	ἔθετο	ἔδοτο	
1 Pl.	ἐθέμεθα	ἐδόμεθα	
2 Pl.	ἔθεσθε	ἔδοσθε	
3 Pl.	ἔθεντο	ἔδοντο	

A κ replaces the σ in the tense-form sign for the aorist of three important μι verbs. They are κ aorists in the active and root aorists in the middle (the aorist middle of ἀφίημι is not given, since it is not used in the LXX or GNT).[24]

23. See further Funk, §411; Mounce, *Morphology*, 102–4.
24. See further Funk, §§412–4120; Mounce, *Morphology*, 101. Smyth (*Grammar*, §777) lists the forms of ἵημι, the root of ἀφίημι. See also table 7, note *a*, under "Principal Parts" below.

Aorist Passive

	πιστεύω	γράφω
1 Sg.	ἐπιστεύθην	ἐγράφην
2 Sg.	ἐπιστεύθης	ἐγράφης
3 Sg.	ἐπιστεύθη	ἐγράφη
1 Pl.	ἐπιστεύθημεν	ἐγράφημεν
2 Pl.	ἐπιστεύθητε	ἐγράφητε
3 Pl.	ἐπιστεύθησαν	ἐγράφησαν

The tense-form sign of the 1 aorist passive is θη, and that of the 2 aorist passive is simply η. The weird thing about aorist passives is that they take active endings, but the person and number are still clear.[25]

Pluperfect Active

	λύω	γράφω
1 Sg.	ἐλελύκειν	ἐγεγράφειν
2 Sg.	ἐλελύκεις	ἐγεγράφεις
3 Sg.	ἐλελύκει(ν)	ἐγεγράφει(ν)
1 Pl.	ἐλελύκειμεν	ἐγεγράφειμεν
2 Pl.	ἐλελύκειτε	ἐγεγράφειτε
3 Pl.	ἐλελύκεισαν	ἐγεγράφεισαν

- An augment is usually added to the perfect stem.
- The tense-form sign κει distinguishes the pluperfect active.
- The second pluperfect simply lacks the κ in the tense-form sign.

Pluperfect Middle/Passive

	λύω
1 Sg.	ἐλελύμην
2 Sg.	ἐλέλυσο
3 Sg.	ἐλέλυτο
1 Pl.	ἐλελύμεθα
2 Pl.	ἐλέλυσθε
3 Pl.	ἐλέλυντο

25. For recent discussion of the significance of θη forms, see app. 5.

Here we have the same ingredients as the pluperfect active, though with middle/passive endings, of course.

Subjunctive Mood

	Pres.	1 Aor.	2 Aor.
Act.	λύω	λύω	λείπω
1 Sg.	λύω	λύσω	λίπω
2 Sg.	λύῃς	λύσῃς	λίπῃς
3 Sg.	λύῃ	λύσῃ	λίπῃ
1 Pl.	λύωμεν	λύσωμεν	λίπωμεν
2 Pl.	λύητε	λύσητε	λίπητε
3 Pl.	λύωσι(ν)	λύσωσι(ν)	λίπωσι(ν)
Mid.			
1 Sg.	λύωμαι	λύσωμαι	λίπωμαι
2 Sg.	λύῃ	λύσῃ	λίπῃ
3 Sg.	λύηται	λύσηται	λίπηται
1 Pl.	λυώμεθα	λυσώμεθα	λιπώμεθα
2 Pl.	λύησθε	λύσησθε	λίπησθε
3 Pl.	λύωνται	λύσωνται	λίπωνται
Pass.			γράφω
1 Sg.	λύωμαι	λυθῶ	γραφῶ
2 Sg.	λύῃ	λυθῇς	γραφῇς
3 Sg.	λύηται	λυθῇ	γραφῇ
1 Pl.	λυώμεθα	λυθῶμεν	γραφῶμεν
2 Pl.	λύησθε	λυθῆτε	γραφῆτε
3 Pl.	λύωνται	λυθῶσι(ν)	γραφῶσι(ν)

A Sample μι Verb: τίθημι

	Pres. Act.	Pres. Mid./ Pass.	Aor. Act.	Aor. Mid.
1 Sg.	τιθῶ	τιθῶμαι	θῶ	θῶμαι
2 Sg.	τιθῇς	τιθῇ	θῇς	θῇ
3 Sg.	τιθῇ	τιθῆται	θῇ	θῆται
1 Pl.	τιθῶμεν	τιθώμεθα	θῶμεν	θώμεθα
2 Pl.	τιθῆτε	τιθῆσθε	θῆτε	θῆσθε
3 Pl.	τιθῶσι	τιθῶνται	θῶσι	θῶνται

- The distinctive characteristic of the subjunctive is the long vowels η and ω. These represent the lengthening of variable vowels.
- The subjunctive uses the same personal endings as the indicative.
- The variable vowel ει lengthens the ε to η, and ι is subscripted: ῃ.
- The main problem with identifying the subjunctive is that some of its forms are identical with other verb forms.
- The present subjunctive of εἰμί is simply the lengthened variable vowel plus the ending of the present active: ὦ, ᾖς, ᾖ, ὦμεν, ᾖτε, ὦσι.

Optative Mood

	Pres.	1 Aor.	2 Aor.
Act.	λύω	λύω	γίνομαι
1 Sg.	λύοιμι	λύσαιμι	γένοιμι
2 Sg.	λύοις	λύσαις	γένοις
3 Sg.	λύοι	λύσαι	γένοι
1 Pl.	λύοιμεν	λύσαιμεν	γένοιμεν
2 Pl.	λύοιτε	λύσαιτε	γένοιτε
3 Pl.	λύοιεν	λύσαιεν	γένοιεν
Mid./Pass.	Mid.	Mid.	
1 Sg.	λυοίμην	λυσαίμην	γενοίμην
2 Sg.	λύοιο	λύσαιο	γένοιο
3 Sg.	λύοιτο	λύσαιτο	γένοιτο
1 Pl.	λυοίμεθα	λυσαίμεθα	γενοίμεθα
2 Pl.	λύοισθε	λύσαισθε	γένοισθε
3 Pl.	λύοιντο	λύσαιντο	γένοιντο

- The optative is rare in the GNT.[26] It is limited primarily to the present and the aorist, both using secondary endings except μι.
- The distinctive characteristic of the optative is an ι added to the variable vowel, though ιε in the active 3 pl.
- The variable vowel in the present is ο combined with the ι.
- The middle 2 sg. ending σο loses its σ when it is added to the variable vowel οι in the present and to σαι in the 1 aorist.

---

26. According to Mounce (*Morphology*, 135), the optative is used 68 times in the NT, only in present and aorist. Of these, εἴη (3 sg. act. Pres. opt. < εἰμί) occurs 12 times, and γένοιτο (3 sg. mid. Aor. opt. < γίνομαι) occurs 17 times, including 15 times in Paul's expression μὴ γένοιτο.

- The μι verbs use ιη in some forms instead of a simple ι. Only εἴη (3 sg. act. Pres. opt. from εἰμί) occurs with any frequency in the GNT.
- The 2 aorist uses the same pattern as the present, but with a 2 aorist stem, of course.[27]

Imperative Mood

The imperative is recognized by its endings, so its endings are another of the core patterns to be familiar with. These are the endings you see on verbs as you are reading, but not all of these forms are the actual endings. For example, the 2 sg. active ending is actually a zero form, and the ε is the variable vowel. So these endings work for reading purposes, which is the focus of this chapter.[28]

Imperative Endings

	Act.	Mid./Pass.
2 Sg.	ε, σον	σο, ου, σαι, θι, τι
3 Sg.	τω	σθω
2 Pl.	τε	σθε
3 Pl.	τωσαν	σθωσαν

In the aorist, the lack of augment is a further sign of the imperative. Because the contract verbs cause problems in some forms of the present imperative, I include their paradigms. Their forms are clear in the aorist, but I include them for comparison.[29]

Present Imperative

Act.	λύω	γεννάω	ποιέω	φανερόω
2 Sg.	λῦε	γέννα	ποίει	φανέρου
3 Sg.	λυέτω	γεννάτω	ποιείτω	φανερούτω
2 Pl.	λύετε	γεννᾶτε	ποιεῖτε	φανεροῦτε
3 Pl.	λυέτωσαν	γεννάτωσαν	ποιείτωσαν	φανερούτωσαν

27. The 2 aorist passive occurs five times in the GNT, all in the 3 sg. -θείη (1 Thess. 5:23; 2 Tim. 4:16; 1 Pet. 1:2; 2 Pet. 1:2; Jude 2).

28. For more precise and detailed descriptions, see Funk, §§0455–4630; and Mounce, *Morphology*, 143–48.

29. In addition to the present and the aorist imperatives, there is also a perfect imperative. It occurs five times in the GNT (Mark 4:39; Acts 15:29; Eph. 5:5; Heb. 12:17; James 1:19). See Mounce, *Morphology*, 146–47; Funk, §462.

	λύω	γεννάω	ποιέω	φανερόω
Mid./Pass.				
2 Sg.	λύου	γεννῶ	ποιοῦ	φανεροῦ
3 Sg.	λυέσθω	γεννάσθω	ποιείσθω	φανερούσθω
2 Pl.	λύεσθε	γεννᾶσθε	ποιεῖσθε	φανεροῦσθε
3 Pl.	λυέσθωσαν	γεννάσθωσαν	ποιείσθωσαν	φανερούσθωσαν

Present Imperative of Some μι Verbs

Act.	ἵστημι	τίθημι	δίδωμι	ἀφίημι
2 Sg.	ἵστη[a]	τίθει	δίδου	ἀφίει
3 Sg.	ἱστάτω	τιθέτω	διδότω	ἀφιέτω
2 Pl.	ἵστατε	τίθετε	δίδοτε	ἀφίετε
3 Pl.	ἱστάτωσαν	τιθέτωσαν	διδότωσαν	ἀφιέτωσαν
Mid./Pass.				
2 Sg.	ἵστασο	τίθεσο	δίδοσο	ἀφίεσο
3 Sg.	ἱστάσθω	τιθέσθω	διδόσθω	ἀφιέσθω
2 Pl.	ἵστασθε	τίθεσθε	δίδοσθε	ἀφίεσθε
3 Pl.	ἱστάσθωσαν	τιθέσθωσαν	διδόσθωσαν	ἀφιέσθωσαν

a. Ἵστη has no ending. The η is a lengthened stem ending.

Note the form of the present imperative of εἰμί, one of the core patterns to know well.

Present Imperative of εἰμί

2 Sg.	ἴσθι
3 Sg.	ἔστω
2 Pl.	ἔστε
3 Pl.	ἔστωσαν

1 Aorist Imperative

Act.	λύω	γεννάω	ποιέω	φανερόω
2 Sg.	λῦσον[a]	γέννησον	ποίησον	φανέρωσον
3 Sg.	λυσάτω	γεννησάτω	ποιησάτω	φανερωσάτω
2 Pl.	λύσατε	γεννήσατε	ποιήσατε	φανερώσατε
3 Pl.	λυσάτωσαν	γεννησάτωσαν	ποιησάτωσαν	φανερωσάτωσαν

	λύω	γεννάω	ποιέω	φανερόω
Mid.				
2 Sg.	λῦσαι[a]	γέννησαι	ποίησαι	φανέρωσαι
3 Sg.	λυσάσθω	γεννησάσθω	ποιησάσθω	φανερωσάσθω
2 Pl.	λύσασθε	γεννήσασθε	ποιήσασθε	φανερώσασθε
3 Pl.	λυσάσθωσαν	γεννησάσθωσαν	ποιησάσθωσαν	φανερωσάσθωσαν

a. According to Mounce (*Morphology*, 145n1), "there is no obvious reason" for the 2 sg. σον and σαι endings.

	2 Aor. Act.	1 Aor. Pass.	2 Aor. Pass.	Perf. Act.
	βάλλω	λύω	γράφω	λύω
2 Sg.	βάλε	λύθητι	γράφηθι	λέλυκε
3 Sg.	βαλέτω	λυθήτω	γραφήτω	λελυκέτω
2 Pl.	βάλετε	λύθητε	γράφητε	λελύκετε
3 Pl.	βαλέτωσαν	λυθήτωσαν	γραφήτωσαν	λελυκέτωσαν
	2 Aor. Mid.			**Perf. Mid./Pass.**
2 Sg.	βαλοῦ			λέλυσο
3 Sg.	βαλέσθω			λελύσθω
2 Pl.	βάλεσθε			λέλυσθε
3 Pl.	βαλέσθωσαν			λελύσθωσαν

Aorist Imperative of Some μι Verbs

	ἵστημι	τίθημι	δίδωμι	ἀφίημι
Act.				
2 Sg.	στῆθι	θές	δός	ἄφες
3 Sg.	στήτω	θέτω	δότω	ἀφέτω
2 Pl.	στῆτε	θέτε	δότε	ἄφετε
3 Pl.	στήτωσαν	θέτωσαν	δότωσαν	ἀφέτωσαν
Mid.				
2 Sg.	στῶ	θοῦ	δοῦ	
3 Sg.	στάσθω	θέσθω	δόσθω	
2 Pl.	στάσθε	θέσθε	δόσθε	
3 Pl.	στάσθωσαν	θέσθωσαν	δόσθωσαν	

Infinitive

An infinitive is recognized by its ending. The following endings form a core pattern to know well.[30]

Infinitive Endings

εν [ειν]   ι [σαι]   ναι   σθαι

- The bracketed forms are the endings as they appear. Ειν is the variable vowel ε contracted with the infinitive ending εν in the present and 2 aorist. Σαι is the tense-form suffix σα of the 1 aorist with the infinitive ending ι. The ending εν contracts differently in the contract verbs, where the stem endings are included in the contraction. For example, an α contract verb will contract with εν to form ᾶν.
- The other two endings, ναι and σθαι, behave themselves and are easy to recognize.
- The present infinitive of εἰμί is εἶναι, which you should learn.

Present Infinitives

	λύω	γεννάω	ποιέω	φανερόω
Act.	λύειν	γεννᾶν	ποιεῖν	φανεροῦν
Mid./Pass.	λύεσθαι	γεννᾶσθαι	ποιεῖσθαι	φανεροῦσθαι

Present Infinitives of Some μι Verbs

	ἵστημι	τίθημι	δίδωμι	δείκνυμι
Act.	ἱστάναι	τιθέναι	διδόναι	δεικνύναι
Mid./Pass.	ἵστασθαι	τίθεσθαι	δίδοσθαι	δείκνυσθαι

1 Aorist Infinitives

	λύω	γεννάω	ποιέω	φανερόω
Act.	λῦσαι	γεννῆσαι	ποιῆσαι	φανερῶσαι
Mid.	λύσασθαι	γεννήσασθαι	ποιήσασθαι	φανερώσασθαι
Pass.	λυθῆναι	γεννηθῆναι	ποιηθῆναι	φανερωθῆναι

30. For a more complete description of infinitive endings, see Funk, §§464–4662; and Mounce, *Morphology*, 148–50.

2 Aorist Infinitive

	βάλλω
Act.	βαλεῖν
Mid.	βαλέσθαι

Aorist Active and Middle Infinitives of Some μι Verbs

	ἵστημι	τίθημι	δίδωμι	ἀφίημι
Act.	στῆναι	θεῖναι	δοῦναι	ἀφεῖναι
Mid.		θέσθαι	δόσθαι	ἀφέσθαι

Perfect Infinitives

	λύω	γεννάω	ποιέω	φανερόω
Act.	λελυκέναι	γεγεννηκέναι	πεποιηκέναι	πεφανερωκέναι
Mid./Pass.	λελῦσθαι	γεγεννῆσθαι	πεποιῆσθαι	πεφανερῶσθαι

Participle

The participle adds to the verb stem one of the three stem formatives (ντ, οτ, μεν), to which are then added adjective endings. The ντ formative signals an active participle or aorist passive, μεν signals a middle or passive participle, and οτ signals a perfect active participle. More specifically:

ντ	Pres. Act.
	Fut. Act.
	Aor. Act.
	Aor. Pass.
μεν	Pres. Mid./Pass.
	Fut. Mid.
	Fut. Pass.
	Aor. Mid.
	Perf. Mid./Pass.
οτ	Perf. Act.

The paradigm of πᾶς, one of the core patterns for adjectives, is the model for participles with ντ. These patterns and the perfect active follow 3-1-3 adjectives. The middle and passive participles that use μεν follow 2-1-2 adjectives. The following "participle box" is a core pattern. It contains the nom. sg. endings and the stem formative for the main paradigms of the participle.

The material in this participle box, in conjunction with an understanding of adjective endings, provides all you need in order to recognize most participles.

Participle Box

	Masc.	Fem.	Neut.	Stem Formative		Stem Formative
Pres./2 Aor. Act.	ων	ουσα	ον	οντ	Mid./Pass.	ομεν
1 Aor. Act.	σας	σασα	σαν	σαντ	Mid.	σαμεν
Aor. Pass.	θεις	θεισα	θεν	θεντ		
Perf. Act.	κως	κυια	κος	κοτ	Mid./Pass.	μεν

- The future is not included; its paradigm is identical to the present but with the σ tense-form sign added.
- The three nom. sg. forms include two of the difficult forms in these paradigms. Specifically, the masc. sg. and neut. sg. forms require special attention because τ cannot end a word, and it drops out when σ is added.[31]

  The neut. sg. uses the zero form, which is the normal neut. sg. ending in the third declension: λυ - οντ - – > λύον.

  The masc. sg. also uses a zero form, which is one of the two options for the masc. sg. in the third declension, but in this case the vowel lengthens, enabling this form to be distinguished from the neut. sg. we just looked at: λυ - οντ - – > λύον > λύων.

  Similarly, in the perfect masc. sg. a ς ending is used, so the τ drops and the vowel lengthens: λε - λυ - κ - οτ - ς > λελυκώς.
- The perfect neut. sg. is irregular,[32] but learning it as part of this pattern means you will be able to recognize it.
- The fem. sg. represents σ added before the stem formatives, which causes the ντ and the οτ to drop out and the vowel to lengthen. This pattern occurs throughout the feminine participle, so use these forms in the participle box to remember this distinctive characteristic of the feminine.
- In 3-1-3 patterns the dat. pl. ending is σι(ν), the σ of which causes the same dropping of the ντ and lengthening of the vowel as in the feminine. So you should use the fem. sg. form in the box to remind yourself of this characteristic as well: λυ - ο - ντ - σι(ν) > λύουσι(ν). These dat. pl. forms are probably easiest to misidentify since they sometimes look like indicative verbs in the 3 pl.

31. This feature also occurs in the feminine forms, discussed below.
32. For attempts at an explanation, see Funk, §249.2; and Mounce, *Morphology*, 157n4.

- The present participle of εἰμί is the same as the endings on the present active participle given below. So the nom. sg. forms are ὤν, οὖσα, ὄν, and the gen. sg. are ὄντος, οὔσης, ὄντος, and so forth.

Present Active Participle

Sg.	Masc.	Fem.	Neut.
Nom.	λύων	λύουσα	λῦον
Gen.	λύοντος	λυούσης	λύοντος
Dat.	λύοντι	λυούσῃ	λύοντι
Acc.	λύοντα	λύουσαν	λῦον
Pl.			
Nom.	λύοντες	λύουσαι	λύοντα
Gen.	λυόντων	λυουσῶν	λυόντων
Dat.	λύουσι(ν)	λυούσαις	λύουσι(ν)
Acc.	λύοντας	λυούσας	λύοντα

Present Middle/Passive Participle

Sg.	Masc.	Fem.	Neut.
Nom.	λυόμενος	λυομένη	λυόμενον
Gen.	λυομένου	λυομένης	λυομένου
Dat.	λυομένῳ	λυομένῃ	λυομένῳ
Acc.	λυόμενον	λυομένην	λυόμενον
Pl.			
Nom.	λυόμενοι	λυόμεναι	λυόμενα
Gen.	λυομένων	λυομένων	λυομένων
Dat.	λυομένοις	λυομέναις	λυομένοις
Acc.	λυομένους	λυομένας	λυόμενα

1 Aorist Active Participle

Sg.	Masc.	Fem.	Neut.
Nom.	λύσας	λύσασα	λῦσαν
Gen.	λύσαντος	λυσάσης	λύσαντος
Dat.	λύσαντι	λυσάσῃ	λύσαντι
Acc.	λύσαντα	λύσασαν	λῦσαν

Pl.	Masc.	Fem.	Neut.
Nom.	λύσαντες	λύσασαι	λύσαντα
Gen.	λυσάντων	λυσασῶν	λυσάντων
Dat.	λύσασι(ν)	λυσάσαις	λύσασι(ν)
Acc.	λύσαντας	λυσάσας	λύσαντα

1 Aorist Middle Participle

Sg.	Masc.	Fem.	Neut.
Nom.	λυσάμενος	λυσαμένη	λυσάμενον
Gen.	λυσαμένου	λυσαμένης	λυσαμένου
Dat.	λυσαμένῳ	λυσαμένῃ	λυσαμένῳ
Acc.	λυσάμενον	λυσαμένην	λυσάμενον
Pl.			
Nom.	λυσάμενοι	λυσάμεναι	λυσάμενα
Gen.	λυσαμένων	λυσαμένων	λυσαμένων
Dat.	λυσαμένοις	λυσαμέναις	λυσαμένοις
Acc.	λυσαμένους	λυσαμένας	λυσάμενα

1 Aorist Passive Participle

Sg.	Masc.	Fem.	Neut.
Nom.	λυθείς	λυθεῖσα	λυθέν
Gen.	λυθέντος	λυθείσης	λυθέντος
Dat.	λυθέντι	λυθείσῃ	λυθέντι
Acc.	λυθέντα	λυθεῖσαν	λυθέν
Pl.			
Nom.	λυθέντες	λυθεῖσαι	λυθέντα
Gen.	λυθέντων	λυθεισῶν	λυθέντων
Dat.	λυθεῖσι(ν)	λυθείσαις	λυθεῖσι(ν)
Acc.	λυθέντας	λυθείσας	λυθέντα

2 Aorist Active Participle

The 2 Aorist Active Participle forms of γίνομαι are as follows.

Sg.	Masc.	Fem.	Neut.
Nom.	γενών	γενοῦσα	γενόν
Gen.	γενόντος	γενούσης	γενόντος
Dat.	γενόντι	γενούσῃ	γενόντι
Acc.	γενόντα	γενοῦσαν	γενόν
Pl.			
Nom.	γενόντες	γενοῦσαι	γενόντα
Gen.	γενόντων	γενουσῶν	γενόντων
Dat.	γενοῦσι(ν)	γενούσαις	γενοῦσι(ν)
Acc.	γενόντας	γενούσας	γενόντα

2 Aorist Middle Participle

The 2 Aorist Middle Participle forms of γίνομαι are as follows.

Sg.	Masc.	Fem.	Neut.
Nom.	γενόμενος	γενομένη	γενόμενον
Gen.	γενομένου	γενομένης	γενομένου
Dat.	γενομένῳ	γενομένῃ	γενομένῳ
Acc.	γενόμενον	γενομένην	γενόμενον
Pl.			
Nom.	γενόμενοι	γενόμεναι	γενόμενα
Gen.	γενομένων	γενομένων	γενομένων
Dat.	γενομένοις	γενομέναις	γενομένοις
Acc.	γενομένους	γενομένας	γενόμενα

2 Aorist Passive Participle

The 2 Aorist Passive Participle forms of γράφω are as follows.

Sg.	Masc.	Fem.	Neut.
Nom.	γραφείς	γραφεῖσα	γραφέν
Gen.	γραφέντος	γραφείσης	γραφέντος
Dat.	γραφέντι	γραφείσῃ	γραφέντι
Acc.	γραφέντα	γραφεῖσαν	γραφέν

Pl.	Masc.	Fem.	Neut.
Nom.	γραφέντες	γραφεῖσαι	γραφέντα
Gen.	γραφέντων	γραφεισῶν	γραφέντων
Dat.	γραφεῖσι(ν)	γραφείσαις	γραφεῖσι(ν)
Acc.	γραφέντας	γραφείσας	γραφέντα

Perfect Active Participle

Sg.	Masc.	Fem.	Neut.
Nom.	λελυκώς	λελυκυῖα	λελυκός
Gen.	λελυκότος	λελυκυίας	λελυκότος
Dat.	λελυκότι	λελυκυίᾳ	λελυκότι
Acc.	λελυκότα	λελυκυῖαν	λελυκός
Pl.			
Nom.	λελυκότες	λελυκυῖαι	λελυκότα
Gen.	λελυκότων	λελυκυιῶν	λελυκότων
Dat.	λελυκόσι(ν)	λελυκυίαις	λελυκόσι(ν)
Acc.	λελυκότας	λελυκυίας	λελυκότα

Perfect Middle/Passive Participle

Sg.	Masc.	Fem.	Neut.
Nom.	λελυμένος	λελυμένη	λελυμένον
Gen.	λελυμένου	λελυμένης	λελυμένου
Dat.	λελυμένῳ	λελυμένη	λελυμένῳ
Acc.	λελυμένον	λελυμένην	λελυμένον
Pl.			
Nom.	λελυμένοι	λελυμέναι	λελυμένα
Gen.	λελυμένων	λελυμένων	λελυμένων
Dat.	λελυμένοις	λελυμέναις	λελυμένοις
Acc.	λελυμένους	λελυμένας	λελυμένα

Principal Parts

The three principal parts of a verb in English are the root or base (which is identical with the infinitive), the simple past, and the past participle. Some English verbs retain one root through the different forms (to study: study, studied, studied), while other verbs have modified roots (to sing: sing, sang, sung) or different roots altogether (to go: go, went, gone).[33] In basic Greek you learned that verbs in Greek can have six principal parts:

1. present active/middle/passive
2. future active/middle
3. aorist active/middle
4. perfect active
5. perfect middle/passive
6. aorist passive

As in English, some Greek verbs retain one root through all six principal parts, while others do not. "Root," or "base," refers to the underlying form from which a verb's tense-forms are derived. "Stem" refers to the basic form in each of the six principal parts. So, for example, the present tense-form stem of βάλλω is βαλλ-, but the root of this verb is *βαλ, which shows up more clearly outside the present tense-form, as we will see. An asterisk (*) is used to indicate a root/base.

Lexicons list verbs by the present tense-form, and we learn vocabulary using the present tense-form, but the actual root is found in the aorist. "The present tense is, in fact, the most 'irregular' of all the tenses and the second aorist is one of the most 'regular.'"[34] So by paying attention to the root and the present tense-form stem, it is often possible to recognize the forms of a verb even though the principal parts undergo changes. Since the present tense-form is often modified from the basic root, it is common to distinguish patterns of principal parts by how the present tense-form changes. There are quite a few patterns and also variations within some of the patterns.

The following list is not comprehensive but represents the major patterns for verbs in the GNT. For some patterns a number of examples are given in order to include the verbs that cause particular difficulty among verbs occurring 50 times or more in the GNT. Funk and Mounce provide comprehensive lists, with detailed discussion of all the patterns and explanations of the morphological changes represented.[35]

---

33. For more detail, see Funk, §301.

34. Mounce, *Morphology*, 73.

35. Funk, §§477–496.5; and Mounce, *Morphology*, 73–78, both of whom make use of Smyth, *Grammar*, §§367–79. Mounce includes analysis of all the verbs of the New Testament. Funk's first two editions included a list of all the verbs in the GNT and the Apostolic Fathers arranged by pattern. This list is now available online at Westar Institute (see bibliography). A more simplified survey of the patterns is given in Wilbert Francis Howard, *Accidence and Word-Formation with an Appendix on Semitisms in the New Testament*, vol. 2 of *A Grammar of New Testament Greek*, by James Hope Moulton, Wilbert Francis Howard, and Nigel Turner (Edinburgh: T&T Clark, 1919, 1920, 1929), 183–85. Mounce has a helpful introduction to verb formation in his

I have listed the root, since comparing the principal parts with the underlying root is often helpful. Scholars do not agree on the form of the roots of some of these verbs, so you will find different roots listed in different resources.[36] For the purposes of reading, the roots—and the patterns themselves—are only means to the end of being able to recognize the tense-form and the verb. So just use them when they help you in that way. For many verbs, if you know the present and either the root or the aorist active form, you can recognize the other forms once you are familiar with the general characteristics of these basic patterns.

You should study these patterns to familiarize yourself with the general characteristics of each pattern. Often the minor changes come in the vowels, so pay special attention to the consonants since they are more constant. In order to be able to read Greek you do not need to memorize all the forms of a verb in detail, though for some of the most irregular verbs you will probably need to do so, especially those that use more than one root. In each case, the point is not to be able to recite from memory lists of principal parts. Rather, for each form in each pattern, ask yourself if you are likely to be able both to recognize the tense-form and to have an idea of what the lexical form might look like when you meet that form while reading.

1. Verbs with roots ending in a vowel and no changes—apart from normal lengthening of variable vowels in contract verbs

Pres.	Fut.	Aor. A/M	Perf. Act.	Perf. M/P	Aor. Pass.	Root
πιστεύω	πιστεύσω	ἐπίστευσα	πεπίστευκα	πεπίστευμαι	ἐπιστεύθην	*πιστευ
ἀγαπάω	ἀγαπήσω	ἠγάπησα	ἠγάπηκα	ἠγάπημαι	ἠγαπήθην	*ἀγαπα
τηρέω	τηρήσω	ἐτήρησα	τετήρηκα	τετήρημαι	ἐτηρήθην	*τηρε
πληρόω	πληρώσω	ἐπλήρωσα	πεπλήρωκα	πεπλήρωμαι	ἐπληρώθην	*πληρο

2. Verbs with roots ending in a labial (π, β, φ), velar (κ, γ, χ), or dental (τ, δ, θ)

A. Verbs with a simple ending, often with minor stem changes

---

basic textbook, *Basics of Biblical Greek*, 3rd ed. (Grand Rapids: Zondervan, 2009), 168–76. A list of the principal parts of all the verbs used in the GNT is included in William C. Trenchard, *The Student's Complete Vocabulary Guide to the Greek New Testament: Complete Frequency Lists, Cognate Groupings & Principal Parts*, rev. ed. (Grand Rapids: Zondervan, 1998), 237–72.

36. Indeed, there are a number of differences among scholars on how to analyze and organize the patterns of the principal parts.

Pres.	Fut.	Aor. A/M	Perf. Act.	Perf. M/P	Aor. Pass.	Root
ἄγω	ἄξω	ἤγαγον	ἦχα	ἦγμαι	ἤχθην	*ἀγαγ
γράφω	γράψω	ἔγραψα	γέγραφα	γέγραμμαι	ἐγράφην	*γραφ
ἔχω	ἕξω	ἔσχον	ἔσχηκα			*σχ
πείθω	πείσω	ἔπεισα	πέποιθα	πέπεισμαι	ἐπείσθην	*πειθ

B. Verbs with the present ending augmented to -πτω, -σσω, -ζω[37]

Pres.	Fut.	Aor. A/M	Perf. Act.	Perf. M/P	Aor. Pass.	Root
ἑτοιμάζω	ἑτοιμάσω	ἡτοίμασα	ἡτοίμακα	ἡτοίμασμαι	ἡτοιμάσθην	*ἑτοιμαδ
καθαρίζω	καθαριῶ[a]	ἐκαθάρισα		κεκαθάρισμαι	ἐκαθαρίσθην	*καθαριδ
κηρύσσω	κηρύξω	ἐκήρυξα	κεκήρυχα	κεκήρυγμαι	ἐκηρύχθην	*κηρυκ
κρύπτω	κρύψω	ἔκρυψα		κέκρυμμαι	ἐκρύβην	*κρυφ
σῴζω	σώσω	ἔσωσα	σέσωκα	σέσωσμαι	ἐσώθην	*σωδ

a. This verb has a liquid form of the future. Some other verbs in this pattern have the more expected form -ισω in the future.

3. Verbs with roots ending in a liquid (λ, ρ) or nasal (μ, ν)

Recall that the future paradigms of liquids and nasals look like ε contract present endings.

A. Verbs with a simple ending, with minor stem changes

Pres.	Fut.	Aor. A/M	Perf. Act.	Perf. M/P	Aor. Pass.	Root
κρίνω	κρινῶ	ἔκρινα	κέκρικα	κέκριμαι	ἐκρίθην	*κριν

B. Verbs with minor stem changes and the present ending augmented by doubling a λ or adding an ι

Pres.	Fut.	Aor. A/M	Perf. Act.	Perf. M/P	Aor. Pass.	Root
ἀποστέλλω	ἀποστελῶ	ἀπέστειλα	ἀπέσταλκα	ἀπέσταλμαι	ἀπεστάλην	*ἀποστειλ
βάλλω	βαλῶ	ἔβαλον	βέβληκα	βέβλημαι	ἐβλήθην	*βαλ
αἴρω	ἀρῶ	ἦρα	ἦρκα	ἦρμαι	ἤρθην	*ἀρ
χαίρω	χαρήσομαι				ἐχάρην	*χαρ

37. The consonantal iota (ι) is a letter that dropped out of use long before the Hellenistic period, but it accounts for the form of some words. See Funk, §§905, 932; Mounce, *Morphology*, 43–45. In this pattern, its addition to the present stem changes a dental to ζ, a velar to σσ, and a labial to πτ.

4. Verbs with minor stem changes and the present augmented by adding σκ or ισκ

Pres.	Fut.	Aor. A/M	Perf. Act.	Perf. M/P	Aor. Pass.	Root
γινώσκω	γνώσομαι	ἔγνων	ἔγνωκα	ἔγνωσμαι	ἐγνώσθην	*γνω
εὑρίσκω	εὑρήσω	εὗρον	εὕρηκα	εὕρημαι	εὑρέθην	*εὑρ

5. Verbs with minor stem changes and the present augmented by adding νυ

Pres.	Fut.	Aor. A/M	Perf. Act.	Perf. M/P	Aor. Pass.	Root
δείκνυμι	δείξω	ἔδειξα	δέδειχα	δέδειγμαι	ἐδείχθην	*δεικ
ἀπόλλυμι[a]	ἀπολέσω	ἀπώλεσα	ἀπόλωλα			*ἀπολεσ, *ἀπολ

a. "When the νυ is added to form the present tense stem, the ν totally assimilates to λ" (Mounce, *Morphology*, 309n5). See Mounce, *Morphology*, 309, for explanations of the irregularities in the other principal parts of this verb.

6. Verbs with stem changes and the present augmented by adding αν

Pres.	Fut.	Aor. A/M	Perf. Act.	Perf. M/P	Aor. Pass.	Root
λαμβάνω[a]	λήμψομαι	ἔλαβον	εἴληφα	εἴλημμαι	ἐλήμφθην	*λαβ
ἀναβαίνω	ἀναβήσομαι	ἀνέβην	ἀναβέβηκα			*βη

a. "If the last vowel of the stem is short, another nasal is inserted after this vowel" (Funk, §485.20); hence the μ in the stem.

7. Verbs whose stems reduplicate in the present, including most μι verbs

Pres.	Fut.	Aor. A/M	Perf. Act.	Perf. M/P	Aor. Pass.	Root
ἀφίημι[a]	ἀφήσω	ἀφῆκα	ἀφεῖκα	ἀφεῖμαι	ἀφέθην	*ἀφε[ι]
γίνομαι[b]	γενήσομαι	ἐγενόμην	γέγονα	γεγένημαι	ἐγενήθην	*γεν
δίδωμι	δώσω	ἔδωκα	δέδωκα	δέδομαι	ἐδόθην	*δο
ἵστημι[c]	στήσω	ἔστησα	ἔστηκα	ἔσταμαι	ἐστάθην	*στη, *στα
πίπτω	πεσοῦμαι	ἔπεσον	πέπτωκα			*πετ, *πτω
τίθημι	θήσω	ἔθηκα	τέθεικα	τέθειμαι	ἐτέθην	*θε

a. This verb is a compound of ἀπό and ἵημι. The reduplication on ἵημι is no longer evident in this form. For details, see Funk, §345.2; and Mounce, *Morphology*, 314n9. There are six compound verbs in the GNT using ἵημι. As the root suggests, a rough rule for these verbs is that if you take everything off the front and back and only an ε in some form (that is, ε, ει, or η) remains, expect the verb to be a compound with ἵημι.

b. Γίνομαι is included here because in earlier Greek the present was reduplicated: γίγνομαι. See Funk, §345.2; Mounce, *Morphology*, 266n1.

c. This verb doubles from στα to σιστα and drops the initial σ. See Funk, §345.2; Mounce, *Morphology*, 88n1.

8. Verb systems that use more than one root
This list includes all the words in the GNT that use more than one root.

Pres.	Fut.	Aor. A/M	Perf. Act.	Perf. M/P	Aor. Pass.	Root
αἱρέω	αἱρήσομαι	εἱλόμην		ᾕρημαι	ᾑρέθην	*αἱρε, *ϝελ[a]
ἔρχομαι	ἐλεύσομαι	ἦλθον	ἐλήλυθα			*ερχ, *ἐλευθ, *ελθ
ἐσθίω	φάγομαι	ἔφαγον				*εσθ, *φαγ
λέγω	ἐρῶ	εἶπον	εἴρηκα	εἴρημαι	ἐρρέθην	*εἰπ, *ϝερ, *ϝεπ
οἶδα	εἰδήσω	ᾔδειν				*οιδ, *ϝιδ
ὁράω	ὄψομαι	εἶδον	ἑώρακα		ὤφθην	*ϝορα, *οπ, *ϝιδ
πάσχω		ἔπαθον	πέπονθα			*παθ, *πονθ
πίνω	πίομαι	ἔπιον	πέπωκα	πέπομαι	ἐπόθην	*πι, *πο, *πω
τρέχω		ἔδραμον				*τρεχ, *δραμ
φέρω	οἴσω	ἤνεγκα	ἐνήνοχα		ἠνέχθην	*φερ, *οι, *ἐνεγκ

a. Like the consonantal iota, the digamma (ϝ) is a letter that dropped out of use by the Hellenistic period, but it accounts for the form of some words. For details, see Funk, §§905, 933; Mounce, *Morphology*, 45–47.

4

MAKING SENSE OF SENTENCES

Courses in basic Greek introduce the major features of grammar and syntax. In this chapter we review some of that material and develop it toward becoming comfortable in Greek. Our goal is to read passages in the order in which the words come to us in the Greek, instead of treating sentences like puzzles and turning them into English order. First we will look at basic structures and word clusters in Greek and then explore three techniques that can help make sense out of difficult passages. As with the other features of Greek, the most important exercise for developing your knowledge and skill is reading, which we will focus on in chapter 5. But you cannot read without knowing how the pieces go together to communicate.

Core Elements in the Basic Sentence Types

Greek sentences can be long and intimidating, but if we take them clause by clause, they are more manageable. Even the longest sentence is composed of clauses, and there are at most only four basic elements in a clause: (1) subject, (2) verb, (3) direct object (that which receives the action of the verb) or complement (with an equative verb like εἰμί), and (4) indirect object (that which receives the object of the verb). A clause may not have all of these elements, but the core of the clause does not contain more than these four elements. This is good news!

Another bit of good news: these elements show up in four basic combinations that account for the vast majority of Greek sentences.[1] These elements can occur in various orders, but the core elements in a clause usually follow one of the following patterns.[2] Recall that the subject is often not explicitly expressed.

Type 1: subject–intransitive verb

ἀπέχει, It is enough. (Mark 14:41)
ἐδάκρυσεν ὁ Ἰησοῦς, Jesus wept. (John 11:35)
πεπλήρωται ὁ καιρός, the time has been fulfilled (Mark 1:15)

Type 2: subject–equative verb–complement: predicate noun or adjective

ἐγώ εἰμι ὁ ἄρτος τῆς ζωῆς, I am the bread of life. (John 6:48)
ἀνὴρ ἁμαρτωλός εἰμι, I am a sinful man (Luke 5:8)
ὁ λόγος σὰρξ ἐγένετο, the Word became flesh (John 1:14)

Type 3: subject–transitive verb–direct object[3]

γινώσκω τὰ ἐμά, I know my own (John 10:14)
ἡμεῖς νόμον ἔχομεν, we have a law (John 19:7)
ἠγάπησεν ὁ θεὸς τὸν κόσμον, God loved the world (John 3:16)
μισεῖ ὑμᾶς ὁ κόσμος, the world hates you (John 15:19)
τὸν Ἰησοῦν ἀνέστησεν ὁ θεός, God raised Jesus (Acts 2:32)
μνημονεύετε τοῦ λόγου, remember the word (John 15:20)
οἱ δοῦλοι αὐτοῦ λατρεύσουσιν αὐτῷ, his slaves will worship him (Rev. 22:3)

1. See Funk, §§500–516. See also David Alan Black, *Linguistics for Students of New Testament Greek: A Survey of Basic Concepts and Applications* (Grand Rapids: Baker, 1988), 102–6; Young, 205–14; K. L. McKay, *A New Syntax of the Verb in New Testament Greek: An Aspectual Approach*, Studies in Biblical Greek 5 (New York: Peter Lang, 1994), 67–72; and Stanley E. Porter, *Idioms of the Greek New Testament*, Biblical Languages: Greek 2 (Sheffield: Sheffield Academic Press, 1992), 292–97. Decker's introductory grammar is the only basic textbook I know of currently available, apart from Funk, which includes such information. See also Rodney J. Decker, *Reading Koine Greek: An Introduction and Integrated Workbook* (Grand Rapids: Baker Academic, 2014), chap. 8. For an introductory textbook with an extremely thorough analysis of sentence structures, see Donald N. Larson, *A Structural Approach to Greek, with Special Emphasis on Learning to Read the Koine Dialect*, 5th ed., 2 vols. (Lincoln, IL: Lincoln Christian College, 1971).

2. Funk (§§520–24) adds type 5: subject–verb–double accusative of object and complement (ψεύστην ποιοῦμεν αὐτόν, "we make him a liar," 1 John 1:10) and type 6: subject–verb–double accusative of person and thing (ἐδίδασκεν αὐτοὺς . . . πολλά, "he taught them many things," Mark 4:2). For double accusatives, see also Wallace, 181–89; Young, 17; and Herbert Weir Smyth, *Greek Grammar*, rev. Gordon M. Messing (Cambridge, MA: Harvard University Press, 1956), §§1612–33.

3. Usually the direct object is an accusative, but some verbs take a genitive or dative, as the last two examples illustrate.

Type 4: subject–transitive verb–direct object–indirect object

προσέφερον αὐτῷ παιδία, they were bringing children to him (Mark 10:13)
σοὶ δώσω τὴν ἐξουσίαν ταύτην ἅπασαν, I will give you all this authority
(Luke 4:6)

Usually you do not need to pay attention to these patterns, since the flow of
the sentence will be clear enough. But if you find a sentence that is confusing,
you can look for one of these patterns at the heart of each clause.

Word Clusters

Each of these four core elements can be expanded, forming little clusters within
a clause. A major part of becoming comfortable in Greek is recognizing word
clusters within clauses. As with the clause types, you usually will not have to
think about the sort of word cluster you are reading once you are familiar with
how words can form clusters. Most of these same clusters can also occur within
phrases, especially prepositional phrases that contain a participle or infinitive.

Expansion of the Subject, Direct Object, and Indirect Object

The subject, direct object, and indirect object can be expanded by means
of the following items:

Adjective (very common)

ὁ λόγος ὁ σός, your word (John 17:17)

Adverb (rare)

ἡ . . . ἄνω Ἰερουσαλήμ, the Jerusalem that is above (Gal. 4:26)

Noun (very common)

Nominative (apposition)

ἐγὼ Ἰωάννης, ὁ ἀδελφὸς ὑμῶν, I, John, your brother (Rev. 1:9)

Genitive (very common with diverse nuances)[4]

τὴν μάχαιραν αὐτοῦ, his sword (Matt. 26:51)

4. For other nuances of the items in this list, see Wallace, Young, or Funk.

Dative (with diverse nuances)

οἱ σοὶ μαθηταί, your disciples (Mark 2:18) (dat. of possession)

Accusative (simple apposition)[5]

Ἀνδρέαν τὸν ἀδελφὸν Σίμωνος, Andrew the brother of Simon (Mark 1:16)

Prepositional phrase (common)

πάτερ ἡμῶν ὁ ἐν τοῖς οὐρανοῖς, our Father in heaven (Matt. 6:9)

Participle (common)

καὶ ὁ πατήρ σου ὁ βλέπων ἐν τῷ κρυπτῷ ἀποδώσει σοι, And your Father who sees in secret will reward you. (Matt. 6:6)

Infinitive (not common)

ἐπλήσθη ὁ χρόνος τοῦ τεκεῖν αὐτήν, the time for her to give birth arrived (Luke 1:57)

Clause

Relative clause (very common)

τὸ ὕδωρ ὃ δώσω αὐτῷ, the water that I will give him/her (John 4:14)

Normal adverbial clause (rare)

ἔρχεται ὥρα ὅτε . . . προσκυνήσετε τῷ πατρί, the hour when you will worship the Father is coming (John 4:21)

Expansion of the Verb

The verbal idea may be conveyed with a simple verb or by a cluster of verbs forming a chain. The most common verb chains include the following:

Periphrastic participle

ἦν . . . διδάσκων αὐτούς, he was teaching them (Matt. 7:29)

τῇ . . . χάριτί ἐστε σεσῳσμένοι, by grace you have been saved (Eph. 2:8)

---

5. The only other use of the accusative to modify something other than a verb is the accusative of respect, which can modify adjectives as well as verbs. τὸν ἀριθμὸν ὡς πεντακισχίλιοι, (woodenly) "about five thousand with respect to number" (John 6:10). See Wallace, 203–4; Young, 20; Funk, §894.6; Smyth, *Grammar*, §1600.

Complementary participle

&ἐπαύσατο λαλῶν, he finished speaking (Luke 5:4)

Supplementary infinitive

ὑμεῖς οὐ δύνασθε ἐλθεῖν, you are not able to come (John 8:21)

A verb or verb chain can be expanded by means of the following items:

Noun

Genitive (common, with diverse nuances)

ἠγοράσθητε . . . τιμῆς, you were bought for a price (1 Cor. 6:20) (gen. of price)

Dative (common, with diverse nuances)

τῇ τρίτῃ ἡμέρᾳ ἐγερθήσεται, on the third day he will be raised (Matt. 17:23) (dat. of time)

Accusative (common, with diverse nuances)

δωρεὰν ἐλάβετε, you received freely (Matt. 10:8) (acc. of manner)

Adjective

μικρὸν καὶ οὐ θεωρεῖτέ με, in a little while you will no longer see me (John 16:19)

Adverb (common)

ἐξετάσατε ἀκριβῶς περὶ τοῦ παιδίου, search carefully for the child (Matt. 2:8)

Prepositional phrase (common)

παρ᾽ αὐτῷ ἔμειναν, they stayed with him (John 1:39)

Participle (common with diverse nuances)

Temporal or causal: νηστεύσας . . . ἐπείνασεν, having fasted . . . he was hungry (Matt. 4:2)

Infinitive (common with diverse nuances)

Purpose: ἦλθες ἀπολέσαι ἡμᾶς; Did you come to destroy us? (Mark 1:24)

The Role of Agreement

Agreement in gender, number, and case is a major way in which clusters are formed, especially between nouns, adjectives, articles, and/or participles. We need to pay special attention to this glue between items within clauses and sentences.

The Role of the Definite Article

The article[6] plays a major role in signaling structure in Greek sentences, especially the organizing of clusters within clauses.[7] Indeed, the Greek article has super powers, since it not only structures Greek sentences, clauses, and phrases but also enables virtually any part of speech to function as an adjective or a noun.[8] It can also add a sense of definiteness to a word and can convey other sometimes subtle but beautiful nuances.[9] While basic Greek courses usually do not explore the more subtle uses of the article, most do cover the key features related to structure signaling and creation of word clusters. In particular, most basic grammars cover the two main attributive positions connecting an adjective to a noun,[10] the predicate position signaling that the verb "to be" is to be supplied, and the bracketing force of the article.

First attributive position: τὴν καλὴν γῆν, the good soil (Matt. 13:23)
Second attributive position: τὴν γῆν τὴν καλήν, the good soil (Matt. 13:8)
Predicate position: οὗτοι οἱ λόγοι πιστοὶ καὶ ἀληθινοί, these words are faithful and true (Rev. 22:6)

The bracketing force of the article is especially important for seeing clusters of words in a clause. For example, in Gal. 3:17 ὁ and νόμος are separated by six words that describe the νόμος:

ὁ μετὰ τετρακόσια καὶ τριάκοντα ἔτη γεγονὼς νόμος
the law which came on the scene 430 years later

6. Since Greek has no indefinite article ("a, an"), we can call it *the definite article* or simply *the article*.

7. For an extensive discussion of the use of the article for structure signaling, see Funk, §§540–51, 680–706.2.

8. For example, the article enables the adverb νῦν, "now," to serve as an adjective or a noun. See BDAG, νῦν 1.a.β, 681.

9. See Funk (§§0710–7160) and Young (chap. 4) for the basic uses. Wallace (206–90) has an extensive coverage of the article, including the significance of its absence.

10. There is also a third attributive position, which is very rare. Apart from John 14:27 (εἰρήνην τὴν ἐμήν, "my peace"), I have found occurrences in the NT only with proper names and substantivized adjectives: e.g., Ἡρῳδίωνα τὸν συγγενῆ μου, "Herodion my kinsman" (Rom. 16:11).

This bracketing enables a speaker or writer to produce a complex description in a single package. Thus, along with the subtle nuances that the article can contribute, attention to the article is crucial for seeing clusters and structures, especially within a clause.

Omission of Elements

In Greek, as in many languages, elements of a phrase, clause, or sentence may be omitted.[11] Sometimes it is simply a matter of not repeating something already said. When you come across a clause or sentence in which something is missing, see whether something should be repeated from the context. Otherwise you must fill in the thought as best you can from the context.

οἱ δὲ λοιποὶ κρατήσαντες τοὺς δούλους αὐτοῦ ὕβρισαν καὶ ἀπέκτειναν.
And the others, seizing his slaves, beat and killed [them]. (Matt. 22:6)

In the above example, the direct object is omitted.

εἴτε γὰρ ἐξέστημεν, θεῷ· εἴτε σωφρονοῦμεν, ὑμῖν.
For if we are out of our minds [it is] for God; if we are in our right minds [it is] for you. (2 Cor. 5:13)

Although English translations supply "it is," we could see here a simple repetition of the verbs in the context: "For if we are out of our minds, we are out of our minds for God; if we are in our right minds, we are in our right minds for you." When simply reading a text, you do not need to supply such words, and you can experience the rhetorical punch.

οὐ γὰρ ἐν λόγῳ ἡ βασιλεία τοῦ θεοῦ ἀλλ᾽ ἐν δυνάμει.
For the kingdom of God [is not/is not a matter of/does not consist in] talk but in power. (1 Cor. 4:20)

A verb must be supplied when you are translating, and the English translations represent several possibilities. Again, when reading, you simply understand the meaning and experience the rhetorical effect.

μόνον μὴ τὴν ἐλευθερίαν εἰς ἀφορμὴν τῇ σαρκί
only [do] not [use] freedom for a base of operations for the flesh (Gal. 5:13)

11. See Funk, §§604–8; BDF §§479–81. Porter (*Idioms*, 287) notes that sometimes something seems like it is missing simply because our expectations are shaped by English.

Above is another example of the omission of a verb, which must be supplied according to the sense of the context, since there is no verb in the context that fits here.

ἵνα καθὼς γέγραπται· ὁ καυχώμενος ἐν κυρίῳ καυχάσθω.
So that, just as it is written, "The one who boasts must boast in the Lord."
(1 Cor. 1:31)

The verb with ἵνα is omitted, but in this case English can omit it as well.

Since some examples of omission correspond with English practice, sorting out a sentence with something missing will be easier at some times than at others. With practice, your comfort with Greek forms of expression will increase, as will your enjoyment of their rhetorical power.

Clauses within a Sentence

Along with recognizing the core elements in a clause, their expansions, and the clusters that words form, we need to be familiar with connections between clauses in a sentence. Either two clauses are coordinate with each other (the second one often introduced by δέ, καί, ἀλλά, πλήν, or ἤ), or one clause is subordinate to the other. Most basic Greek courses introduce these coordinate clauses as well as the main forms of subordinate clauses. Below are some examples of the types of clauses and the Greek words that typically introduce them:

- Temporal (ὅτε, ἐπεί, ἕως, πρίν, ὡς)
- Local (οὗ, ὅθεν, ὅπου)
- Purpose (ἵνα, ὡς, ὅπως)
- Result (ὥστε, ἵνα)
- Causal (ὅτι, ἐπεί)
- Comparative (ὡς, ὥσπερ, καθώς)
- Concessive (καίπερ)
- Conditional (εἰ, ἐάν, εἰ μή)
- Direct discourse and indirect discourse (Both direct and indirect discourse function like a direct object and can be thought of as a "content" clause.)

Remember that participles can serve in most of these functions, and infinitives in many of them.[12] We will explore clauses further when discussing sentence mapping later in this chapter and in appendix 1.

---

12. Basic Greek texts usually introduce these uses of participles and infinitives. An intermediate grammar will fill in further details. For examples, see Wallace, 587–655; Young, chaps. 10, 11.

Word Order

Familiarity with the basic structures just covered is essential for reading Greek. But the actual order in which things come in a sentence can vary quite a bit, as every first-year student knows. A clause might have verbs, subjects, direct objects, and indirect objects in any order, and so we need to be ready to receive the flow of thought however it may come. Simply reading a text does not require a knowledge of which order is more common, but some familiarity with the patterns of normal word order increases the enjoyment of reading Greek. It also helps us understand the author's flow of thought and main concerns better, since departure from the normal pattern suggests emphasis.[13] Such nuance is usually impossible to convey in a translation, since it is often less intense than an English equivalent would be.

While Greek word order is flexible, the basic principle is quite simple. Greek flows in a linear fashion, with the most important element in a clause or phrase introduced first, followed by other core elements or modifiers.[14] So in a clause, the first core element is normally the verb,[15] and in a phrase, the first element is the head term.[16] That is, a modifier such as an adjective, genitive, or demonstrative pronoun (not in the nominative) normally follows the noun it modifies.[17]

This simple principle must be supplemented with attention to a variety of other factors at work in actual passages that effect what is normal and what is "marked" (i.e., unusual and thus significant in some way). Attention to the nuances of word order are connected to issues of discourse analysis and various forms of emphasis, as we will see. Furthermore, the genre of a passage, the author's style, and the nature of the relation between the author and the audience all play a role, among other factors.[18] Indeed, often several forms of

13. "Paul made strategic use of the Greek language through a wide range of devices for providing various levels of highlighting to help readers more easily recognize his points" (Fredrick J. Long, *II Corinthians: A Handbook on the Greek Text*, Baylor Handbook on the Greek New Testament [Waco: Baylor University Press, 2015], xviii).

14. Contrast Latin, e.g., in which the verb commonly comes at the end of the sentence.

15. Among the core elements, the verb is usually first in a clause, but other elements are often at or near the beginning, such as conjunctions and "interrogatives, clause negatives, words of succession (πρῶτον, ἔπειτα, εἶτα), most pronouns including demonstratives in the nominative case, νῦν, τότε, αὐτός (self), ἄλλος and ἕτερος, ἀμφότεροι, πολύς, πολλάκις, εἷς" (Porter, *Idioms*, 289).

16. Porter, *Idioms*, 296, citing BDF §472(2); see also Andrew W. Pitts, "Greek Word Order and Clause Structure: A Comparative Study of Some New Testament Corpora," in *The Language of the New Testament: Context, History, and Development*, ed. Stanley E. Porter and Andrew W. Pitts, Early Christianity in Its Hellenistic Context 3 (Leiden: Brill, 2013), 340–42.

17. Porter, *Idioms*, 290–91.

18. Pitts, "Greek Word Order," 330, 340–42; Long, *II Corinthians*, xxxix.

emphasis are working together in a passage.[19] To complicate matters further, features that are emphatic in one form of discourse may not be so in another.[20] Thus it is not surprising that there are a number of different approaches to word order among scholars, as well as many open questions and disputed points.[21] While there are a number of factors to take into account in order to catch the dynamics at work in a passage, the following norms provide a starting point when considering word order.

1. *Order between main clauses and subordinate clauses.* Certain subordinate clauses have a tendency to come either before or after a main clause.[22]

Subordinate – Main

Conditional, concessive, and certain temporal clauses (e.g., with ὅτε or ὅταν) usually come before a main clause. When a conditional or concessive clause or one of these forms of temporal clauses comes after the main clause, it is marked in some way.

Main – Subordinate

Purpose, result, causal, content (ὅτι), local, comparative, and certain temporal clauses (e.g., with ἕως or ἄχρι) usually come after a main

19. Long (*II Corinthians*, xxix) says that "an important principle of emphasis" is that "*one will often find more than one emphatic indicator to mark elements for prominence*" (emphasis original).

20. Ibid., xxxv.

21. Surveys of the discussion of word order in biblical Greek are included in Ivan Shing Chung Kwong, *The Word Order of the Gospel of Luke: Its Foregrounded Messages*, Library of New Testament Studies 298 (London: T&T Clark, 2005), chaps. 1–2; Pitts, "Greek Word Order," 311–13; Stanley E. Porter, *Linguistic Analysis of the Greek New Testament: Studies in Tools, Methods, and Practice* (Grand Rapids: Baker Academic, 2015), 348–53; and Long, *II Corinthians*, xxxix–xliii. Further resources for word order include David Alan Black, *Learn to Read New Testament Greek*, 3rd ed. (Nashville: B&H, 2009), 31, 201–4; Young, 214–18; BDF §§472–78; Robertson, *Grammar*, 417–25; Nigel Turner, *Syntax*, vol. 3 of *A Grammar of New Testament Greek*, by James Hope Moulton, Wilbert Francis Howard, and Nigel Turner (Edinburgh: T&T Clark, 1963), 347–50. In *Style*, vol. 4 of *A Grammar of New Testament Greek*, by Moulton, Howard, and Turner (Edinburgh: T&T Clark, 1976), Nigel Turner discusses word order as well as many other issues, author by author, in the GNT. Turner emphasizes the influence of Hebrew constructions in the GNT through the LXX. In his *Christian Words* (Edinburgh: T&T Clark, 1980), he makes the same point about the vocabulary of the GNT. He believes the language is the ordinary language of ordinary people but greatly influenced by the LXX (see *Words*, xii–xiii). However, many scholars would say that the language of the LXX itself is basically common Greek and that the influence of the LXX on the language of the GNT is primarily through some of the religious and theological terms. See Karen H. Jobes and Moisés Silva, *Invitation to the Septuagint*, 2nd ed. (Grand Rapids: Baker Academic, 2015), 199–204, 218–21. After a major study of Greek and Hebrew verbal aspect in the Pentateuch, T. V. Evans notes some distinctives in the LXX but concludes, "The use of aspect, tense, and mood in the Greek Pentateuch represents essentially idiomatic Greek, in accord with the usage of the early Koine vernacular" (*Verbal Syntax in the Greek Pentateuch: Natural Greek Usage and Hebrew Interference* [Oxford: Oxford University Press, 2001], 259).

22. Young, 216.

clause. When one of these clauses comes before the main clause, it is highlighted in some way.

The following chart illustrates the normal position of subordinate clauses in relation to the main clause:

$$
\left.\begin{array}{l}
\text{Conditional} \\
\text{Concessive} \\
\text{Temporal (e.g., ὅτε, ὅταν)}
\end{array}\right\}
\text{Main Clause}
\left\{\begin{array}{l}
\text{Purpose} \\
\text{Result} \\
\text{Causal} \\
\text{Content (ὅτι)} \\
\text{Local} \\
\text{Comparative} \\
\text{Temporal (e.g., ἕως, ἄχρι)}
\end{array}\right.
$$

2. *Order within clauses.* It has often been said that the normal order in a Greek clause is verb-subject-object (including direct and indirect objects). But this norm can be misleading, since in many clauses the subject is embedded in the verb rather than explicitly stated.[23] Within clauses (both primary and secondary), as well as in participle and infinitive clauses, the verb tends to come before an object. When the subject is stated, it tends to come before the verb.[24] Accordingly, when an object is moved to the front, it includes some emphasis.

3. *Order within phrases.* Within phrases the normal order is for the head term to come first, followed by any modifiers, including relative clauses.[25] The main exceptions are words like πᾶς, πρῶτος, and numerals, which usually come before the head term.[26]

4. *Shifted words.* Often the words in a cluster will be together in a clause, but at other times one or more words are separated from the rest of the cluster, which signals emphasis.

μειζοτέραν τούτων οὐκ ἔχω χαράν
I have no greater joy than this (3 John 4)

The attributive modifier μειζοτέραν τούτων is separated from the word it modifies, χαράν, as a way of emphasizing the modifier.

---

23. Porter, *Idioms*, 293; Pitts, "Greek Word Order," 343; Long, *II Corinthians*, xl.

24. Pitts, "Greek Word Order," 337–42. Porter (*Idioms*, 295–96) says that the expressed subject often serves "either to draw attention to the subject of discussion or to mark a shift in the topic, perhaps signaling that a new person or event is the center of focus. Then comment is made upon this topic by means of the predicate. The subject gives new or emphatic information and the predicate elucidates it."

25. Porter, *Idioms*, 292.

26. Pitts, "Greek Word Order," 325–29.

Κύριε, οὐκ εἰμὶ ἱκανὸς ἵνα μου ὑπὸ τὴν στέγην εἰσέλθῃς
Lord, I am not worthy that you should come under my roof (Matt. 8:8)

The genitive μου modifies the object of the prepositional phrase, but it is given before the prepositional phrase itself. This shift is a poignant expression of the centurion's sense of unworthiness, which is probably impossible to convey in English. Luke's account of this same story uses the normal order:

ἵνα ὑπὸ τὴν στέγην μου εἰσέλθῃς (Luke 7:6)

Discourse Features

Along with these grammatical structures, discourse structures can signal emphasis and other nuances.[27] For example, while both δέ and καί introduce coordinate clauses and their particular nuance is conveyed by the context, their discourse functions can differ. In general, δέ chunks the text and signals some level of development from one thought to the next, while καί simply links two grammatically equal units.[28]

So, for example, Eph. 4:20–24 is one sentence in *SBLGNT* and NA[28], but in the midst of it, δέ occurs (4:23). The three infinitives provide the content of what the Ephesians were taught, forming a chiasm, as noted by many commentators.

A ἀποθέσθαι, put off the old man
  B ἀνανεοῦσθαι δέ, be renewed in the spirit of your mind
A′ καὶ ἐνδύσασθαι, put on the new man

27. See Jeffrey T. Reed, *A Discourse Analysis of Philippians: Method and Rhetoric in the Debate over Literary Integrity*, Journal for the Study of the New Testament Supplement Series 136 (Sheffield: Sheffield Academic, 1997); Robert A. Dooley and Stephen H. Levinsohn, *Analysing Discourse: A Manual of Basic Concepts* (Dallas: SIL International, 2001); Stephen H. Levinsohn, *Discourse Features of New Testament Greek: A Coursebook on the Information Structure of New Testament Greek*, 2nd ed. (Dallas: SIL, 2000); and Steven E. Runge, *Discourse Grammar of the Greek New Testament: A Practical Introduction for Teaching and Exegesis* (Peabody, MA: Hendrickson, 2010). In *The Lexham Discourse Greek New Testament* (Bellingham, WA: Lexham, 2008), Runge marks occurrences of the various discourse features he discusses in *Discourse Grammar*. Long makes significant use of the contributions of Reed, Levinsohn, and Runge, while also suggesting important corrections (see *II Corinthians*, xxxiv–xxxviii, xl–xliii). For helpful introductions to discourse analysis, see Peter Cotterell and Max Turner, *Linguistics and Biblical Interpretation* (Downers Grove, IL: InterVarsity, 1989), 205–17; and George Guthrie, "Discourse Analysis," in *Interpreting the New Testament: Essays on Methods and Issues*, ed. David Alan Black and David S. Dockery (Nashville: Broadman & Holman, 2001), 253–71. For sample studies, see David Alan Black, with Katharine Barnwell and Stephen Levinsohn, eds., *Linguistics and New Testament Interpretation: Essays on Discourse Analysis* (Nashville: Broadman & Holman, 1992); and several of the essays included in Stanley E. Porter and Matthew Brook O'Donnell, eds., *The Linguist as Pedagogue: Trends in the Teaching and Linguistic Analysis of the Greek New Testament* (Sheffield: Sheffield Phoenix, 2009).

28. Levinsohn, *Discourse Features*, 71–93; Runge, *Discourse Grammar*, 17–36.

This chiasm is formed by the meaning of the words, and it is enhanced by the present infinitive between the two aorist infinitives. Within this chiasm, the function of δέ is usually seen as adversative ("but"), which is correct. But δέ also chunks this tight chiasm, with the following καί binding the second two infinitives together. So there is more than one level of organization to the flow of thought in this sentence.

Verb tense-form can also signal shifts in a narrative discourse.[29] For example, the aorist is often used to move the story along, while the imperfect is often used to fill in details within a scene. A few illustrations are given in the discussion of Luke 5 in chapter 7. Attending to such details helps us see how an author views the flow of the narrative or the development of thought in an epistle.

Emphasis through Specific Words

1. *Emphatic words.* Certain words usually carry at least some level of emphasis.[30]

- Adverbs (e.g., ἀληθῶς, εὐθύς)
- Emphatic personal pronouns (ἐμοῦ, ἐμοί, ἐμέ, etc.)
- Emphatic possessive adjectives (σός, ἡμέτερος, etc.)
- Nominative personal pronoun (αὐτός, αὐτή, etc.)
- Intensive adverbs (οὐχί, νυνί)
- Double negatives (οὐ μή)

Similarly, some particles such as δή and γέ are "nuance words"[31] that function like verbal gestures, adding flavor or emphasis. Note, for example, the description of γέ in BDAG (190):[32]

γέ (Hom.+; apolog. exc. Ar.) enclit. particle, appended to the word or words it refers to; as in Hom.+ it serves to "focus the attention upon a single idea, and

---

29. See Levinsohn, *Discourse Features*, 172–77, 197–213; Runge, *Discourse Grammar*, 125–43; Constantine R. Campbell, *Verbal Aspect, the Indicative Mood, and Narrative: Soundings in the Greek of the New Testament*, Studies in Biblical Greek 13 (New York: Peter Lang, 2007), 239–47. See the very helpful, brief survey of the function of verbal aspect, conjunctions, and word order in Luke's Gospel in Martin M. Culy, Mikeal C. Parsons, and Joshua J. Stigall, *Luke: A Handbook on the Greek Text*, Baylor Handbook on the Greek New Testament (Waco: Baylor University Press, 2010), xxiii–xxxiii.

30. These first six examples are from Black, *Learn*, 202.

31. Funk, §014.4.

32. BDAG's reference to Denniston is to J. D. Denniston, *The Greek Particles*, 2nd ed., rev. K. J. Dover (London: Gerald Duckworth, 1950). See also Margaret E. Thrall, *Greek Particles in the New Testament: Linguistic and Exegetical Studies* (Grand Rapids: Eerdmans, 1962); and A. T. Robertson, *A Grammar of the Greek New Testament in the Light of Historical Research* (Nashville: Broadman, 1934), 1142–55.

place it, as it were, in the limelight: differing thus from δή, which emphasizes the reality of a concept (though in certain respects the usages of the two particles are similar)" (Denniston 114). In oral utterance it would be accompanied by a change in pitch of voice at certain points in the context, and a translator may use an adverb or indicate the point through word order, choice of typeface, or punctuation *at least, even, indeed*, etc.

2. Lexical emphasis. Themes are highlighted through the repetition of key words and their cognates within a particular text. Such patterns can occur at the level of paragraphs, sections, or an entire document.[33] Key words that occur only once or a few times can also be particularly significant as authors develop their thought.[34]

These features of word order, discourse, and other signals of emphasis are only some of the ways authors guided their readers' thoughts and feelings. Fredrick Long lists thirty-five such signals.[35] His commentary on 2 Corinthians provides a good, brief introduction to this form of analysis and is a stimulating example of sustained attention to such features in a complete document.

Three Techniques for Sorting Out a Sentence or Passage

Having surveyed some of the main features of clause and sentence structure helpful for gaining fluency, we come now to several specific techniques you might use to sort out the flow of difficult sentences or passages. These techniques, especially sentence mapping, are very helpful for exegesis and meditation, that is, when you are paying close attention to the details of a passage. When you are simply reading, you will probably use such techniques only when you cannot see what is going on in the Greek.

I will use Rev. 5:8–10 to illustrate these techniques. Here is the Greek text, along with a translation and some detailed notes to help you get into the text quickly, so we can use it to focus on a description of the three techniques.

[8]καὶ ὅτε ἔλαβεν τὸ βιβλίον, τὰ τέσσαρα ζῷα καὶ οἱ εἴκοσι τέσσαρες πρεσβύτεροι ἔπεσαν ἐνώπιον τοῦ ἀρνίου, ἔχοντες ἕκαστος κιθάραν καὶ φιάλας χρυσᾶς γεμούσας θυμιαμάτων, αἵ εἰσιν αἱ προσευχαὶ τῶν ἁγίων· [9]καὶ ᾄδουσιν ᾠδὴν καινὴν λέγοντες· Ἄξιος εἶ λαβεῖν τὸ βιβλίον καὶ ἀνοῖξαι τὰς σφραγῖδας αὐτοῦ, ὅτι ἐσφάγης καὶ ἠγόρασας τῷ θεῷ ἐν τῷ αἵματί σου ἐκ πάσης φυλῆς καὶ γλώσσης καὶ λαοῦ καὶ ἔθνους, [10]καὶ ἐποίησας αὐτοὺς τῷ θεῷ ἡμῶν βασιλείαν καὶ ἱερεῖς, καὶ βασιλεύουσιν ἐπὶ τῆς γῆς.

33. Long, *II Corinthians*, 271. Long highlights lexical emphasis throughout 2 Corinthians.
34. Ibid., xxxix.
35. Ibid., xviii, described in the glossary, 265–76.

[8]When he took the book, the four living creatures and the twenty-four elders fell down before the Lamb, each one having a harp and golden bowls full of incense, which are the prayers of the saints. [9]And they sing a new song, saying, "You are worthy to take the book and to open its seals, because you were slain and you purchased for God with your blood people from every tribe and tongue and people and nation. [10]You made them to be a kingdom and priests to our God; and they reign upon the earth."

In the following analysis of the above passage, I begin with a marked text. I am *not* advocating this way of marking as a tool to use. The three techniques I will describe later are much less complex and time consuming than what follows here. But this more detailed form of marking and my description of the grammar provide help in preparation for looking at the techniques I do want to suggest.

In this marked text, I have used brackets to bring out the clusters and the functions of the core words. At the heart of a clause is the verb, so I have underlined the verbs. Conjunctions that join clauses are also underlined. The identification of the cases is given between the lines, though I have not labeled cases of adjectives modifying nouns, nor objects of prepositions. Double angle brackets (<< >>) identify main clauses; single angle brackets (< >) identify subordinate clauses and other minor clauses (for example, relative clauses and adjectival participles, which act like adjectives but can have clausal characteristics because of the participle). Square brackets ([ ]) identify clusters within clauses.

Revelation 5:8–10

<< <   [ACC   ]> [NOM
[8]καὶ ὅτε ἔλαβεν τὸ βιβλίον,   τὰ τέσσαρα ζῷα καὶ οἱ εἴκοσι τέσσαρες

    NOM   ]   [   ]<   [NOM][ACC
πρεσβύτεροι ἔπεσαν ἐνώπιον τοῦ ἀρνίου, ἔχοντες ἕκαστος κιθάραν καὶ

ACC   ]><   GEN   > < NOM   [NOM
φιάλας χρυσᾶς   γεμούσας θυμιαμάτων,   αἵ εἰσιν αἱ προσευχαὶ τῶν

GEN] > >> <<   [ACC   ] <   > < NOM   [
ἁγίων·   [9]καὶ ᾄδουσιν ᾠδὴν καινὴν λέγοντες· Ἄξιος εἶ λαβεῖν τὸ

ACC]   [ACC   GEN]> <   [DAT]
βιβλίον καὶ ἀνοῖξαι τὰς σφραγῖδας αὐτοῦ, ὅτι ἐσφάγης καὶ ἠγόρασας τῷ θεῷ

[GEN] [   ]
ἐν τῷ αἵματί σου ἐκ πάσης φυλῆς καὶ γλώσσης καὶ λαοῦ καὶ ἔθνους, [10]καὶ

        ACC [DAT GEN][ACC   ACC]   [
ἐποίησας αὐτοὺς τῷ θεῷ ἡμῶν βασιλείαν καὶ ἱερεῖς, καὶ βασιλεύουσιν ἐπὶ τῆς

   ]> >>
γῆς.

Notes

$\overset{<<\quad<}{^8\underline{καὶ\ ὅτε\ ἔλαβεν}}$

The passage begins with two conjunctions. Usually this means there are two clauses, one clause embedded in the other. Here καί connects the sentence with what went before, and a temporal subordinate clause is given first, before the rest of the main clause.

$\overset{[\quad ACC\quad] >}{τὸ\ βιβλίον,}$

This article + noun cluster is the direct object. Since it is neuter, this form could be a nominative, but the context indicates that the scroll is being received/taken, not doing the receiving/taking. This word concludes the subordinate temporal clause, since the next words (τὰ τέσσαρα ζῷα) signal a new clause. For while the neuter τὰ τέσσαρα ζῷα could be an accusative and thus a continuation of the direct object of ἔλαβεν, there would usually be a conjunction to join two direct objects. So τὰ τέσσαρα ζῷα is probably going with another verb.

$\overset{[\qquad NOM \qquad\qquad\qquad NOM\qquad]}{τὰ\ τέσσαρα\ ζῷα\ καὶ\ οἱ\ εἴκοσι\ τέσσαρες\ πρεσβύτεροι}$

I have put NOM above the two nouns that are at the heart of this cluster. All but one of the other words in the cluster agree in gender, number, and case with one of these nouns, τέσσαρα in the neuter agreeing with τὰ ζῷα, and τέσσαρες in the masculine agreeing with πρεσβύτεροι. εἴκοσι is indeclinable (it does not change form), but its location between the article and the other masculine nominatives and its meaning indicate that it goes with οἱ πρεσβύτεροι. The modifiers of πρεσβύτεροι are embedded between the article οἱ and its noun πρεσβύτεροι. This string of nominatives makes us expect it to be the subject of the next clause. There is no conjunction introducing this clause, because we already saw the conjunction at the beginning of the verse, that is, καί.

ἔπεσαν

This is a 3 pl. verb matching the compound subject. It is a 2 aorist, but the usual ending, ον, has been replaced with a 1 aorist ending. This happens to several verbs in their 2 aorist forms in the Hellenistic period. Lexicons and grammars help you sort out such irregularities.[36]

$\overset{[\qquad\qquad]}{ἐνώπιον\ τοῦ\ ἀρνίου,}$

I did not label this genitive, since it is simply the object of the preposition.

---

36. For this mixture of 1 and 2 aorist paradigms, see Funk, §4122.

<
ἔχοντες

Since this participle is in the nominative, either it is serving as an adjective modifying one (or both) of the nominative nouns already present in the clause, or it is introducing an adverbial participle clause, giving more information about the circumstances of the clause it is modifying. Since it is masculine, it is most likely telling us something about the elders (πρεσβύτεροι, masc.), though it is possible that the participle includes the four living creatures as part of the compound subject, even though that word, ζῷα, is in the neuter.

[NOM]
ἕκαστος

It is a little unusual to have a nominative within a participle clause, but this word serves to emphasize that each of the elders (and, perhaps, the creatures) had a lyre/harp and bowls filled with incense.

[ACC   ACC   ]>
κιθάραν καὶ φιάλας χρυσᾶς

These two accusatives provide the direct object of the participle. The second has an adjective modifier, χρυσᾶς, also in the accusative in agreement in gender, number, and case. I have placed an angle bracket here to signal the shift to another participle, but actually the next participle and the relative clause that follows are both part of this participle clause with ἔχοντες, since they modify elements within the ἔχοντες clause.

<
γεμούσας

This feminine accusative plural participle agrees with φιάλας and modifies it like an adjective. Since this participle functions as an adjective, it is not a clause. However, I have put angle brackets around it since it forms a verbal cluster.

    GEN   >
θυμιαμάτων,

I have labeled this genitive since it gives the content of the action of the participle. Verbs meaning "to fill" frequently use a genitive of content.[37]

< NOM
αἵ

This relative pronoun is in the nominative because it is the subject of its own clause. A relative pronoun usually takes its gender and number from

---

37. BDF, §172, appears to treat this genitive as a direct object, but more frequently it is understood to be a genitive of content. See Wallace, 92–94, 131; Funk, §889.3.

the word it is referring back to (its "antecedent"), since a relative clause acts like an adjective to say something about an item in the sentence. So here this feminine plural form suggests it is referring to φιάλας, the bowls, or perhaps the lyres and the bowls together. Since elsewhere in Scripture (e.g., Ps. 141:2) and in later tradition, incense represents prayers, most interpreters I have consulted think the relative pronoun has been changed to match προσευχαί in its own clause, or φιάλας earlier, even though the reference is to θυμιαμάτων, a neuter. This sort of thing happens from time to time. It is known as the "attraction of the relative" since the relative pronoun gets attracted into the form of some word in the context. Such attraction usually is a change in the case, but it can also happen with the gender. It is interesting that in Rev. 8:3 both prayers and incense are mentioned and distinguished from one another, with the incense offered along with the prayers or perhaps added to the prayers.

εἰσιν

This is the verb for the relative clause. It is an equative verb ("$x = y$"), so we expect a nominative for both the subject and the predicate.

[NOM   GEN   ] > >>
αἱ προσευχαὶ τῶν ἁγίων·

Here the predicate nominative after the equative verb forms a little cluster with a genitive modifier. The single angle bracket signals the end of the relative clause, and the double bracket signals the conclusion of the main clause that began with καί at the beginning of the verse, the main verb of which was ἔπεσαν.

<<
⁹καὶ ᾄδουσιν

The new sentence begins with a conjunction that connects it loosely to what went before. Αΐδουσιν[38] is the first of several main verbs in this compound sentence.

[ACC   ]
ᾠδὴν καινὴν

This is the direct object of ᾄδουσιν, along with an adjective modifier.

---

38. Note the common practice of changing an iota subscript to a regular iota when used with a capital letter. Such an iota is referred to as iota adscript.

<   >

λέγοντες·

This form is a nominative adverbial participle that serves to introduce discourse, usually direct discourse. I have marked it with angle brackets as if it were a clause by itself, but more properly it goes with the discourse that follows. I simplified the brackets to avoid the clutter of additional levels of embedded clauses.

< NOM

Ἄξιος

This is the predicate nominative of the equative verb εἶ.

εἶ

The verb in this reported speech has an embedded subject, "you" (sg.).

λαβεῖν

This epexegetic infinitive explains the term ἄξιος.

[ACC   ]

τὸ βιβλίον

This is the direct object of the infinitive.

καὶ ἀνοῖξαι

This is another epexegetic infinitive.

[ACC   GEN   ] >

τὰς σφραγῖδας αὐτοῦ,

The direct object of ἀνοῖξαι has a genitive modifier.

<

ὅτι ἐσφάγης

The conjunction introduces a subordinate clause modifying εἶ, giving the reason why he is worthy. The verb is an aorist passive, with a tense-form suffix of η instead of the more common θη. This is the first of a series of four verbs that go with this ὅτι. Within this long subordinate clause each verb has its own set of modifiers that could be bracketed off (apart from this first verb that has no modifiers). I have not added this further level of brackets within the subordinate clause.

καὶ <u>ἠγόρασας</u>

This is another verb that is part of the ὅτι clause, providing more of the reason he is worthy. The direct object is not given, so it must be supplied from the context: "persons."

[DAT]
τῷ θεῷ

This dative modifying ἠγόρασας is an example of a "dative of advantage": the purchase of these persons was for God.

[GEN]
ἐν τῷ αἵματί σου

Here is a prepositional phrase with a genitive modifier. I did not label the dative, since that is simply the object of the preposition, but I did label the genitive, since it has been added to a basic prepositional phrase. This prepositional phrase modifies ἠγόρασας.

[   ]
ἐκ πάσης φυλῆς καὶ γλώσσης καὶ λαοῦ καὶ ἔθνους,

This is another prepositional phrase with an adjective modifier; πάσης probably applies to all the nouns in this prepositional phrase. This phrase modifies the direct object of ἠγόρασας. This object is implied rather than stated.[39]

¹⁰καὶ <u>ἐποίησας</u>

The conjunction introduces a new verb within this long ὅτι clause.

ACC
αὐτοὺς

The direct object of ἐποίησας is part of a double accusative construction (see below).

[DAT   GEN]
τῷ θεῷ ἡμῶν

This is another dative of advantage, with a genitive modifier. This cluster modifies ἐποίησας.

[ACC   ACC]
βασιλείαν καὶ ἱερεῖς,

These two accusatives together form the second part of a double accusative construction, with αὐτούς providing the first part. The verb ποιέω belongs to a

---

39. In the sentence map given below, I insert [τινας] to stand for this implied object.

group of verbs that can take two accusatives, one for the object and the other for an object complement. "He made them a kingdom and priests," means, "He made them [object] *to be/become* a kingdom and priests [complements]." So it is as if the verb "to be" or "to become" is implied. We have the same construction in English, as in "I will make you [object] fishers of men/people [complement]."

καὶ <u>βασιλεύουσιν</u>

Here is another verb in this ὅτι clause.

[   ] > >>
ἐπὶ τῆς γῆς.

This is a simple prepositional phrase, modifying βασιλεύουσιν. The single angle bracket signals the end of the ὅτι clause, and the double angle brackets signal the end of the compound sentence that began at the beginning of verse 9.

With a good understanding of our sample passage, let us now look at three ways to work with a text to sort out its structures.

Technique 1: Chunking

I will begin with the simplest technique. This common and effective approach to sorting out Greek sentences involves marking or rewriting a sentence to break down the text into its basic sense units.[40] Punctuation provides help, and further divisions can be made by following the structure of the clauses, phrases, and other clusters found in a sentence. Any coherent unit, such as a direct object, can be marked or, if you are rewriting, can have its own line. In this way sense units and clusters are highlighted, making pronunciation and reading easier. How far to divide a sentence into separate lines depends on what the individual reader finds helpful. Here is one possible chunking of the first verse in our sample passage, in both formats:

[8]καὶ ὅτε ἔλαβεν | τὸ βιβλίον, | τὰ τέσσαρα ζῷα καὶ οἱ εἴκοσι τέσσαρες πρεσβύτε-ροι | ἔπεσαν | ἐνώπιον τοῦ ἀρνίου, | ἔχοντες | ἕκαστος | κιθάραν καὶ φιάλας χρυσᾶς | γεμούσας θυμιαμάτων, | αἵ εἰσιν αἱ προσευχαὶ τῶν ἁγίων

[8]καὶ ὅτε ἔλαβεν
τὸ βιβλίον,
τὰ τέσσαρα ζῷα καὶ οἱ εἴκοσι τέσσαρες πρεσβύτεροι

40. Examples similar to some of what I offer here may be found in B. D. Hoyos, *Latin, How to Read It Fluently: A Practical Manual* (Amherst, MA: Classical Association of New England, 1997, www.canepress.org), chaps. 4–6; see also Jonathan Robie, "Phrasing a Greek Text" (online; see bibliography). On this site, Robie provides a link to a "rough phrasing," as he calls it, of the Greek New Testament, based simply on punctuation.

ἔπεσαν
ἐνώπιον τοῦ ἀρνίου,
ἔχοντες
ἕκαστος
κιθάραν καὶ φιάλας χρυσᾶς
γεμούσας θυμιαμάτων,
αἵ εἰσιν αἱ προσευχαὶ τῶν ἁγίων

To this simple scan you could add explanatory notes to some or all of its features. For my example, I will use three columns. The analysis in my sample is more thorough than you probably would need most of the time. Again, I will give only the first verse, since that is enough to give you an idea of the technique.

Column 1

Number the clauses within each sentence in order to show the clause structures. Compound clauses could be indicated with letters (1a, 1b, etc), though there are none in this first verse. Minor clausal elements (participles, infinitives, and relative clauses) are numbered with lowercase Roman numerals. Use a space to separate sentences.

Column 2

The text itself is broken down by sense units.

Column 3

Labels are given indicating the role of each unit. More detailed descriptions may be added, if desired.

1	⁸καὶ ὅτε ἔλαβεν	*subordinate clause*
	τὸ βιβλίον,	*dir. obj.*
2	τὰ τέσσαρα ζῷα	*compound subj.*
	καὶ οἱ εἴκοσι τέσσαρες πρεσβύτεροι	
	ἔπεσαν	*main verb*
	ἐνώπιον τοῦ ἀρνίου,	*prep. phrase*
2.i	ἔχοντες	*adv. ptc.*
	ἕκαστος	*nom. subj. of ptc.*
	κιθάραν καὶ φιάλας χρυσᾶς	*dir. objs.*
2.ii	γεμούσας θυμιαμάτων,	*adj. ptc. w. φιάλας*
2.iii	αἵ εἰσιν αἱ προσευχαὶ τῶν ἁγίων	*rel. clause w. φιάλας or θυμιαμάτων*

Technique 2: Sentence Scanning

Another common way to sort out Greek sentences is by marking the main structures and substructures. You can do this in a paper copy or a digital copy, or you could print the passage with several spaces between lines for these markings and other notes. Here is a simple set of marks you could use.

| | Put a vertical line between clauses.
[ ] | Put square brackets around verbal clusters within clauses, including relative clauses, adverbial participles, and adverbial infinitives.
< > | For particularly complex sentences, angle brackets can set off units within larger clauses.
( ) | Put parentheses around prepositional phrases, adjectival participles, and any other major word clusters you find helpful to mark.

You could also double underline finite verbs (verbs that have person and number) and single underline other verb forms (infinitives and participles).

⁸καὶ | ὅτε ἔλαβεν τὸ βιβλίον, | (τὰ τέσσαρα ζῷα καὶ οἱ εἴκοσι τέσσαρες πρεσβύτεροι) ἔπεσαν (ἐνώπιον τοῦ ἀρνίου), [ἔχοντες ἕκαστος κιθάραν καὶ φιάλας χρυσᾶς (γεμούσας θυμιαμάτων)], [αἵ εἰσιν αἱ προσευχαὶ τῶν ἁγίων]·

⁹καὶ ᾄδουσιν ᾠδὴν καινὴν [λέγοντες] | Ἄξιος εἶ (λαβεῖν τὸ βιβλίον) καὶ (ἀνοῖξαι τὰς σφραγῖδας αὐτοῦ), | ὅτι ἐσφάγης καὶ ἠγόρασας τῷ θεῷ (ἐν τῷ αἵματί σου) (ἐκ πάσης φυλῆς καὶ γλώσσης καὶ λαοῦ καὶ ἔθνους), ¹⁰καὶ ἐποίησας αὐτοὺς τῷ θεῷ ἡμῶν βασιλείαν καὶ ἱερεῖς, καὶ βασιλεύουσιν (ἐπὶ τῆς γῆς).

I put parentheses around the long nominative subject in verse 8 and around the infinitives and their objects in verse 9, though this is merely an option. I have not put lines between the verbs in the long compound ὅτι clause in 9b–10, but you could add them if helpful.

This marking system is meant to be simple and flexible, so you should adapt these markings as need arises. For example, a preposition with an articular infinitive for its object might be marked for the prepositional phrase and the function of the infinitive:

καὶ (μετὰ [τὸ παραδοθῆναι τὸν Ἰωάννης]) ἦλθεν ὁ Ἰησους, And after John was taken into custody Jesus came (Mark 1:14)[41]

41. See the discussion of this verse in app. 1.

Sometimes creative rhetoric in a passage requires creative application of this technique. In Gal. 4:2 Paul interrupts a prepositional phrase to insert the verb of the clause. In this case, hyphens may help clarify the structure of the sentence.

ἀλλὰ (ὑπὸ ἐπιτρόπους -) ἐστὶ (- καὶ οἰκονόμους) (ἄχρι τῆς προθεσμίας τοῦ πατρός).
But he is under guardians and managers until the time set by his father.

These markings are not an end in themselves. In a course, the professor will indicate how you are to use this technique, but when working on your own, you should experiment to find what is most helpful to you. Whether you mark the text on a computer or on paper, you could also add notes about vocabulary, difficult parsings, and points of grammar.

Technique 3: Sentence Mapping

Many books on exegesis describe some form of rewriting a passage in order to see the flow of thought. Such techniques are very valuable for exegesis and other forms of detailed study of a passage such as in meditation, covered in chapter 6. Rewriting can also help you sort out difficult passages when reading. Here I offer my own approach to this exercise. I have tried to provide a method that is as simple as possible yet allows a passage to be analyzed on several levels of detail and enables you to see the original order of the Greek. This method has the additional advantage of working equally well in English or in Greek. The basic principles can often be applied in more than one way. This flexibility enables you to create a map that is clearest to you.

I have tried to describe this technique clearly here and in more detail in appendix 1, but this is dense material and requires slow and careful study. Students in class often find the details easier to grasp when presented orally. So I have provided videos that introduce the main points of this technique. See the website for this book.

In sentence mapping, the core elements of each clause (subject, verb, direct object, and indirect object) are kept on the same line, and the other elements of the sentence are aligned or indented to show their relation to these core elements. I work with three possible levels of maps. A level 1 map shows the relations between clauses in the sentences of a passage, a level 2 map adds the role of prepositional phrases in the sentences, and a level 3 map highlights the role of all the elements in a sentence; for example, an adjective or a genitive would be placed under the noun it modifies. I have found the level 2 map is usually the most helpful for exegesis, though a level 3 map can be valuable for particularly complex material. In appendix 1 I provide detailed guidelines for creating sentence maps of all three levels in both Greek and English.

Level 2 Sentence Map: Revelation 5:8–10

8   ⌐ καὶ ὅτε ἔλαβεν τὸ βιβλίον,
  τὰ τέσσαρα ζῷα καὶ οἱ εἴκοσι τέσσαρες πρεσβύτεροι ἔπεσαν
                                      ἐνώπιον τοῦ ἀρνίου,

  ἔχοντες ἔκαστος κιθάραν καὶ φιάλας χρυσᾶς
                   γεμούσας θυμιαμάτων,
              ⌐—— or ——⌐
            αἵ εἰσιν αἱ προσευχαὶ τῶν ἁγίων·

9   καὶ ᾄδουσιν ᾠδὴν καινὴν
      λέγοντες,
         Ἄξιος εἶ λαβεῖν τὸ βιβλίον
              καὶ ἀνοῖξαι τὰς σφραγῖδας αὐτοῦ,
         ὅτι   ἐσφάγης
             καὶ ἠγόρασας τῷ θεῷ [τινας]
               ἐν τῷ αἵματί σου
                    ἐκ πάσης   φυλῆς
                                καὶ γλώσσης
                                καὶ λαοῦ
                                καὶ ἔθνους,

10   καὶ ἐποίησας αὐτοὺς τῷ θεῷ ἡμῶν βασιλείαν καὶ ἱερεῖς,
                    καὶ βασιλεύουσιν
                       ἐπὶ τῆς γῆς.

- From this example you can see that each line usually will contain either a clause or a prepositional phrase, though you can modify how the principles of this method are applied depending on what you find helpful in a given passage. For example, here I have not kept all of the objects of the preposition ἐκ on the same line at the end of verse 9.
- The core elements within each clause line will include, if present, the conjunction, subject, verb, negative adverb, direct object, and indirect object.
- Prepositional phrases consist of the preposition and its object.
- In both clauses and prepositional phrases, additional elements included will usually be adjective and genitive modifiers, if present.
- Other items may appear, such as adverbials, but adjectives and genitives are the most common, as illustrated in our passage.

- In my discussion I noted that αἵ (v. 8) might refer to either φιάλας or θυμιαμάτων, and the map allows both options to be represented.

Examples of More Complex Scanning and Mapping

The following examples illustrate the use of scanning and mapping for more complex sentences.

- Very wooden English translations are included merely to help you sort out the Greek more quickly. These renderings are closer to an interlinear than to an actual translation.

Acts 2:22–24

Scan

²²Ἄνδρες Ἰσραηλῖται, <u>ἀκούσατε</u> τοὺς λόγους τούτους. | Ἰησοῦν τὸν Ναζωραῖον, [ἄνδρα <u>ἀποδεδειγμένον</u> (ἀπὸ τοῦ θεοῦ) (εἰς ὑμᾶς) (δυνάμεσι καὶ τέρασι καὶ σημείοις)] [οἷς <u>ἐποίησεν</u> (δι' αὐτοῦ) ὁ θεὸς (ἐν μέσῳ ὑμῶν)], [καθὼς αὐτοὶ <u>οἴδατε</u>], ²³[τοῦτον (τῇ <u>ὡρισμένῃ</u> βουλῇ καὶ προγνώσει τοῦ θεοῦ) ἔκδοτον <(διὰ χειρὸς ἀνόμων) <u>προσπήξαντες</u>> <u>ἀνείλατε</u>], ²⁴[ὃν ὁ θεὸς <u>ἀνέστησεν</u> (λύσας τὰς ὠδῖνας τοῦ θανάτου), (καθότι οὐκ <u>ἦν</u> δυνατὸν <u>κρατεῖσθαι</u> αὐτὸν ὑπ' αὐτοῦ)]·

- There are only two main verbs in this sentence, ἀκούσατε and ἀνείλατε, so only one vertical line is used. The other finite verbs are in relative clauses and subordinate clauses.
- Verse 23 is complex enough to need the angle brackets to set off <(διὰ χειρὸς ἀνόμων) <u>προσπήξαντες</u>>, an adverbial participle clause within a larger clause.

English Map

22   Israelite men, listen to these words:

      Jesus
      the Nazarene
      a man
          attested
                by God
             to you
              through miracles ⌐
              and wonders   ⌐
              and signs   ⌐

and signs   ⌐
                 that God did
                         through him
                         in your midst
                         as you yourselves know,

23 this one   you took out
              having been given over   or >|
                     by the determined decision   ⌐
                        and plan/foreknowledge   ⌐
                                              of God
                                                            ⌐_____⌐
                                 by nailing [him]
                                     by the hand
                                         of lawless ones

24   whom God raised up
                  having loosened the pains
                           of death
                  because it was not possible for him to be held
                                                      by it.

Greek Map

22 Ἄνδρες Ἰσραηλῖται, ἀκούσατε τοὺς λόγους τούτους.

Ἰησοῦν
τὸν Ναζωραῖον,
ἄνδρα
    ἀποδεδειγμένον
            ἀπὸ τοῦ θεοῦ
          εἰς ὑμᾶς
        δυνάμεσι   ⌐
        καὶ τέρασι   ⌐
        καὶ σημείοις ⌐
                    οἷς ἐποίησεν . . .[1] ὁ θεὸς . . .[2] . . .[3]
                        [1]δι' αὐτοῦ
                        [2]ἐν μέσῳ ὑμῶν,
                        [3]καθὼς αὐτοὶ οἴδατε,

23 τοῦτον . . .¹ . . .² . . .³   ἀνείλατε,

    ¹. . . ἔκδοτον   or >|

      τῇ ὡρισμένῃ βουλῇ καὶ προγνώσει τοῦ θεοῦ

                                                    ³προσπήξαντες

                                                    ²διὰ χειρὸς ἀνόμων

24   ὃν ὁ θεὸς ἀνέστησεν

        λύσας τὰς ὠδῖνας τοῦ θανάτου,

          καθότι οὐκ ἦν δυνατὸν κρατεῖσθαι αὐτὸν

                    ὑπ' αὐτοῦ·

- The map allows the passage to be analyzed in greater detail than the scan.
- We can see that verse 22 begins with an introductory clause and then continues with an elaborate description of Jesus, all flowing from the accusative Ἰησοῦν.
- This description of Jesus is picked up by the resumptive τοῦτον in verse 23, which is the direct object of ἀνείλατε.
- But before we get to the main verb in verse 23, there is a further description of Jesus as ἔκδοτον and also an adverbial participle, προσπήξαντες, which tells us more about the action of the main verb.
- There is some question about the function of ἔκδοτον. As it stands, it seems to tell us more about τοῦτον, as if it were followed by γενόμενον. In fact, γενόμενον with an adjective is a common construction in Acts (see 7:32; 10:4; 12:23; 16:27). Some manuscripts, however, have ἔκδοτον λαβόντες, which would take ἔκδοτον as part of a participial clause modifying the verb.[42] While the construction as we have it places ἔκδοτον with τοῦτον, I have noted the alternative in the map.
- I have not placed τοῦ θεοῦ under the word it modifies in verse 23, since this is a level 2 map. But in the English translation this genitive is a prepositional phrase, so it is placed under the word it modifies.
- The sentence continues in verse 24 with another relative clause, describing Jesus in further detail in terms of God's action on his behalf.
- Actions by God and by Jesus's opponents are mentioned, but the flow of the Greek is all centered on Jesus in a quite remarkable fashion.

42. On both of these options for ἔκδοτον, see C. K. Barrett, *Acts*, International Critical Commentary (Edinburgh: T&T Clark, 1994), 1:142.

Acts 9:1–2

Scan

¹[Ὁ δὲ Σαῦλος <ἔτι <u>ἐμπνέων</u> ἀπειλῆς καὶ φόνου (εἰς τοὺς μαθητὰς τοῦ κυρίου)>, <<u>προσελθὼν</u> τῷ ἀρχιερεῖ ²<u>ἠτήσατο</u> (παρ' αὐτοῦ) ἐπιστολὰς (εἰς Δαμασκὸν) (πρὸς τὰς συναγωγάς)], |[ὅπως <ἐάν τινας <u>εὕρῃ</u> (τῆς ὁδοῦ <u>ὄντας</u>, ἄνδρας τε καὶ γυναῖκας)>, (<u>δεδεμένους</u>) <u>ἀγάγῃ</u> (εἰς Ἰερουσαλήμ)].

- The scan shows there is one main verb in this sentence (<u>ἠτήσατο</u>); three adverbial participles (<u>ἐμπνέων</u>, <u>προσελθὼν</u>, and <u>δεδεμένους</u>); an attributive participle (<u>ὄντας</u>); two subordinate clauses, one inside the other (ὅπως and ἐάν); and five prepositional phrases.

English Map

```
              ┌¹still breathing threat and murder
              └ against the disciples
                              of the Lord
                ┌²going to the high priest
And Saul . . .¹ . . .² requested . . .³      letters
                ³from him           for Damascus
                                  to the synagogues


                          ┌⁴if he might find some people
                                      who were of the Way
                                men and women
        so that . . .⁴ [them] . . .⁵ he might bring
              ⁵bound                to Jerusalem
```

Greek Map

```
        ┌¹ἔτι ἐμπνέων ἀπειλῆς καὶ φόνου
        └εἰς τοὺς μαθητὰς τοῦ κυρίου,
        ┌²προσελθὼν τῷ ἀρχιερεῖ

Ὁ δὲ Σαῦλος . . .¹ . . .² ἠτήσατο    . . .³    ἐπιστολὰς
              ³παρ' αὐτοῦ       εἰς Δαμασκὸν
                          πρὸς τὰς συναγωγάς,


                      ┌⁴ἐάν τινας εὕρῃ
                              τῆς ὁδοῦ ὄντας,
                              ἄνδρας τε καὶ γυναῖκας,
        ὅπως . . .⁴ [αὐτούς] . . .⁵    ἀγάγῃ
              ⁵δεδεμένους      εἰς  Ἰερουσαλήμ.
```

- Two adverbial participles set the scene for Saul's request for letters. These are offset from one another so that both can point independently to the verb they modify. They are not lined up flush, since they are not in apposition to each other.
- The purpose clause (ὅπως) is itself modified by the conditional clause (ἐάν).
- Normally a blank line signals a new sentence, but sometimes it can be used to clarify a cluttered sentence. Accordingly, I have added an extra line after the first two participles and also between ἐάν and the line before it to clarify that the conditional modifies what follows.
- The phrase ἄνδρας τε καὶ γυναῖκας is in apposition to τινας, so it is lined up flush with it, using a tab.
- I have supplied the omitted direct object of ἀγάγῃ, [αὐτούς], in order to have a place to link the modifier δεδεμένους.

For comparison, here is a map of this sentence in the ESV.

```
                        ⌐¹ still breathing threats and murder
                                against the disciples
                                        of the Lord,
  1  But Saul, . . .¹   went
                            to the high priest
  2                      and asked him
                                for letters
                                    to the synagogues
                                        at Damascus,

                                    ⌐¹if he found any belonging to the Way,
                                            men or women,
                        so that . . .¹ he might bring them
                                            bound
                                        to Jerusalem.
```

Conclusion

As you become skilled in these three techniques, you will discover which of them is most useful for you personally. Mapping is the most detailed. For simply sorting out a complex sentence while reading, you may find either the chunking or the scanning technique sufficient.

As you gain fluency, you will have less need for chunking, scanning, or mapping when reading Greek. However, the attention necessary to do a map is related to the attention used in meditation, so not only is work on a map very valuable when sorting out a difficult sentence or analyzing the thought of a passage in exegetical detail, but it also often draws your attention to specific items for meditation, which we come to in chapter 6.

5

Gaining Familiarity
and Fluency

In the introduction, we saw the importance of reading Greek. In each of
the chapters since then, I have emphasized reading, while offering other
more concentrated exercises for working on specific parts of Greek. Now we
come to the crucial practice for developing familiarity with Greek and moving
toward fluency. I recommend that you move toward fluency one passage at a
time. How, then, do you approach a passage?

From Puzzling to Fluency, Passage by Passage

Step 1: Puzzling

When you first approach your passage, skim over it to see what you recognize. If very little is familiar to you, then you will need to sort out the
necessary details of parsing, vocabulary, and grammar and put them together.
This approach is like working through a piece of music, measure by measure,
learning to play it while still in the earlier stages of mastering the instrument.

A professor of Classics, William Harris, refers to this initial work as providing
the background necessary for the foreground. Here are his recommendations

for Latin students, and they apply equally well to Greek. He suggests they pick a really good poem and focus on that.

> Read through ONE poem first, using where necessary grammar and dictionary and work through the whole traditional mode. I suggest getting this firmly in mind, and then setting it aside in an effort to forget it, which means consigning it to somewhere in the unconscious mind. Language works that way, you read concentrating actively on the words and sounds of your text, while your grammatical apparatus is operating "in the background" as we say in computer language. This is how language works. No background means no comprehension. But background pushed into the foreground means no real reading at all.[1]

In other words, once you have sorted out this data in your passage, you can begin to encounter the text itself and move from puzzling to reading. Harris notes it is best to begin with passages that are of particular interest and value to you. Obviously, it does not need to be a poem; any passage would be fine.

Step 2: Scanning

As your knowledge of Greek develops, you will not need to start with puzzling, since you will be able to recognize many items in a passage from an initial scan. You can simply survey a sentence to see its structures and then fill in any needed details. The following six "Reading Rules for Latin" by Dexter Hoyos, another professor of Classics, are a good example of such an approach.

> RULE 1: A new sentence or passage should be read[2] through completely, several times if necessary, so as to see all its words in context.
> RULE 2: As you read, register mentally the ending of every word so as to recognise how the words in the sentence relate to one another.
> RULE 3: Recognise the way in which the sentence is structured: its Main Clause(s), subordinate clauses and phrases. Read them in sequence to achieve this recognition and re-read the sentence as often as necessary, *without translating it*.
> RULE 4: Now look up unfamiliar words in the dictionary; and once you know what all the words can mean, re-read the Latin to improve your grasp of the context and so clarify what the words in this sentence do mean.
> RULE 5: If translating, translate only when you have seen exactly how the sentence works and what it means. Do not translate in order to find out what the sentence means. Understand first, *then* translate.

1. William Harris, "The Sin of Transverbalizing . . . or Translating as you Read!" Available online (see bibliography).
2. "Be read" here means to be pronounced and understood, not translated, as becomes clear in the later rules.

RULE 6:

   a. Once a subordinate clause or phrase is begun, it must be completed syntactically before the rest of the sentence can proceed.

   b. When one subordinate construction embraces another, the embraced one must be completed before the embracing one can proceed.

   c. A Main Clause must be completed before another Main Clause can start.[3]

If you want to apply this advice to a passage in Greek, what should you look for? Here is a summary of the most important items to keep in mind. You will see that most, perhaps all, of these key items are things you learned in basic Greek, which should be an encouragement. As you develop fluency, you have no need to attend to these details, since you receive their information automatically. But for sentences that are difficult, you can look for these elements to sort things out.

1. How many *clauses* are there? As you try to notice the clusters of words in a sentence, you will have a better understanding of the sentence, and clauses are the biggest clusters in a sentence. In fact, some sentences are simply one clause (though this is not common in Greek). Indeed, in context a sentence can be a single adverb (οὔ, "no" in John 1:21) or a single noun in the genitive (Καίσαρος, "Caesar's" in Matt. 22:21)! So as you survey a sentence, watch for *conjunctions* (since they initiate clauses) and *verbs* (since the verb is the heart of a clause).

2. Watch for *infinitives* and *participles*, since they are often the core of a cluster of words.

3. Are there any *prepositional phrases*? Prepositional phrases are another important form of word cluster in a sentence. When you come across a preposition, you expect the next words to go with that preposition, forming the prepositional phrase. The preposition and the words that go with it (known as the "object of the preposition") are read as a unit.

4. What *nouns* are present, and what is the case of each? This is where knowing the endings is crucial, especially the ability to recognize the case, since that indicates the job the noun does in the sentence.

   • *The most important uses of the cases* are the nominative for the subject of the verb, the accusative for the direct object of the verb, the dative for the indirect object of the verb, and the genitive to modify a noun or verb.

---

3. B. D. Hoyos, "The Ten Basic Reading Rules for Latin" (emphasis original). Available online (see bibliography). I give only the first six rules here, since they apply most directly to Greek.

- Equative verbs (such as εἰμί and γίνομαι) usually mean "to be" or "to become." These verbs have a *nominative* for both the subject and the complement—they do not use an accusative, because these verbs do not describe action, so there is no direct object. These verbs produce sentences like "*x* is *y*" or "*x* becomes *y*." Thinking of these verbs as producing an "*x* = *y*" kind of thought may help you remember that they use a nominative for both the "*x*" and the "*y*."[4]

- Besides serving as a direct object, the *accusative* can also function as the subject of an infinitive.[5] Additionally, some Greek verbs can take two accusatives, but because this construction also occurs in English (e.g., "He taught them many things"), you should have no trouble recognizing it.[6]

- The *dative* has other possible functions besides indirect object. The most important ones include the direct object with some verbs,[7] location, and means/instrument. So when you come across a dative that is not part of a prepositional phrase, it is most often an indirect object, a direct object, a locative for place or time, or the means or instrument.

- Most *genitives* modify a noun, so if you spot a genitive, it probably forms a little cluster with the noun it modifies. Such genitives can come either before or after the word they modify. The genitive also is used for the object of certain verbs and as the subject of a genitive absolute participle construction.

- You will learn many more uses of each of the cases as you progress in Greek, though many of the nuances are more important in exegesis and meditation than in reading. The ones I have just listed are the most common, so you should know them well.

5. An *adjective* may either serve as a noun or modify a noun. When an adjective modifies a noun, that adjective and noun form a small word cluster.

6. The other main type of word in a sentence is the *adverb*, including the negatives οὐ and μή. These serve as modifiers to the main elements in

---

4. There are constructions in which the complement is not in the nominative case: e.g., in the double accusative of object and complement referred to below in note 6.

5. This accusative is actually an accusative of respect. See the discussion on Luke 1:57 in app. 1.

6. See chap. 4, note 2. An example of the double accusative of object and complement is discussed below in connection with Rev. 5:10.

7. These verbs are "usually transitive in English," and the dative is used "to denote the sole complement or object (i.e. when no other object is present)" (Funk, §1130).

a sentence, usually the verb, and they do not form word clusters by themselves.

7. As you survey a sentence, watch especially for the *article*, since it often connects words together into clusters and performs other important functions, such as substantivizing adjectives and participles, as we have seen.

Once you have examined a sentence, sorting out parsings and noting word groups and the overall structure, then fill in the vocabulary. For each unfamiliar word, before looking up the information make the best educated guess you can. Reading actively like this is very important because it helps you make connections, pay more attention, and thus internalize answers when you get them, instead of just getting puzzle pieces and hurrying on.

Step 3: Rereading

Once you have sorted out the passage sentence by sentence, you should immediately reread the passage several times. *This step is crucial for becoming comfortable in Greek.* As you read the text, work at picking up the meaning as it comes in the Greek order, paying attention to the signals just discussed. Pronounce the text aloud at least once or twice. If there are structures or clusters that were difficult to sort out, use this repetition to become more comfortable with them. Such repetition builds vocabulary and parsing ability, helps you become comfortable with the Greek flow of thought, and increases your ability to engage the passage's message directly. You are moving from puzzling, to translating quickly, to reading.

As you reread, especially the first several times through the passage, you probably will mentally use English translations of the words, somewhat like a mental interlinear. But as you continue to reread and get familiar with the flow and the vocabulary, you will find that you are moving toward a focus on the meaning of the Greek words without translating into English.

It is particularly valuable to do some of this rereading word by word. Train yourself to walk through a text word by word.[8] At each word ask yourself what a Greek hearer/reader would find in this word to convey meaning to him or her, using the following questions. These questions focus on both the

---

8. Such an approach is advocated by William Gardner Hale. I have modified his description of how to analyze a word as given in his *The Art of Reading Latin: How to Teach It* (Boston: Ginn, 1887), 5–17; and *Aims and Methods in Classical Study* (Boston: Ginn, 1888), 26–37. See also his more general discussion in "An Experiment in the Teaching of First and Second Year Latin," *Classical Journal* 1, no. 1 (December 1905): 7–18. These resources are available online (see bibliography). I recommend reading at least the first several pages of *The Art of Reading Latin* for a valuable (and humorous) explanation and example of this approach.

lexical contribution of the individual word and its role in the structures of a clause or sentence.

1. *Inflection and Part of Speech*: What do the word's parsing and part of speech suggest about its role in the sentence or clause?
2. *Position*: How does this word fit in the structure of the sentence?
   • What light does this word throw on the sentence up to this point? Does it clarify something that was uncertain earlier in the sentence?
   • What light does it throw on what lies ahead in the sentence? What are the possible constructions ahead in the light of this word?
   • Does the word require a specific construction to complete its meaning?
3. *Signification*: What are the main options for the meaning of the word?

Attention to each word as it comes in the way outlined here will greatly increase your familiarity and comfort with Greek and help move you toward fluency. In the early stages of your life in Greek, you will need to puzzle through passages, but eventually this word-by-word approach can become your initial scan—you are simply reading the text. As your experience in more complex texts increases and you become more familiar with vocabulary and morphology, you will need to pause and puzzle less and less.

Rapid Reading

After you have worked through several passages and you begin to develop a feel for Greek through the rereading exercises, it is helpful to spend some time trying to read rapidly—something like C. S. Lewis's experience that was mentioned in the introduction. Scan a text or read it word by word without pausing to get all the details sorted out. Then read a translation to see how close you got to its meaning. Such rapid reading helps you learn to pick up the signals in the text more quickly.

Software programs are especially helpful for rapid reading. They provide multiple tabs or pages, so you can have one of your tabs in BibleWorks, Accordance, or Logos set up to read a text in this fashion. One procedure you might try is to work through the text verse by verse, with the current verse on the screen. Read over the verse, making as much sense of it as you can along the lines of Hoyos's rules and the word-by-word approach, without looking at a translation. Then fill in any vocabulary or parsing that you do not know by mousing over the words. Once you think you have the main idea, check a translation, note any major errors you may have made, and move on.

If your main interest is in the GNT, then you might want to do your rapid reading in a New Testament book, but it is also valuable to encounter less familiar texts. I recommend reading the Psalter and the Apostolic Fathers, both of which are valuable in themselves and also in their connection with the GNT.

Fluency beyond the Passage—What Is Your Goal?

Perhaps your goal is familiarity with a set of favorite passages. If so, you can work through them with the three steps just described. It can be helpful to write brief notes on the parsing, vocabulary, and grammar needed to read each text. Be sure to include in the notes only what you need in order to read the text, since it is easy to set the plow too deep and get bogged down. There are obviously many ways to collect, store, and access such notes. I find that writing these brief fluency notes by hand slows me down and allows me to pay attention to the data instead of just processing it. So you might consider keeping a paper notebook instead of an electronic document. These personal notes will enable you to reread the passage repeatedly in the future with increasing ease.

After you have worked through some favorite passages, you may want to choose a book to work through. Now your goal is fluency in a whole book! A notebook becomes even more valuable, since it is harder to remember all the necessary details for a large amount of text.

If your goal is to become fluent in the GNT, then you can break this goal down into pieces, aiming at fluency sentence by sentence, paragraph by paragraph, chapter by chapter, book by book. Even if you never become fluent in the whole GNT, you will be familiar with the passages you have read, and you will enjoy the benefits they bring to your life.

Perhaps your goal is even bigger: to become fluent in a large body of literature, such as the LXX or even major collections of texts in Homeric Greek, Classical Greek (fifth century BC Attic texts), Hellenistic Greek, or Patristic Greek. Obviously it takes time to become comfortable in Greek, especially to gain such general fluency. If you want to become fluent—able to pick up a text and read it rapidly, accurately, automatically, and in keeping with its rhythmical structures—there is no substitute for spending lots of time reading.[9] You will need to have a good grasp of the forms that words can take and a relatively large vocabulary, and you will need to read extensively in a variety of genres and authors.[10]

9. For these elements of fluency, see the introduction.
10. There are readers for each of these bodies of literature, which provide helpful starting points. See note 15 below.

Resources for Reading Greek

There are wonderful resources for help with all these aspects of reading we have been considering. But be careful. They need to be used wisely or they will actually decrease your knowledge of Greek!

Software and the Internet

Software programs such as BibleWorks, Accordance, and Logos provide not only the biblical texts but also a number of other Greek texts as well, along with translations. All the words in a text are coded, so mousing over a word in the Greek provides the parsing of the word as well as a lexical entry. Syntactical and discourse help for the GNT is also available through Logos and the web.[11]

On the internet[12] the most comprehensive set of texts, from Homer and Classical authors through the Patristic period, is found in the *Thesaurus Linguae Graecae*. Unfortunately, access to this resource is very expensive. On the *Perseus* website Homer and many Classical texts (Greek and Latin), as well as the New Testament (Westcott-Hort edition), are available for free, along with English translations and other reference material. As with the software programs, the Greek texts in *TLG* and *Perseus* are tagged so you can click on a word and get its parsing, a basic definition, and links to several lexicons, including both LS and the larger LSJ. You can also look up words directly in the lexicons on *Perseus*, so this site is valuable even if you do not plan to read Homer or Classical texts.[13] The grammar by Smyth is also available through *Perseus*, which is especially helpful when you are reading outside the GNT.

Older public domain resources are available on a number of websites, some of which also provide parsing help.[14] More extensive and up-to-date help for learning Greek and reading the GNT is also available. Since these sites go in and out of existence, I suggest that you check the links on the following sites to see what is currently available:

11. For such help, see http://opentext.org/. This resource and several others are available in Logos software. See Dean Deppe, *The Lexham Clausal Outlines of the Greek New Testament* (Bellingham, WA: Logos Bible Software, 2006); Albert L. Lukaszewski and Mark Dubis, *The Lexham Syntactic Greek New Testament* (Bellingham, WA: Logos Bible Software, 2009); Stanley Porter, Matthew Brook O'Donnell, Jeffrey T. Reed, et al., *The OpenText.org Syntactically Analyzed Greek New Testament* (Bellingham, WA: Logos Bible Software, 2006); and Stanley E. Porter, Matthew Brook O'Donnell, Jeffrey T. Reed, et al., *The OpenText.org Syntactically Analyzed Greek New Testament: Clause Analysis; OpenText.org Clause Analysis* (Bellingham, WA: Logos Bible Software, 2006).

12. URLs for the resources in this paragraph are in the bibliography.

13. In a video (see website for this book) I demonstrate how to look up a word in a lexicon on *Perseus*.

14. For example, http://biblehub.com.

http://www.ntgateway.com/greek-ntgateway/greek-new-testament-texts/
http://www.ibiblio.org/bgreek/forum/index.php
http://www.biblicalgreek.org/links/

Books

A number of Greek readers provide help for selected passages in the GNT and many bodies of Greek literature.[15] There also are several books designed to help you read the GNT rapidly. *The UBS Greek New Testament: A Reader's Edition*[16] and Zondervan's *A Reader's Greek New Testament*[17] present the Greek text, with footnotes providing meanings of words used fewer than 30 times and a lexicon for words used more than 30 times. The UBS reader also includes parsing help. It gives the text of UBS[4]/NA[28], while the Zondervan volume gives the text followed by *Today's New International Version*, with footnotes to indicate where this text differs from UBS[4]/NA[27]. The UBS reader gives definitions chosen for each specific context, while the Zondervan reader lists multiple definitions for each word.

Another good resource, *A New Reader's Lexicon of the Greek New Testament*,[18] lists verse by verse the vocabulary used fewer than 50 times. Usually more than one definition is given, though they are all context specific and usually follow BDAG. The book does not include the Greek text or a list of vocabulary used 50 times or more; nor does it help with parsings. A companion book provides the same information for reading the Apostolic Fathers.[19]

15. See, e.g., F. C. Conybeare and St. George Stock, *Grammar of Septuagint Greek with Selected Readings from the Septuagint according to the Text of Swete* (1905; repr., Peabody, MA: Hendrickson, 1988); Rodney J. Decker, *Koine Greek Reader: Selections from the New Testament, Septuagint, and Early Christian Writers* (Grand Rapids: Kregel, 2007); Joint Association of Classical Teachers' Greek Course, *A World of Heroes: Selections from Homer, Herodotus and Sophocles* (Cambridge: Cambridge University Press, 1979); Joint Association of Classical Teachers' Greek Course, *The Intellectual Revolution: Selections from Euripides, Thucydides and Plato* (Cambridge: Cambridge University Press, 1980); William D. Mounce, *A Graded Reader of Biblical Greek* (Grand Rapids: Zondervan, 1996); Rodney A. Whitacre, *A Patristic Greek Reader* (Grand Rapids: Baker Academic, 2007); and Allen Wikgren, in collaboration with Ernest Cadman Colwell and Ralph Marcus, *Hellenistic Greek Texts* (Chicago: University of Chicago Press, 1947). For a reader containing poetry from Homer to the twentieth century, see Constantine A. Trypanis, ed., *The Penguin Book of Greek Verse* (New York: Penguin, 1971).

16. *The UBS Greek New Testament: A Reader's Edition* (Stuttgart: Deutsche Bibelgesellschaft, 2014).

17. Richard J. Goodrich and Albert L. Lukaszewski, eds., *A Reader's Greek New Testament*, 2nd ed. (Grand Rapids: Zondervan, 2007). This resource is also available bound with a Hebrew Bible with similar helps: A. Philip Brown II, Bryan W. Smith, Richard J. Goodrich, and Albert L. Lukaszewski, eds., *A Reader's Hebrew and Greek Bible* (Grand Rapids: Zondervan, 2010).

18. Michael H. Burer and Jeffrey E. Miller, eds., *A New Reader's Lexicon of the Greek New Testament* (Grand Rapids: Kregel, 2008).

19. Daniel B. Wallace, Brittany C. Burnette, and Terri Darby Moore, eds., *A Reader's Lexicon of the Apostolic Fathers* (Grand Rapids: Kregel, 2013).

Finally, a particularly helpful resource is the more comprehensive set of notes by Zerwick and Grosvenor, *An Analysis of the Greek New Testament.*[20] This book offers brief help for parsing, vocabulary, and grammar for every verse in the New Testament. You could be on a desert island and read the GNT with only this book.[21]

Caution

These amazing resources obviously can greatly speed up your reading of a text, but just getting the data and dashing on will not necessarily improve your knowledge of Greek—such "data processing," as it were, is not the same as reading! You need to think about what you are seeing in the text. In the past, when people had to sort out parsings on their own and look up words in a print lexicon, it could be frustrating to look up the same word repeatedly if one's memory was not very retentive. This problem would make it hard to develop fluency, but the very slowness of the process gave opportunity to pay attention. Now you have to build in opportunity for paying attention. On occasion you might work through a passage without digital helps, using just a print lexicon and a set of paradigms.[22] When you do use digital resources, I suggest that you not look up a parsing or definition until you have spent at least ten seconds of hard work trying to sort it out from your memory. This mental work engages your mind so the answer has more of a chance to register and be retained.

These resources can be a great help if used wisely. They can also be a crutch that leads you to neglect the exercise of your Greek muscles, causing them to atrophy.[23]

Concluding Encouragement

Spending some time in both rapid and more careful reading pays the greatest dividends. You can set aside blocks of time to read passages, or you can set aside short periods, even just five minutes several days a week.

20. Maximilian Zerwick and Mary Grosvenor, *An Analysis of the Greek New Testament*, 5th ed. (Rome: Biblical Institute Press, 2010).

21. Zerwick, *Analysis*, cites Maximilian Zerwick, *Biblical Greek: Illustrated by Examples* (Rome: Biblical Institute Press, 1963), for discussion of particular grammatical details. *Analysis* is very useful, regardless of whether you have access to the additional resource by Zerwick.

22. *CGEL* lists irregular verb forms. Abbott-Smith includes appendixes with lists of irregular verbs and unusual verb forms.

23. For further thoughts on the values and dangers of software and tips for using it, see Constantine R. Campbell, *Keep Your Greek: Strategies for Busy People* (Grand Rapids: Zondervan, 2010), chap. 3.

For many people, the rapid reading of blocks of text will be an occasional exercise, while their main work in Greek day by day will be in particular passages in which they have a strong interest. They gain fluency passage by passage and reap the benefits immediately, while building knowledge of the language as they go along.

The main thing is to keep in the Greek. Working in the Greek for even a few minutes a day will enable you to keep the language fresh and know for yourself its value and joy.

UTILIZING GREEK IN MEDITATION

We now move from gaining fluency to engaging a text with depth. From learning how to see the sweep of a whole forest, we now consider how to examine closely a single tree. From guzzling we move to sipping.

The Basic Technique in Meditation

I have suggested that you work on fluency one passage at a time. This focus on a single passage moves seamlessly to meditation, for now in meditation we read a given passage repeatedly, sounding it out and turning over its details. In chapter 5 we saw William Harris's suggestions for working through a Latin passage on an initial level. Now here is his description of the further process, again equally relevant for Greek texts and not just poetry.

> Then memorize the poem you have selected, so you can speak and read it aloud from memory when the book is closed, when you are walking down the street or watching a sunset in another mood. Now you have something in Latin which has become a part of your mind, without the grammatical claptrap rearing up between you and the words. Walking around, away from the book, talk it through again. And again . . . and again. But sooner or later, at some critical point in your progression, you will be hearing and visualizing the images, the

thoughts. At this point, you are dealing directly with Meanings [*sic*] as you read, and you will be started off on the right road.[1]

Thus meditation is an extension of the crucial first step in exegesis, careful observation.[2] Meditation consists in reading and rereading a passage reflectively, even to the point of memorizing it, as Harris encourages. I remember at the annual meeting of the Society of Biblical Literature one year hearing Martin Hengel give a talk in which he held up his GNT and said, "It is a small book. You can memorize it." That would be a stretch for most of us, but memorizing verses, and even passages, is within reach and pays great dividends both for learning Greek and for life. You can rehearse them at any time, gaining not only inspiration but also the opportunity to have new insights into the text. This slow, thoughtful rereading and then recitation from memory allows the text to seep into your mind and imagination in very powerful ways that touch the heart, the will, and the emotions.[3]

As we see from Harris's example, such reflective reading is not specifically a religious exercise. People from all religions and no religion find passages that speak to them, which they memorize and turn to for inspiration, comfort, and guidance. Likewise, people focus on passages in different ways. I will mention two approaches in particular.

Approach 1: Meditation and Silence

An ancient Christian practice, which is shared with other religions, makes use of a word or passage to enter God's presence in silence. Such prayer has a number of names, including the prayer of the heart and contemplative prayer. There are several forms, including centering prayer, the Jesus Prayer, and passage meditation, among others.

In passage meditation you memorize a passage that is meaningful to you; its length does not matter. Then you set aside a period of time to recite this passage; usually 20–30 minutes is recommended. It is helpful to have reflected on the meaning of the passage before meditating on it, but during this time of prayer you do not reflect on the meaning of the words or analyze them. Rather,

---

1. William Harris, "The Sin of Transverbalizing . . . or Translating as you Read!" (online; see bibliography).

2. Manuals for interpretation stress observation and often cite the delightful and inspiring story "The Student, the Fish, and Agassiz." Available online, http://people.bethel.edu/~dhoward /resources/Agassizfish/Agassizfish.htm. This website includes information about the background of the story and its various versions.

3. Indeed, observation and rereading are part not only of exegesis and meditation but also of any careful reading. "Good readers re-read many things many times" (James W. Sire, *How to Read Slowly: A Christian Guide to Reading with the Mind* [Colorado Springs: WaterBrook, 1978], 21).

you sit in silence and stillness, repeating the words inwardly and focusing on their sound within the context of silence. When your attention gets distracted, you simply return to the recitation. In this practice you do actually engage the meaning of the words and what they point to, but on a level deeper than thought and emotion. "When you concentrate on the sounds of each word, you will also be concentrating on the meaning of the passage."[4] The words help us shift our attention off ourselves and become attentive to God's constant presence.

In other forms of such prayer, you use the same procedure as in passage meditation, but instead of focusing on a passage, you focus on a single word like God, *Abba*, Jesus, *maranatha*, or any other word or short phrase or sentence that provides a point of alignment with God. In passage meditation you change passages every now and then, but in most of these other approaches you may keep the same word, phrase, or sentence for years, or even for your entire life.

Although there are many books devoted to such prayer,[5] its practice is extremely simple. Obviously most people practice it using texts in their own language, but using Greek texts for passage meditation or for one of these other ways of praying can be very edifying.[6]

Approach 2: Meditation on the Passage Details

In this second approach, you do focus on the meanings and associations of the text—whether on the general thought of the passage, a few particular

4. Eknath Easwaran, *Passage Meditation: Bringing the Deep Wisdom of the Heart into Daily Life*, 3rd ed. (Tomales, CA: Nilgiri, 2008), 43. Easwaran's writings are very helpful. He often draws on Christian sources, though he comes from a Hindu context and some of his comments are not reflective of general Christian views. See related resources at http://www.easwaran.org /learning-how-to-meditate.html.

5. I find the writings of John Main especially helpful. See John Main, *Word into Silence: A Manual for Christian Meditation* (1980; repr., Norwich, England: Canterbury, 2006); and his *Word Made Flesh: Recovering a Sense of the Sacred through Prayer* (1993; repr., Norwich, England: Canterbury, 2009). There are many other excellent works, including Lev Gillet, *The Jesus Prayer*, rev. ed. (Crestwood, NY: St. Vladimir's Seminary Press, 1987), esp. 93–106; Thomas Keating, *Open Mind, Open Heart: The Contemplative Dimension of the Gospel*, 20th anniversary ed. (New York: Continuum, 2006); Martin Laird, *Into the Silent Land: A Guide to the Christian Practice of Contemplation* (Oxford: Oxford University Press, 2006); Martin Laird, *A Sunlit Absence: Silence, Awareness, and Contemplation* (Oxford: Oxford University Press, 2011); and George Maloney, *Prayer of the Heart: The Contemplative Tradition of the Christian East*, rev. ed. (Notre Dame, IN: Ave Maria, 2008).

6. In addition to the Aramaic word *maranatha* recommended by John Main, I value three short Greek expressions in particular: (1) Αββα ὁ πατήρ (Gal. 4:6; Rom. 8:15), (2) Εὐλογητὸς ὁ θεὸς καὶ πατὴρ τοῦ κυρίου ἡμῶν Ἰησοῦ Χριστοῦ (2 Cor. 1:3; Eph. 1:3; 1 Pet. 1:3), and (3) ὁ ὤν, the divine name according to Exod. 3:14. See the discussion of Rev. 1:4 later in this chapter, and note Rev. 1:4, 8; 4:8; 11:17; 16:5. For a prayer word during the day, I often use the vocative form Ἰησοῦ. For this word, I use the Modern Greek pronunciation in which both ι and η are pronounced *ee* (as in "seek"). So Ἰησοῦ comes out *ee-sou*, and these two sounds fit the thin quality of the in-breath and the fuller quality of the out-breath nicely.

images or words, or even the whole of the passage on a more detailed level. In the ancient church such meditation is often associated with the practice of finding several senses in a text. In contrast, the focus of many people today is on the grammatical-historical sense of the text. It is possible to combine these ancient and modern practices, so I will briefly discuss them both and then offer some examples. I hope the discussion will encourage you to practice meditation on passages in whatever form you find appropriate and helpful.

Ancient Christian Meditation and the Senses of Scripture

In the ancient world, reading was usually done out loud, so reading was not just a visual and mental exercise but also vocal, aural, and muscular. Such speaking and listening to the text resulted in "a muscular memory of the words pronounced and an aural memory of the words heard. . . . To meditate is to attach oneself closely to the sentence being recited and weigh all its words in order to sound the depths of their full meaning. It means assimilating the content of a text by means of a kind of mastication which releases its full flavor."[7] In the ancient church, believers ruminated on passages in the context of the whole of Scripture. The words and images in a passage were part of networks of associations, with the whole of Scripture forming a great code, all of which was seen in relation to Christ.[8] Thus the context for interpretation was not simply the book in which the passage occurred but primarily the whole Bible.

Furthermore, for those in the ancient church, words and images could convey meaning on several levels. John Cassian (360–435) speaks of Scripture as providing historical knowledge and three kinds of spiritual knowledge.[9] The historical "embraces the knowledge of past and visible things," and allegory[10] builds on the historical "because what really occurred is said to have prefigured the form of another mystery." Among the ancients the allegorical

7. Jean Leclercq, *The Love of Learning and the Desire for God: A Study of Monastic Culture*, trans. Catharine Misrahi, rev. ed. (New York: Fordham University Press, 1974), 90.

8. An allusion to Northrop Frye, *The Great Code: The Bible and Literature* (New York: Harcourt, Brace, Jovanovich, 1982). His literary study of the Bible dovetails with the ancients' view of the Bible at many points. "Wherever we stop, the unity of the Bible as a whole is an assumption underlying the understanding of any part of it. This unity is not primarily, we repeat, a metonymic consistency of doctrine addressed to our faith: it is a unity of narrative and imagery and what we have called implicit metaphor" (62). "The typological organization of the Bible does present the difficulty, to a secular literary critic, of being unique: no other book in the world, to my knowledge, has a structure even remotely like that of the Christian Bible" (80).

9. All quotes in this paragraph are from John Cassian, *The Conferences*, trans. and ed. Boniface Ramsey, Ancient Christian Writers 57 (New York: Paulist Press, 1997), 14.8 (pp. 509–11). Cassian's text is also available in NPNF² 11:437–38.

10. Ἀλληγορία, "an allegory, i.e., description of one thing under the image of another" (LS 37). The verb form, ἀλληγορέω, occurs in Gal. 4:24.

sense usually points to the person and work of Christ and the church. Anagogy[11] "mounts from spiritual mysteries to certain more sublime and sacred heavenly secrets." The anagogical reference is usually to the invisible heavenly realities now and/or the future final state. "Tropology[12] is moral explanation pertaining to correction of life and to practical instruction." Cassian illustrates these four "figures," as he calls them, with the use of the term "Jerusalem" in Scripture. "According to history it is the city of the Jews. According to allegory it is the church of Christ. According to anagogy it is that heavenly city of God 'which is the mother of us all.'[13] According to tropology it is the soul of the human being, which under this name is frequently either reproached or praised by the Lord."

A similar view of the senses of Scripture is found in Augustine of Hippo (354–430)[14] and the ancient church in general. Thomas Aquinas (1225–74) lays out these senses at the beginning of his *Summa Theologica*, noting that the literal, historical sense is the basic sense and is presupposed by the spiritual senses.[15] Augustine of Dacia (d. 1282) summarizes the senses nicely: "The letter teaches events, allegory what you should believe, morality what you should do, anagogy what mark you should be aiming for."[16]

Leaders of the ancient church emphasized the place of prayer and one's right relationship with God for hearing God in and through the text. The connection between meditation on Scripture and prayer is seen in the ancient practice of *lectio divina*. The repeated reading with attentiveness that I have mentioned forms the first two elements in *lectio divina*, namely *lectio*, listening/reading, and *meditatio*, meditation—ruminating as we ponder the details of the passage. In the context of this pondering we can practice the third element of *lectio divina*, *oratio*—praying as we reflect on the passage. Such prayer might include offering adoration, confession, thanksgiving, and/or intercession in response to what we are hearing through the passage. The fourth element, *contemplatio*, contemplation, is not further thought or emotion in light of the passage but a resting in God's presence in silence and stillness in the context of what we have heard in the passage. That is, in *contemplatio*

11. From ἀναγωγή, "a leading up." Cf. ἀνάγω.

12. From τρόπος, "manner or way," including the way in which a person behaves or lives. See BDAG, τρόπος 2, 1017.

13. Cassian here alludes to Gal. 4:26. He illustrates each of the four senses from Gal. 4 and then adds further illustrations, mostly from Paul. It was common in the ancient church to appeal to Paul for how to read Scripture. See Margaret M. Mitchell, *Paul, the Corinthians and the Birth of Christian Hermeneutics* (Cambridge: Cambridge University Press, 2010).

14. *The Literal Meaning of Genesis*, 1.1.

15. *Summa Theologica*, 1.1.10.

16. "Littera gesta docet, quid credas allegoria, moralis quid agas, quo tendas anagogia." Quoted from *Rotulus pugillaris* in Henri de Lubac, *The Four Senses of Scripture*, vol. 1 of *Medieval Exegesis*, trans. Mark Sebanc (Grand Rapids: Eerdmans, 1998; French original, 1959), 1.

an image or a theme or a particular word of the text provides a framework or ground or orientation for stepping back from all thoughts and emotions and simply opening ourselves to the actual presence of God, instead of our thoughts and feelings about God.[17] So *lectio divina* leads to the silent prayer we saw in approach 1.

There is much more to be said about the ancient views of the Bible, its interpretation, and its engagement through *lectio divina*, but this brief description must suffice for present purposes.[18] During the Reformation some elements of the ancient views were rejected and others were modified, and even more so after the Enlightenment. But large parts of the church have continued these views and practices, and even in the post-Reformation church there are striking examples.[19] In our own time there is renewed interest in these early views and practices throughout much of the church.[20]

17. John of the Cross has a delightful description of the four parts of *lectio divina* using Jesus's saying about asking, seeking, and knocking (Matt. 7:7; Luke 11:9): "Seek in reading and you will find in meditation; knock in prayer and it will be opened to you in contemplation" ("Maxims on Love" no. 79, in *The Collected Works of St. John of the Cross*, trans. Kieran Kavanaugh and Otilio Rodriguez [Washington, DC: ICS, 1973], 680). This saying itself is an example of reading according to the spiritual senses rather than the literal/historical.

18. For excellent introductions to ancient Christian views of the Bible and its interpretation, see John J. O'Keefe and R. R. Reno, *Sanctified Vision: An Introduction to Early Christian Interpretation of the Bible* (Baltimore: Johns Hopkins University Press, 2005); Frances M. Young, *Virtuoso Theology: The Bible and Interpretation* (Eugene, OR: Wipf & Stock, 2002), originally published under the title *The Art of Performance: Towards a Theology of Holy Scripture* (London: Darton, Longman & Todd, 1990); Christopher A. Hall, *Reading Scripture with the Church Fathers* (Downers Grove, IL: InterVarsity, 1998); and Michael Graves, *The Inspiration and Interpretation of Scripture: What the Early Church Can Teach Us* (Grand Rapids: Eerdmans, 2014). Two of the most insightful works I know of for this topic are Frances M. Young, *Biblical Exegesis and the Formation of Christian Culture* (Cambridge: Cambridge University Press, 1997; repr., Peabody, MA: Hendrickson, 2002); and Andrew Louth, *Discerning the Mystery: An Essay on the Nature of Theology* (Oxford: Clarendon, 1983). Among the many books on *lectio divina*, see Stephen J. Binz, *Conversing with God in Scripture: A Contemporary Approach to Lectio Divina* (Ijamsville, MD: The Word among Us, 2008); and Michael Casey, *Sacred Readings: The Ancient Art of* Lectio Divina (Liguori, MO: Liguori Publications, 1995).

19. For example, Frye comments:

> For the preacher's purpose the immediate context of the sentence is as likely to be three hundred pages off as to be the next or the preceding sentence. Ideally, every sentence is the key to the whole Bible. This is not a factual statement about the Bible, but it helps to explain the practice of preachers who knew what they were doing, like some of those in seventeenth-century England. In the sermons of John Donne [1572–1631], for example, we can see how the text leads us, like a guide with a candle, into the vast labyrinth of Scripture, which to Donne was an infinitely bigger structure than the cathedral he was preaching in. (*Code*, 208–9)

George Herbert (1593–1633) provides a particularly good example. See my article "George Herbert and Biblical Theology," *Trinity Journal for Theology and Ministry* 3, no. 1 (Spring 2009): 67–88. Available online (see bibliography).

20. The references in note 18 illustrate this point, as do many recent titles from major evangelical publishers, especially Baker, Eerdmans, and InterVarsity.

Meditation and Exegesis

How do these ancient views and practices relate to modern grammatical-historical exegesis? Some modern interpreters share little, if anything, in common with precritical interpreters.[21] Other modern interpreters do not use the spiritual senses of Scripture but do have views similar to the ancients' views of the Bible as a coherent inspired revelation providing knowledge of the person of God, the purposes of God, and the pattern of life that is in alignment with God.[22] So some modern approaches to the Bible overlap with elements of the assumptions behind *lectio divina*. Likewise, many modern discussions of *lectio divina* point out the value of grammatical-historical exegesis for our understanding of the ancients' literal/historical sense of Scripture, and they also note how this form of interpretation comes into play in our *lectio* and *meditatio*.[23] But in fact, as mentioned earlier, you can practice *lectio divina* without reference to any of the precritical views of the ancient church.

Similarly, you can reflect on insights in the Greek text without reference to *lectio divina* at all. A. T. Robertson, for example, published a six-volume collection of details in the Greek text that he found interesting.[24] He included a variety of types of data, specifically focused on the research of the day.

> These volumes do not claim to be formal commentary. Nowhere is the whole text discussed, but everywhere those words are selected for discussion which seem to be richest for the needs of the reader in the light of present-day knowledge. A great deal of the personal equation is thus inevitable. My own remarks will be now lexical, now grammatical, now archaeological, now exegetical, now illustrative, anything that the mood of the moment may move me to write that may throw light here and there on the New Testament words and idioms.[25]

21. James L. Kugel (*How to Read the Bible: A Guide to Scripture, Then and Now* [New York: Free Press, 2007]) gives fascinating examples of ancient and modern approaches to texts and includes reflections on the tension of trying to value both the ancient and the modern views.

22. See especially the numerous current studies associated with Biblical Theology and the theological interpretation of the Bible. For examples, see T. Desmond Alexander, Brian S. Rosner, D. A. Carson, and Graeme Goldsworthy, eds., *New Dictionary of Biblical Theology: Exploring the Unity and Diversity of Scripture* (Downers Grove, IL: InterVarsity, 2000); and Kevin J. Vanhoozer, Craig G. Bartholomew, Daniel J. Treier, and N. T. Wright, eds., *Dictionary for Theological Interpretation of the Bible* (Grand Rapids: Baker Academic, 2005).

23. I use "literal/historical" for the ancient view and "grammatical-historical" for the modern since there is overlap, but also significant difference, between them. See Young, *Biblical Exegesis*, esp. 186–89.

24. *Word Pictures in the New Testament*, 6 vols. (Nashville: Broadman, 1930–33).

25. Ibid., 1:ix.

Similarly, a recent collection of fifty-two short "devotions" on passages in the Greek text of the New Testament by thirty-two authors highlights a variety of features in the passages.

> Some insights focus on particular words and their role in the passage, while others highlight background studies or provide a theological reading of the passage. Some contributions diagram the passage, others trace important literary patterns such as chiasms, and still others draw attention to the connections between the Old and New Testament. Each devotion draws students into translating a short passage and understanding why this or that insight matters greatly for our life and ministry.[26]

These devotions give an idea of some of the many ways Greek can be helpful. Lexical and grammatical observations are the most frequent subjects in this volume.

Another helpful set of brief "exegetical insights" by twenty-two different authors is included by William D. Mounce in his *Basics of Biblical Greek*.[27] These insights are given at the beginning of most of the chapters and almost always focus on points of grammar discussed in that chapter.

Thus, while at the outset of this chapter we heard William Harris advocate moving beyond "grammatical claptrap" to the direct engagement with the meanings and images of a passage, these recent devotions and insights often focus on points of grammar. They illustrate some of the fruit of exegesis and the way Greek can illumine the text.

A Hybrid Approach

In a hybrid of the ancient and the modern approaches, grammatical-historical exegesis is foundational for understanding a text. The details you reflect on and turn into prayer as you meditate on a passage often correspond to the fruit of exegesis, especially the meanings of words and "grammatical claptrap" such as the possible nuances of cases, the middle voice, the definite article, and verbal aspect and *Aktionsart*.[28] But in your personal engagement with the text, you might also make use at times of the three spiritual senses by exploring how words or images may be taken as references to Christ, the church, and/or the life of discipleship. In this approach the idea is not to spiritualize the details

26. J. Scott Duvall and Verlyn D. Verbrugge, eds., *Devotions on the Greek New Testament: 52 Reflections to Inspire & Instruct* (Grand Rapids: Zondervan, 2012).

27. William D. Mounce, *Basics of Biblical Greek: Grammar*, 3rd ed. (Grand Rapids: Zondervan, 2009).

28. For the middle voice, aspect, and *Aktionsart*, see app. 5.

of the passage through abstraction but rather to work with the details in the context of the church's faith, the *regula fidei*.[29] In this approach there need not be one right interpretation.[30]

> So when one person has said "Moses thought what I say," and another "No, what I say," I think it more religious in spirit to say "Why not rather say both, if both are true?" And if anyone sees a third or fourth and a further truth in these words, why not believe that Moses discerned all these things? For through him the one God has tempered the sacred books to the interpretations of many, who could come to see a diversity of truths.[31]

Thus, this approach is not a method, nor does a method of interpretation validate a given reading of the passage, as in modern exegesis. Rather, in this approach a reading is valid if it is congruent with the biblical faith, which is grounded in the church's reception of the biblical revelation as a whole.

Take for example Ps. 137:9, "Blessed shall he be who takes your little ones and dashes them against the rock!" (ESV). This psalm is set during the Babylonian exile (v. 1), and the grammatical-historical sense of verse 9 is obviously a desire for literal children to be smashed, as the Babylonians had done to the Israelite children (v. 8). A spiritual reading common in the ancient church takes Babylon as an image of the enemy of God (drawing on biblical usage such as 1 Pet. 5:13; Rev. 17–18) and then applies this on a personal level. In this way Babylonian babies are taken as evil thoughts arising within us. The rock is taken as a reference to God, in keeping with its frequent use in the Old Testament (e.g., Deut. 32:4; Ps. 19:14), or more specifically to Christ (1 Cor. 10:4). Read in this way, this verse provides an image for what to do with temptations and sinful thoughts when they first arise—dash them against the rock, which is Christ. This verse thus provides powerful imagery for prayer and discipleship, and it leads you on to consider how you go about dashing thoughts against

---

29. *Regula fidei* means "the rule of faith," a term used beginning in the second century. It represents the common teaching of the church, but it is not a clearly articulated set of beliefs like the creeds. "The essential message was fixed by the facts of the gospel and the structure of Christian belief in one God, reception of salvation in Christ, and experience of the Holy Spirit; but each teacher had his own way of stating or elaborating these points" (Everett Ferguson, "Rule of Faith," in *Encyclopedia of Early Christianity*, ed. Everett Ferguson [New York: Garland, 1990], 804–5).

30. Rowan Greer notes that "the Rule of faith is a negative rather than a positive principle. That is, it excludes incorrect interpretations but does not require a correct one. Of a given passage there may be many interpretations that are valid because they do not contradict the Rule of faith, but we cannot be sure of its true meaning. . . . The unity of valid scriptural interpretation does not require uniformity" (James L. Kugel and Rowan A. Greer, *Early Biblical Interpretation*, Library of Early Christianity [Philadelphia: Westminster, 1986], 197).

31. Saint Augustine, *Confessions*, trans. Henry Chadwick (Oxford: Oxford University Press, 1991), 12.31(42), 270–71.

>‑ρ‑‑ρ‑ρ

the rock of Christ. The reading is valid in that it is congruent with the biblical faith in general. This figural reading opens up ways of engaging the text that differ from those of a grammatical-historical reading. While at times some ancient Christian teachers would focus only on this spiritual sense to the neglect or even rejection of the literal-historical sense, such a response is not necessary; we can engage both the grammatical-historical and the figural.[32]

Also in keeping with the views and practices of the ancient church, you might sometimes play with multiple meanings of words.[33] That is, not only may a word have multiple referents, as in the spiritual senses, but also more than one meaning of a word may be of interest. In exegesis we seek the one best interpretation of a word or point of grammar,[34] but in ancient interpretation it was common to reflect on multiple meanings of a term if they expressed truths about Christ. For example, Origen (185–254) examines six possible meanings of the word ἀρχή in John 1:1 and sifts through them for the one he thinks is best for that passage, somewhat like a modern exegete would do. But Origen also reflects on how the other senses are also relevant for understanding Christ.[35]

In a similar fashion, in meditation you might sometimes explore different possible readings of a word or point of grammar. For example, in passages in which Paul refers to πίστις Χριστοῦ and related terms, exegetes struggle to decide whether Paul is referring to faith in Christ (Χριστοῦ as an objective genitive) or to Christ's own faith/faithfulness (subjective genitive). When you are meditating on such passages, it can be fruitful to reflect on what each of these interpretations would say to you. If you find value in both interpretations, you could test your reflections by Paul's thought in general and the larger

32. The grammatical-historical reading obviously includes attention to the figural in poetic passages, but imagery is actually pervasive throughout the biblical genres. In particular, our language for spiritual realities is primarily metaphorical. Paul's "in Christ" is a spatial metaphor. Indeed, much of our language in general is metaphorical. See George Lakoff and Mark Johnson, *Metaphors We Live By*, with a new afterword (Chicago: University of Chicago Press, 2003). This fact has great significance for those who teach and preach. See Warren W. Wiersbe, *Teaching and Preaching with Imagination: The Quest for Biblical Ministry* (Grand Rapids: Baker, 1994).

33. Here we see an example of a difference between ancient and modern views, mentioned in note 23 above. Developments in hermeneutical thought are leading to a renewed interest in the ancient approaches to the text, as noted by Young (*Biblical Exegesis*) and Louth (*Discerning the Mystery*), among many others.

34. See, e.g., Moisés Silva, *Biblical Words and Their Meaning: An Introduction to Lexical Semantics*, rev. and exp. (Grand Rapids: Zondervan, 1995), 148–56. Silva notes that sometimes an author intends ambiguity, but he thinks this is rare, and in any case, "context serves to *eliminate* multiple meanings" (150, emphasis original). As examples of scholars who embrace more ambiguity, he cites Nigel Turner, *Grammatical Insights into the New Testament* (Edinburgh: T&T Clark, 1965); and Maximilian Zerwick, *Biblical Greek: Illustrated by Examples* (Rome: Biblical Institute Press, 1963).

35. *Commentary on the Gospel of John* 1.16–22 (*ANF* 10:305–8). See the helpful discussion of this passage in O'Keefe and Reno, *Sanctified Vision*, 53–56.

biblical revelation. Thus, in meditation you can often ponder alternate readings when there is doubt about the intended sense, or even when it is fairly plain.

Similarly, etymologies and other word associations noted in chapter 2 can be suggestive for meditation. Before utilizing etymology in this way, however, you must understand its limitations and the proper role etymology can play in determining the meaning of a word in context.[36] This knowledge helps you distinguish an insight into the meaning of the word from a devotional association that may be suggestive to you personally.

Such meditation may bring new insights into the exegesis of the passage, but that would be a by-product of meditation. The focus in meditation is on what the text says to you personally, and how you should pray in the light of this engagement with the text. Thus, such meditation is a part of prayer, as it was for the ancients. You are listening through the text in the presence of Christ.

The ultimate fruit of this practice is its effect in our lives. The nuances and insights gained in this way are nourishing and transformative, but they are also often quite personal. While insights from meditation can sometimes be shared with others through teaching, preaching, and/or personal sharing from Scripture, the main fruit is borne in our life, whether or not it is something useful to others.

Examples of Meditation

The following examples illustrate a mixture of the ancient and modern approaches just outlined. Given the nature of meditation, these are my personal reflections.

Matthew 11:28–30

28   Δεῦτε πρός με πάντες οἱ κοπιῶντες καὶ πεφορτισμένοι,
      κἀγὼ ἀναπαύσω ὑμᾶς.

29   ἄρατε τὸν ζυγόν μου ἐφ᾽ ὑμᾶς
      καὶ μάθετε ἀπ᾽ ἐμοῦ,
          ὅτι πραΰς εἰμι καὶ ταπεινὸς τῇ καρδίᾳ,
          καὶ εὑρήσετε ἀνάπαυσιν ταῖς ψυχαῖς ὑμῶν
30   ὁ γὰρ ζυγός μου χρηστὸς
          καὶ τὸ φορτίον μου ἐλαφρόν ἐστιν.

36. See, e.g., Silva, *Biblical Words*, and the exegetical resources cited in chap. 2.

28   Come to me, all who labor and are heavy laden,
and I will give you rest.

29   Take my yoke upon you,
and learn from me,
     for I am gentle and lowly in heart,
     and you will find rest for your souls.
30   For my yoke is easy,
      and my burden is light. (ESV)

δεῦτε. All of the translations I consulted translate this word with the verb "come."[37] Interestingly, in Greek it is not a verb but rather the adverb δεῦρο with a second person plural ending added! As Danker notes in BDAG,[38] it serves as a hortatory particle. In meditating on the word, I played with the two senses of δεῦρο: spatial, "here," and temporal, "now." "The basic idea is position in the presence of the speaker with focus on immediacy; hence temporality and peremptoriness are related aspects."[39] So we respond here and now. "Here-now to me, all you who are laboring and are heavy laden." This would not be a good translation, but it expresses the point of my meditation. The very combination expresses the more general idea of living consciously here with Christ in the present moment. There seems to be something biblical in the slogan from the 1960s, "Be here now." "Here-now toward me" is a striking summary of the orientation of *contemplatio*. So δεῦτε πρός με is a wonderful text for the passage meditation of approach 1; indeed, this whole passage is such.

πάντες οἱ κοπιῶντες καὶ πεφορτισμένοι. I often reflect on the verb tense-forms, noting here the progressive aspect of κοπιῶντες and that πεφορτισμένοι is stative.[40] So we have an activity and a state. These are people in the midst of laboring, and they are weighed down by loads or burdens that have been placed on them. The perfect tense-form can be middle or passive, so these

37. For these examples I have consulted the following twelve translations, representing a variety of translation strategies: the Common English Bible (2011), English Revised Version (1885), English Standard Version (2011), Holman Christian Standard Bible (2009), New American Bible (2010), New American Standard Bible (1995), NET Bible (2004), New International Version (2011), New Jerusalem Bible (1985), New Living Translation (2007), New Revised Standard Version (1989), and Revised English Bible (1989).

38. BDAG 220.

39. *CGEL* 87.

40. As noted in app. 5, there is debate over whether the perfect tense is stative in its aspect or stative due to the particular lexeme.

burdens have been placed by others or by themselves. The passive is exegetically more likely, but in meditation I might include reflection on self-imposed burdens as well.

κἀγώ. There is probably a bit of emphasis in this pronoun. Jesus says, "You are laboring, and you have had burdens loaded on you, and it is I who can give you rest." Jesus expresses a strong self-reference throughout these verses. Exegetically the contrast is probably with the scribes and Pharisees, but in meditation we can explore other referents that play such a role for us. This exercise is similar to the way many manuals for exegesis approach the application of a passage.[41]

ἄρατε . . . καὶ μάθετε. Aorist imperatives are often used for specific things to be done by specific people in a specific setting.[42] But since Jesus is speaking to all who are laboring and weighed down, the aorists here signal a general instruction viewed as a whole, in keeping with the perfective aspect of the aorist.[43] These two actions are the prerequisites for finding the rest Jesus speaks of.

ὅτι. All of the English translations I have consulted translate ὅτι as "for," interpreting Jesus's gentleness and lowliness of heart as the reason for learning from him. But after a verb like μανθάνω ("I learn"), the ὅτι could well give the content of what is to be learned.[44] We will find rest as we enter into Jesus's own way of humility as one who is πραΰς and ταπεινὸς τῇ καρδίᾳ. Jesus's dealing with both his disciples and his opponents was often not gentle, but in his heart orientation toward the Father he was always πραΰς καὶ ταπεινὸς τῇ καρδίᾳ.

πραΰς. This word is translated "gentle" by nine of the translations and "meek" by two (ERV and NAB).[45] Danker describes its sense as "characterized

41. E.g., J. Scott Duvall and J. Daniel Hays, *Grasping God's Word*, 3rd ed. (Grand Rapids: Zondervan, 2012), 43–45, 235–47.

42. See Constantine R. Campbell, *Basics of Verbal Aspect in Biblical Greek* (Grand Rapids: Zondervan, 2008), 92.

43. See Constantine R. Campbell, *Verbal Aspect and Non-indicative Verbs: Further Soundings in the Greek of the New Testament*, Studies in Biblical Greek 15 (New York: Peter Lang, 2008), 86–91. Wallace understands such aorist imperatives to be constatives that stress "the solemnity and urgency of the action" (720). But Young is probably correct that the urgency is "derived from the situation and the authority of the speaker . . . not from the tense form" (143).

44. After noticing in meditation that ὅτι could give the content, I found that some commentaries mention this option, including Alfred Plummer, *An Exegetical Commentary on the Gospel according to St. Matthew* (1910; repr., Grand Rapids: Eerdmans, 1956), 170; W. D. Davies and Dale C. Allison, *The Gospel according to Saint Matthew*, International Critical Commenary (Edinburgh: T&T Clark, 1991), 2:290; and Grant R. Osborne, *Matthew*, Zondervan Exegetical Commentary on the New Testament (Grand Rapids: Zondervan, 2010), 443. Plummer favors seeing ὅτι as content, Osborne rejects that view, and Davies and Allison merely note the two options. Ironically, Osborne's helpful discussion of the passage could actually be seen as supporting the view that ὅτι gives the content of what disciples are to learn.

45. The twelfth translation, the NLT, reverses the usual translations for these words: "because I am humble and gentle at heart."

by a temperate attitude."[46] For meditation purposes I have found it very fruitful to reflect on the use of this term in some Classical Greek texts for an animal that has been tamed.[47] All the power is there, but it is under the control of a master. Thinking of this term as "God-tamed" is very suggestive and fits with biblical teaching about humility and discipleship. Jesus himself is the chief example of one who says to God, "Not my will but yours be done." If ὅτι gives us the lesson we are to learn, then that lesson is Jesus's heart toward the Father. The image of the yoke fits with this picture as well. Such alignment with God and the motif of rest tie in with major biblical themes worth reflecting on.

Revelation 1:4

Right at the outset of the book of Revelation, there is a point of grammar that is theologically and spiritually suggestive to me.

> Ἰωάννης
> τοῖς ἑπτὰ ἐκκλησίαις ταῖς ἐν τῇ Ἀσίᾳ·
> χάρις ὑμῖν καὶ εἰρήνη [ ]
> > ἀπὸ ὁ ὢν καὶ ὁ ἦν καὶ ὁ ἐρχόμενος,
> > ἀπὸ τῶν ἑπτὰ πνευμάτων
> > > ἃ ἐνώπιον τοῦ θρόνου αὐτοῦ,

> John
> To the seven churches which are in Asia;
> Grace and peace [be] to you
> > from The One Who Is and Who Was
> > > and Who Is Coming
> > and from the seven spirits
> > > that are before his throne

In the book of Revelation John's grammar is idiosyncratic. For example, in this verse he has two prepositional phrases with ἀπό: ἀπὸ ὁ ὢν καὶ ὁ ἦν καὶ ὁ ἐρχόμενος καὶ ἀπὸ τῶν ἑπτὰ πνευμάτων. In the second prepositional phrase he puts the object of the preposition in the genitive, as is normal. But in the first prepositional phrase he uses the nominative for the object of the preposition instead of the genitive! This expression is probably the equivalent of the

---

46. *CGEL* 296.
47. See LSJ 1459. William Barclay develops this thought nicely in *New Testament Words* (Philadelphia: Westminster, 1964), 240–42.

Tetragrammaton. It seems that John views the expression of the Name as so heavy that even the grammar is affected, bent around this Reality.

Along with this point of grammar about the nominative case, there is also much to meditate on in the title ὁ ὢν καὶ ὁ ἦν καὶ ὁ ἐρχόμενος. Its very form is striking—two participles and a finite verb, each substantivized by an article! The first participle, ὁ ὢν, is the term used in Exod. 3:14 in the LXX for the Divine Name.[48]

καὶ εἶπεν ὁ θεὸς πρὸς Μωυσῆν
    ἐγώ εἰμι ὁ ὢν
καὶ εἶπεν
    οὕτως ἐρεῖς τοῖς υἱοῖς Ισραηλ
        ὁ ὢν ἀπέσταλκέν με πρὸς ὑμᾶς

And God said to Moyses,
    "I am The One Who Is."
And he said,
    "Thus shall you say to the sons of Israel,
        The One Who Is has sent me to you.'"
          (NETS)

Compare this translation from NETS with the older translation of the LXX by Brenton:[49]

And God spoke to Moses, saying,
    I am THE BEING;
and he said,
    Thus shall ye say to the children of Israel,
        THE BEING has sent me to you.

Neither of these translations is really an adequate rendering of ὁ ὢν, though each catches part of it. This expression of eternal Being is then combined in Rev. 1:4 with a finite verb for past existence, which is substantivized by the article, ὁ ἦν! To these is added a participle expressing dynamic movement within time, ὁ ἐρχόμενος. Grammar here is being stretched to express the inexpressible.

---

48. Thus the LXX does not use ἐγώ εἰμι for the Divine Name in this passage, contrary to what many people think, but ἐγώ εἰμι ("I am") may be used for the Divine Name elsewhere in the LXX (see, e.g., Isa. 43:10).

49. Lancelot C. L. Brenton, *The Septuagint with Apocrypha: Greek and English* (London: Samuel Bagster and Sons, 1851).

Revelation 3:20

ἰδοὺ ἕστηκα ἐπὶ τὴν θύραν
καὶ κρούω

    ⌐ ἐάν τις   ἀκούσῃ τῆς φωνῆς μου
                καὶ ἀνοίξῃ τὴν θύραν,
καὶ εἰσελεύσομαι πρὸς αὐτὸν
καὶ δειπνήσω μετ' αὐτοῦ
καὶ αὐτὸς μετ' ἐμοῦ.

Behold, I stand at the door
and knock.

    ⌐ If anyone   hears my voice
                and opens the door,
I will come in to him
and eat with him,
and he with me.

ἕστηκα . . . καὶ κρούω. We have a perfect tense-form (stative aspect or *Aktionsart*) and a present tense-form (imperfective aspect). The perfect of ἵστημι emphasizes the present state of standing or being present.[50] Jesus is present at the door and remains there continuing to knock.

τῆς φωνῆς μου. The word φωνή can refer to a sound or a voice. All the translations I consulted take it as his voice, but it could be the sound of the knocking. There is much to reflect on what it means to hear the φωνή of Jesus, and what it means to open the door. This imagery is very helpful when one is engaged in *contemplatio*, waiting upon God in stillness and silence, attentive and listening for the voice, or at least the knock.

Exegetically, the door in this passage is that of a church that seems apostate. Jesus is on the outside knocking, and individuals within the church who are able to hear Jesus are offered the chance to receive him and have intimate fellowship with him. One of the characteristics of the Johannine literature in the New Testament is the interweaving of the corporate and the individual. On the level of meditation, this verse has been used from the early days of the church to refer to Jesus knocking at the heart of individuals, either unbelievers, pointing to evangelism, or believers, pointing to intimate personal union with Christ.

50. BDAG 482: ἵστημι C.1: "to be in a standing position, *I stand, I stood* of bodily position. . . . C.2: to be at a place, *stand (there), be (there)*, w. the emphasis less on 'standing' than on 'being, existing.'"

Revelation 15:4

τίς οὐ μὴ   φοβηθῇ, κύριε,   ⌐
             καὶ δοξάσει τὸ ὄνομά σου,   ⌐
                                               ὅτι μόνος ὅσιος;

Who will not fear, Lord,   ⌐
             and glorify your Name,   ⌐
                                               for [you] alone [are] ὅσιος?

The word ὅσιος is usually used of humans, "pert. to being without fault relative to deity, *devout, pious, pleasing to God, holy.*"[51] So it is an unusual term to use for God, though it does appear for God in the LXX of Deut. 32:4 and Ps. 144:17 (145:17 MT). The passage in Deuteronomy is in the deuteronomic Song of Moses (cf. Exod. 15), and Ps. 144 is thematically very similar to this section of Revelation. So perhaps one or both of these passages are echoed in this word in this heavenly song. All of the English translations I checked use "holy," which obscures the fact that there is an unusual word here. BDAG says that when ὅσιος is used of God, it pertains to "the standard for what constitutes holiness,"[52] but this also obscures the fact that the word refers to devotion and piety. Stephen Smalley says, "The 'holiness' of God denotes not his sinlessness, the opposite of which would be a theological impossibility, but the distinction between his nature in its wholeness, as sovereign and powerful, and that of his creation in its incompleteness and injustice."[53] This point is true, but seems to be working more with the nuances of ἅγιος.

The translation of Ps. 144:17 in NETS captures how striking this word is: "Just is the Lord in all his ways, and devout in all his works" (δίκαιος κύριος ἐν πάσαις ταῖς ὁδοῖς αὐτοῦ καὶ ὅσιος ἐν πᾶσιν τοῖς ἔργοις αὐτοῦ). What would it mean for God to be devout? The interpretations of BDAG, Smalley, and others are probably along the right lines exegetically, but it is worth meditating on. Here the hymn is addressed to "Lord God, the Almighty" (κύριε ὁ θεὸς ὁ παντοκράτωρ, v. 3), but it is possible that it is addressed to the Lamb as well. The high Christology throughout Revelation and the interweaving of the hymns to God and to the Lamb in Rev. 4–5 would then come through here as well. The song in Rev. 15:3–4 is called "the song of the Lamb" (τὴν ᾠδὴν τοῦ ἀρνίου, v. 3), and τοῦ ἀρνίου may be subjective, a song sung by the Lamb, but it could be objective and thus another song to the Lamb.[54] If both

51. BDAG 728.
52. Ibid.
53. Stephen S. Smalley, *The Revelation to John: A Commentary on the Greek Text of the Apocalypse* (Downers Grove, IL: InterVarsity, 2005), 388.
54. So Smalley, *Revelation*, 386.

the Lamb and God are in view, then the aptness of ὅσιος may become clear. The devoutness of God glimpsed in the OT has been revealed in Jesus. This word, ὅσιος, may remind us that the deity of Christ reveals truths about the Godhead. Here we see that being the subject of devotion and the object of devotion are both found within the Deity. Our being ὅσιος depends on him, since, as our verse says, he alone is ὅσιος. Such christological reflections would not be part of a grammatical-historical interpretation of this text, but they are not unlike some meditations in the ancient church.

1 Clement 2.1

Clement begins his letter to the Corinthians by speaking of their earlier condition of spiritual health before recent troubles arose. *First Clement* 2.1 is part of his description:

Πάντες τε ἐταπεινοφρονεῖτε
μηδὲν ἀλαζονευόμενοι
ὑποτασσόμενοι μᾶλλον ἢ ὑποτάσσοντες
ἥδιον διδόντες ἢ λαμβάνοντες
τοῖς ἐφοδίοις τοῦ θεοῦ ἀρκούμενοι
καὶ προσέχοντες τοὺς λόγους αὐτοῦ
ἐπιμελῶς ἐνεστερνισμένοι ἦτε τοῖς σπλάγχνοις
καὶ τὰ παθήματα αὐτοῦ ἦν πρὸ ὀφθαλμῶν ὑμῶν.

Moreover, you were all humble
and free from arrogance,
submitting rather than demanding submission,
more glad to give than to receive,
and content with the provisions that God supplies.
And giving heed to his words,
you stored them up diligently in your hearts,
and kept his sufferings before your eyes.[55]

One of the things in this sentence that caught my attention was the word translated "provisions." This is a good translation of τοῖς ἐφοδίοις, but the etymology of ἐφόδιον is striking (ἐπί + ὁδός, "for the way/path"). BDAG says the word means *travel allowance, provisions for a journey* and then touches on the figurative use in our passage: "fig. of the provisions which Christ gives

55. Michael W. Holmes, ed. and trans., *The Apostolic Fathers: Greek Texts and English Translations*, 3rd ed. (Grand Rapids: Baker Academic, 2007), 47.

his followers for the journey of life 1 Cl 2:1."[56] This word reminds me of the "waybread" of the Elves in Tolkien's *Lord of the Rings*. A Wikipedia article on references to food and drink in *The Lord of the Rings* helps unpack further some of the reflections I have had meditating on this word in *1 Clement*.

> Appearing in *The Lord of the Rings* and *Silmarillion* material, **lembas** is a special bread made by the *Elves*, also called **waybread** in the *Common Speech*. Shaped into thin cakes, it is very nutritious, stays fresh for months when kept unbroken in its original leaf-wrappings, and is used for sustenance on long journeys. . . . Commentators have noted that *lembas* has *Eucharistic* overtones in accordance with *Roman Catholic* teachings. *Lembas* literally sustains the *hobbits'* lives, strength and will, while the Eucharist is the spiritual "Bread of Life." Also, Gollum and other evil creatures cannot abide *lembas*, while Catholics are instructed not to receive the Eucharist if in the state of *mortal sin*. Further, the Eucharist is sometimes called *viaticum*, a *Latin* term meaning "for the way," literally the spiritual food for the Christian's arduous journey through earthly life to heaven. The term *viaticum* was more commonly heard in Tolkien's day than today. In a private letter, Tolkien acknowledged that *lembas* bore religious significance.[57]

Note that *viaticum* is similar in etymology to ἐφόδιον.[58] While etymology does not determine meaning, as noted in chapter 2, it can often be worth meditating on.

I found the whole final part of *1 Clement* 2.1 engaging. It is translated as a separate sentence above, though, as you see, in Greek it is the final clause of the one sentence.

┌ καὶ προσέχοντες τοὺς λόγους αὐτοῦ
ἐπιμελῶς ἐνεστερνισμένοι ἦτε τοῖς σπλάγχνοις
καὶ τὰ παθήματα αὐτοῦ ἦν πρὸ ὀφθαλμῶν ὑμῶν

┌ and giving heed to his words,
you stored them up diligently in your hearts,
and kept his sufferings before your eyes.

Again, Holmes's translation is fine, but reading the Greek reflectively nourishes like waybread. For example, προσέχω signifies very careful attention. BDAG lists three meanings and places this passage under the second meaning,

---

56. BDAG 419 (bold and italics original).
57. "List of Middle-Earth Food and Drink," Wikipedia, http://en.wikipedia.org/wiki/List_of_Middle-earth_food_and_drink.
58. *Viaticum* is the neuter of *viaticus*, "of a journey," from *via*, "way."

"to pay close attention to someth., *pay attention to, give heed to, follow.*"[59] It seems, however, that it could just as well be an example of the third meaning, "to continue in close attention to someth., *occupy oneself with, devote* or *apply oneself to,*"[60] since devoting yourself to God's words fits with storing them up in your heart. Προσέχοντες is a present participle, so the aspect of the verb is of continuous, ongoing activity occurring at the same time as the main verb, ἐνεστερνισμένοι ἦτε, a perfect middle participle with the imperfect form of εἰμί to form a pluperfect: "you had stored up for yourselves."

The word translated "hearts" is not the common word for heart, καρδία, but a more graphic one, σπλάγχνον, one's inward parts, especially the viscera.[61] And the word for "store up," ἐνστερνίζομαι, is also graphic. BDAG says that it means "to store away within oneself" and translates our passage "you had carefully stored away in the depths of your being."[62] The imagery in this word is fruitful for meditation.

Even the adverb ἐπιμελῶς caught my attention since it is part of a significant word family for "care," "concern," "worry"; for example, μέλομαι, which BDAG indicates means "be an object of care, be a cause of concern."[63] The only use of this adverb in the New Testament is in Jesus's parable about the woman who lost one of ten silver coins and searched diligently/carefully for it (Luke 15:8).

So in the light of this data, I turned over in my mind this final part of the sentence in *1 Clement* 2.1, encouraged by its image of engagement with God's word in the depths of my being in the context of ongoing, continuous, careful attention to / occupying myself with his words. It speaks of the very exercise of meditation I am discussing. It is a wonderful expression of the similar sentiment found in Ps. 119:11 (118:11 LXX).

> I have stored up your word in my heart, that I might not sin against you. (ESV)
> ἐν τῇ καρδίᾳ μου ἔκρυψα τὰ λόγιά σου ὅπως ἂν μὴ ἁμάρτω σοι. (LXX)
> In my heart I hid your sayings, so that I may not sin against you. (NETS)

Finally, at the end of *1 Clement* 2.1 the combination of this attention to the words of God with the sufferings of Christ (though Christ is not named, so the sufferings are associated with God) is food for reflection and transformation as well. The cross is the great revelation of God to keep before our eyes as we travel through this world.

59. BDAG 880 (italics original).
60. Ibid.
61. See BDAG 938.
62. Ibid.
63. BDAG 628.

Conclusion

Some of these points for meditation are in keeping with exegesis, and some go beyond it. All of them are meaningful to me, but you may not resonate with all of them—or with any of them! I encourage you to meditate on passages in whatever form seems appropriate to you and speaks most directly to you. In this way we not only improve our knowledge of Greek and become more fluent; we also gain benefits from the Greek for "the rest of our lives," in both senses of that expression!

7

PRACTICE PASSAGES

Once you have worked through the first six chapters in this book and the appendixes, I encourage you to focus on a passage of your choice and start developing your fluency, passage by passage. If you would like a bit more help before doing so, the three passages in this chapter offer you a chance to practice the skills described in this book. For each passage several levels of notes provide various forms of help.

Text with Basic Reading Helps

The first set of notes is a copy of the text with vocabulary and parsing helps. Words occurring fewer than 30 times in the GNT are included. For a list of words occurring 30 times or more, see the website for this book.

Passage Scan

For each passage, a scan is provided, using the markings introduced in chapter 4, which help highlight the structures of the Greek sentences.

Sentence Map

A level 2 map provides yet further analysis for each passage. In a level 2 map, main clauses, subordinate clauses, and prepositional phrases are given their own line. Often participles and infinitives are also on a separate line, depending on their function. These various items are arranged to show how they are related to each other in the sentence. If you are familiar with the material on maps in chapter 4 and appendix 1, these maps should clarify the flow of each sentence.

Guided Tour of the Passage

A further set of notes offers a guided tour of the passage by way of commentary on the map. In any clause the core elements may include the subject, verb, direct object, and indirect object. The notes assume you can recognize these elements, as well as conjunctions, negative adverbs (οὐ, μή), and adjectives. The notes focus on genitives, participles, infinitives, and any unusual features.

Bonus Coverage

A final set of notes provides comments on a few of the words and structures in each passage, using the approaches described in this book to go into a bit more depth. Often I comment on verbal aspect and *Aktionsart*, especially in Luke 5, for which see appendix 5. These notes only touch on a few of the many issues present in each passage. For additional help beyond these notes, you should consult translations, commentaries, and other reference works.[1]

I suggest you begin with the three steps described in chapter 5. Look over the passage and then use the reading helps as needed for puzzling and scanning. If you find bits that are still puzzling, use the passage scan, the sentence map, and the guided tour to sort them out. Once you have understood the passage, reread it several times and then check out the bonus coverage notes.

Once you have worked through these practice passages, you will be ready to launch into a favorite text and reap the benefits of knowing Greek.[2]

---

1. The notes in the NET Bible often discuss details in the Greek. Volumes in the Baylor Handbook on the Greek New Testament (Baylor University Press) and volumes in the Exegetical Guide to the Greek New Testament (B&H Academic) offer fairly extensive help for issues in the Greek.
2. You can choose any Greek passage, of course, but as you get started, you may find helpful one or more of the readers listed in chap. 5, note 15.

1 John 2:1–6

Text with Basic Reading Helps

¹Τεκνία³ μου, ταῦτα γράφω ὑμῖν ἵνα μὴ ἁμάρτητε.⁴ καὶ ἐάν τις ἁμάρτῃ, παράκλητον⁵ ἔχομεν πρὸς τὸν πατέρα Ἰησοῦν Χριστὸν δίκαιον, ²καὶ αὐτὸς ἱλασμός⁶ ἐστιν περὶ τῶν ἁμαρτιῶν ἡμῶν, οὐ περὶ τῶν ἡμετέρων⁷ δὲ μόνον ἀλλὰ καὶ περὶ ὅλου τοῦ κόσμου. ³Καὶ ἐν τούτῳ γινώσκομεν ὅτι ἐγνώκαμεν⁸ αὐτόν, ἐὰν τὰς ἐντολὰς αὐτοῦ τηρῶμεν. ⁴ὁ λέγων ὅτι Ἔγνωκα αὐτόν καὶ τὰς ἐντολὰς αὐτοῦ μὴ τηρῶν ψεύστης⁹ ἐστίν, καὶ ἐν τούτῳ ἡ ἀλήθεια οὐκ ἔστιν· ⁵ὃς δ' ἂν τηρῇ αὐτοῦ τὸν λόγον, ἀληθῶς¹⁰ ἐν τούτῳ ἡ ἀγάπη τοῦ θεοῦ τετελείωται.¹¹ ἐν τούτῳ γινώσκομεν ὅτι ἐν αὐτῷ ἐσμεν· ⁶ὁ λέγων ἐν αὐτῷ μένειν ὀφείλει καθὼς ἐκεῖνος περιεπάτησεν¹² καὶ αὐτὸς περιπατεῖν.

Passage Scan

¹Τεκνία μου, ταῦτα γράφω ὑμῖν | ἵνα μὴ ἁμάρτητε. | καὶ ἐάν τις ἁμάρτῃ, | παράκλητον ἔχομεν (πρὸς τὸν πατέρα) Ἰησοῦν Χριστὸν δίκαιον, | ²καὶ αὐτὸς ἱλασμός ἐστιν (περὶ τῶν ἁμαρτιῶν ἡμῶν), <οὐ (περὶ τῶν ἡμετέρων) δὲ μόνον> <ἀλλὰ καὶ (περὶ ὅλου τοῦ κόσμου)>.

³Καὶ (ἐν τούτῳ) γινώσκομεν | ὅτι ἐγνώκαμεν αὐτόν, | ἐὰν τὰς ἐντολὰς αὐτοῦ τηρῶμεν. | ⁴[ὁ λέγων <ὅτι Ἔγνωκα αὐτὸν> καὶ τὰς ἐντολὰς αὐτοῦ μὴ τηρῶν] ψεύστης ἐστίν, | καὶ (ἐν τούτῳ) ἡ ἀλήθεια οὐκ ἔστιν· ⁵[ὃς δ' ἂν τηρῇ αὐτοῦ τὸν λόγον], ἀληθῶς (ἐν τούτῳ) ἡ ἀγάπη τοῦ θεοῦ τετελείωται. | (ἐν τούτῳ) γινώσκομεν | ὅτι (ἐν αὐτῷ) ἐσμεν· | ⁶[ὁ λέγων (ἐν αὐτῷ) μένειν] ὀφείλει [καθὼς ἐκεῖνος περιεπάτησεν] καὶ αὐτὸς περιπατεῖν.

3. voc. pl. neut. < τεκνίον, ου, τό, child
4. 2 pl. act. Aor. subjn. < ἁμαρτάνω, I sin
5. acc. sg. masc. < παράκλητος, ου, ὁ, counselor, encourager, intercessor
6. nom. sg. masc. < ἱλασμός, οῦ, ὁ, means of forgiveness and appeasement
7. gen. pl. masc. < ἡμέτερος, α, ον, our
8. 1 pl. act. Pf. ind. < γινώσκω, I know
9. nom. sg. masc. < ψεύστης, ου, ὁ, liar
10. adv., ἀληθῶς, truly
11. 3 sg. pass. Pf. ind. < τελειόω, I make perfect
12. 3 sg. act. Aor. ind. < περιπατέω, I walk

Sentence Map

1 Τεκνία μου, ταῦτα γράφω ὑμῖν
                        ἵνα μὴ ἁμάρτητε.

                  ⌜ καὶ ἐάν τις ἁμάρτῃ,
    παράκλητον ἔχομεν
                        πρὸς τὸν πατέρα

    Ἰησοῦν Χριστὸν
    δίκαιον.

2 καὶ αὐτὸς ἱλασμός ἐστιν
                              περὶ τῶν ἁμαρτιῶν ἡμῶν,
    [αὐτὸς ἱλασμός ἐστιν]
                        οὐ περὶ τῶν ἡμετέρων δὲ μόνον
                        ἀλλὰ καὶ περὶ ὅλου τοῦ κόσμου.

3 Καὶ . . .¹ γινώσκομεν
                    ὅτι ἐγνώκαμεν αὐτόν, . . .²
              ¹ἐν   τούτῳ
                    ²ἐὰν τὰς ἐντολὰς αὐτοῦ τηρῶμεν.

4 ὁ λέγων
        ὅτι Ἔγνωκα αὐτόν
    καὶ τὰς ἐντολὰς αὐτοῦ μὴ τηρῶν ψεύστης ἐστίν,

    καὶ . . . ἡ ἀλήθεια οὐκ ἔστιν·
                        ἐν τούτῳ

5   ⌜¹ὃς δ' ἂν τηρῇ αὐτοῦ τὸν λόγον,
                                      ²ἐν τούτῳ
    . . .¹ ἀληθῶς . . .² ἡ ἀγάπη τοῦ θεοῦ τετελείωται.

    . . .³ γινώσκομεν
                    ὅτι . . . ἐσμεν·
                          ἐν αὐτῷ
              ³ἐν τούτῳ

6 ὁ λέγων . . .¹ . . .² ὀφείλει . . .³ καὶ αὐτὸς περιπατεῖν.
        ²μένειν   ³καθὼς ἐκεῖνος περιεπάτησεν,
        ¹ἐν αὐτῷ

Guided Tour of the Passage

2:1. The first sentence adds a vocative to the main clause. The second sentence includes Ἰησοῦν Χριστόν in apposition to the direct object παράκλητον, while another appositive, δίκαιον, describes Jesus.

2:2. Ἡμῶν modifies the object of the preposition. The οὐ-ἀλλά construction is introduced by δέ, five places from the beginning. This construction could have been placed under the verb, but since δέ usually introduces clauses, it seems here to imply a repetition of the first clause, which is included in brackets on the map.

2:3. The conditional clause in apposition is explaining τούτῳ, and αὐτοῦ modifies the direct object in the conditional clause.

2:4. The subject of the first clause is composed of two participles sharing a single article, so the subject extends from ὁ to τηρῶν. This construction implies a unity between the participles; here they are referring to the same person.[13] Αὐτοῦ modifies the direct object of τηρῶν. Ψεύστης is a predicate noun.

2:5. The indefinite relative clause includes a genitive modifying the direct object. The first main clause includes the adverb ἀληθῶς and a genitive modifying the subject.

2:6. The subject is a substantival participle that has an infinitive (indicating indirect discourse) for the content of what is said. Ὀφείλει has a complementary infinitive, περιπατεῖν. The fronting of the comparative clause adds focus on the way of living exemplified by Jesus (ἐκεῖνος). Καί is adjunctive, "also." After the καθώς clause, αὐτός picks up the subject of the main verb again (the resumptive use).

The punctuation in *SBLGNT* interprets τούτῳ in verse 5 as referring forward to verse 6, with verse 6 in apposition to τούτῳ, explaining the means by which we know we are in him. In NA[28] there is a raised dot after τετελείωται, which suggests τούτῳ refers back to what has just been said in verse 5. A map can show both of these options:

```
. . .¹ γινώσκομεν
      ὅτι . . . ἐσμεν·
                  ἐν αὐτῷ
      ¹ἐν τούτῳ

6 |<or——   ὁ λέγων . . .¹ . . .² ὀφείλει, . . .³ καὶ αὐτὸς περιπατεῖν.
              ²μένειν                          ³καθὼς ἐκεῖνος περιεπάτησεν
              ¹ἐν αὐτῷ
```

13. This is an example of the Granville Sharp Rule. See Wallace, 270–90, esp. 274–75, and much more extensively, Daniel B. Wallace, *Granville Sharp's Canon and Its Kin: Semantics and Significance*, Studies in Biblical Greek 14 (New York: Peter Lang, 2009).

Bonus Coverage

2:1. ἵνα μὴ ἁμάρτητε. This clause gives the purpose for John's writing. The aspect of the aorist is perfective, and the *Aktionsart* here is probably summary, the most common use of the aorist.[14] It views the action as a whole, with no added nuance of pointing to its beginning or ending or ongoing progression. The aspect of the present is imperfective, so a present tense-form here probably would have included the nuance of not continuing in sin or not allowing sinful habits to characterize one's life. John, however, assumes that habitual sin has been broken (1 John 3:7–10), so here committing a sin reflects an *occasion* of failure rather than an ongoing lifestyle. Thus, while John rejects the views of those who claim sinlessness (1 John 1:8–10), he also has no place for a lax complacency regarding sin.

πρὸς τὸν πατέρα. When πρός is used for being in company with someone,[15] it can include an element of relationship or interaction, and not just proximity. In this context, then, the word suggests that the Paraclete and the Father are not just near one another but are in some form of personal relationship. The same word is used of the relationship between the Word and God in John 1:1–2. As another example, when Jesus is rejected at Nazareth, the townsfolk say, "Are not his sisters here with us?" (πρὸς ἡμᾶς, Mark 6:3; Matt. 13:56). In this context πρός carries the nuance that they are with us and known to us.

2:2. καὶ αὐτὸς ἱλασμός ἐστιν. The word ἱλασμός may refer to propitiation (removing God's wrath), or expiation (removing sin). Both ideas fit the context, and it is possible that both elements are usually present to some extent. Accordingly, some translations use a comprehensive term like "atoning sacrifice" (NIV), and the gloss in the reading notes also includes both ideas, "means of forgiveness and appeasement." Because ἱλασμός is anarthrous (lacking an article), one might be tempted to think John refers to "*a* means of forgiveness and appeasement," that is, one among others. But here we have an anarthrous predicate nominative coming before an equative verb, and thus an example of Colwell's Rule. Wallace summarizes the implication of this rule: "An anarthrous pre-verbal PN [predicate nominative] is normally qualitative, sometimes definite, and only rarely indefinite."[16] So "*a* means" would have

---

14. Constantine R. Campbell, *Basics of Verbal Aspect in Biblical Greek* (Grand Rapids: Zondervan, 2008), 86–87. The categories of verbs in Wallace and Young correspond for the most part with the *Aktionsarten*. They both refer to the summary *Aktionsart* as the constative use of the aorist (Wallace, 518; Young, 122).

15. BDAG, πρός 3.g, 875.

16. Wallace, 262. See Wallace's whole discussion (256–70), which presents the further research after Colwell on which Wallace's inference rests. For Colwell's original article, see E. C. Colwell, "A Definite Rule for the Use of the Article in the Greek New Testament," *Journal of Biblical Literature* 52 (1933): 12–21. Available online (see bibliography).

to be very clearly signaled by the context since this use is rare. Wallace cites this verse as an example of the definite use; John is referring to *the* means by which God has dealt with our sin.[17]

This interpretation certainly fits with John's theology, and Wallace's test for distinguishing qualitative and definite uses helps us reflect on what John is saying. "One of the ways to test whether a PN [predicate nominative] is qualitative or definite is to swap the S [subject] with the PN. If the sentence makes the same sense, then the PN is definite since the construction involves a convertible proposition."[18] So our means of forgiveness and appeasement is he. In other words, John is saying something about Jesus himself and not just something he did. Westcott compares this statement with others in the NT (Col. 3:4; 1 Cor. 1:31): "He does not simply guide, teach, quicken: He is 'the Way, the Truth, the Life' (John 14:6). It follows that the efficacy of His work for the individual depends upon fellowship with Him."[19] Thus this bit of grammar reflects major themes in John's thought.

2:3. γινώσκομεν, ἐγνώκαμεν. The present tense-form often has a progressive sense as its *Aktionsart*.[20] The perfect represents a state[21] and often views an event as something that has happened in the past with ongoing results of some sort.[22] Γινώσκω is a stative verb to begin with. Putting these nuances together, we may have something like "by this we are in a state of knowing that we stand in a state of having come to know him." This obviously is not a good translation but may catch the flavor of the tenses.[23] Note that two different meanings of γινώσκω are here side by side, as seen by the object of each. The first is knowledge of a fact, "be in receipt of information w. focus on awareness."[24] The second is knowledge of a person, "have a personal relationship involving recognition of another's identity or value."[25]

17. Ibid., 264.

18. Ibid., 264n24.

19. Brooke Foss Westcott, *The Epistles of St John: The Greek Text with Notes*, 3rd ed. (1892; repr., Grand Rapids: Eerdmans, 1966), 44.

20. Campbell, *Basics*, 63–64; Wallace, 518; referred to as the descriptive present in Young, 107.

21. There is debate over whether the perfect is stative in its aspect or as an *Aktionsart*. See app. 5.

22. Wallace, 501. This nuance of the perfect is also debated, as noted in app. 5.

23. The alternative would be that the perfect expresses simply the present state of knowing, but this fails to account for the shift of the same stative verb from present to perfect.

24. *CGEL*, γινώσκω 1, 79.

25. *CGEL*, γινώσκω 3, 80.

Luke 5:1–11

Text with Basic Reading Helps

^{1}Ἐγένετο^{26} δὲ ἐν τῷ τὸν ὄχλον ἐπικεῖσθαι^{27} αὐτῷ καὶ ἀκούειν τὸν λόγον τοῦ θεοῦ καὶ αὐτὸς ἦν ἑστὼς^{28} παρὰ τὴν λίμνην^{29} Γεννησαρέτ,^{30} ^{2}καὶ εἶδεν δύο πλοῖα ἑστῶτα^{31} παρὰ τὴν λίμνην, οἱ δὲ ἁλιεῖς^{32} ἀπ' αὐτῶν ἀποβάντες^{33} ἔπλυνον^{34} τὰ δίκτυα.^{35} ^{3}ἐμβὰς^{36} δὲ εἰς ἓν τῶν πλοίων, ὃ ἦν Σίμωνος,^{37} ἠρώτησεν^{38} αὐτὸν ἀπὸ τῆς γῆς ἐπαναγαγεῖν^{39} ὀλίγον, καθίσας^{40} δὲ ἐκ τοῦ πλοίου ἐδίδασκεν τοὺς ὄχλους. ^{4}ὡς δὲ ἐπαύσατο^{41} λαλῶν, εἶπεν πρὸς τὸν Σίμωνα· Ἐπανάγαγε^{42} εἰς τὸ βάθος^{43} καὶ χαλάσατε^{44} τὰ δίκτυα ὑμῶν εἰς ἄγραν.^{45} ^{5}καὶ ἀποκριθεὶς^{46} Σίμων εἶπεν· Ἐπιστάτα,^{47} δι' ὅλης νυκτὸς κοπιάσαντες^{48} οὐδὲν ἐλάβομεν,^{49} ἐπὶ δὲ τῷ ῥήματί σου χαλάσω^{50} τὰ δίκτυα. ^{6}καὶ τοῦτο ποιήσαντες συνέκλεισαν^{51} πλῆθος ἰχθύων^{52} πολύ, διερρήσσετο^{53} δὲ τὰ δίκτυα αὐτῶν. ^{7}καὶ κατένευσαν^{54} τοῖς μετόχοις^{55} ἐν τῷ ἑτέρῳ πλοίῳ τοῦ ἐλθόντας^{56} συλλαβέσθαι^{57} αὐτοῖς· καὶ ἦλθον

26. 3 sg. mid. Aor. ind. < γίνομαι, I happen
27. Pres. mid. inf. < ἐπίκειμαι, I press around
28. nom. sg. masc. act. Pf. ptc. < ἵστημι, I stand. Since the perfect of ἵστημι is used with a present meaning, this pluperfect periphrastic construction has the sense of an imperfect.
29. acc. sg. fem. < λίμνη, ης, ἡ, lake
30. Γεννησαρέτ, ἡ, indeclinable, Gennesaret
31. acc. pl. neut. act. Pf. ptc. < ἵστημι. This participle is either attributive or the complement in a double accusative construction of object and complement.
32. nom. pl. masc. < ἁλιεύς, έως, ὁ, fisherman
33. nom. pl. masc. act. Aor. ptc. < ἀποβαίνω, I get out
34. 3 pl. act. Impf. ind. < πλύνω, I wash
35. acc. pl. neut. < δίκτυον, ου, τό, fish net
36. nom. sg. masc. act. Aor. ptc. < ἐμβαίνω, I go/get in/into
37. gen. sg. masc. < Σίμων, ωνος, ὁ, Simon
38. 3 sg. act. Aor. ind. < ἐρωτάω, I ask
39. Aor. act. inf. < ἐπανάγω, go out, put out (to sea)
40. nom. sg. masc. act. Aor. ptc. < καθίζω, I sit
41. 3 sg. mid. Aor. ind. < παύω, I stop
42. 2 pl. act. Aor. impv. < ἐπανάγω, I go out, put out (to sea)
43. acc. sg. neut. < βάθος, ους, τό, depth, deep (water)
44. 2 pl. act. Aor. impv. < χαλάω, I let down
45. acc. sg. fem. < ἄγρα, ας, ἡ, catching, a catch
46. nom. sg. masc. pass. Aor. ptc. < ἀποκρίνομαι, I answer
47. voc. sg. masc. < ἐπιστάτης, ου, ὁ, master. For this vocative form, see Funk, §205.3.
48. nom. pl. masc. act. Aor. ptc. < κοπιάω, I work hard, toil
49. 1 pl. act. Aor. ind. < λαμβάνω, I take, catch
50. 1 sg. act. Fut. ind. < χαλάω, I let down
51. 3 pl. act. Aor. ind. < συγκλείω, I enclose
52. gen. pl. masc. < ἰχθύς, ύος, ὁ, fish
53. 3 sg. pass. Impf. ind. < διαρρήγνυμι/διαρήσσω, I tear
54. 3 pl. act. Aor. ind. < κατανεύω, I signal
55. dat. pl. masc. < μέτοχος, ον, sharing in; as a noun, partner
56. acc. pl. masc. act. Aor. ptc. < ἔρχομαι, I come
57. Aor. mid. inf. < συλλαμβάνω, I help (see BDAG, συλλαμβάνω 4, 955)

καὶ ἔπλησαν[58] ἀμφότερα[59] τὰ πλοῖα ὥστε βυθίζεσθαι[60] αὐτά. [8]ἰδὼν[61] δὲ Σίμων Πέτρος προσέπεσεν[62] τοῖς γόνασιν[63] Ἰησοῦ λέγων Ἔξελθε[64] ἀπ᾽ ἐμοῦ, ὅτι ἀνὴρ ἁμαρτωλός εἰμι, κύριε· [9]θάμβος[65] γὰρ περιέσχεν[66] αὐτὸν καὶ πάντας τοὺς σὺν αὐτῷ ἐπὶ τῇ ἄγρᾳ τῶν ἰχθύων ὧν συνέλαβον,[67] [10]ὁμοίως[68] δὲ καὶ Ἰάκωβον καὶ Ἰωάννην υἱοὺς Ζεβεδαίου, οἳ ἦσαν κοινωνοὶ[69] τῷ Σίμωνι. καὶ εἶπεν πρὸς τὸν Σίμωνα ὁ Ἰησοῦς· Μὴ φοβοῦ·[70] ἀπὸ τοῦ νῦν ἀνθρώπους ἔσῃ[71] ζωγρῶν.[72] [11]καὶ καταγαγόντες[73] τὰ πλοῖα ἐπὶ τὴν γῆν ἀφέντες[74] πάντα ἠκολούθησαν αὐτῷ.

Passage Scan

[1]Ἐγένετο δὲ (ἐν [τῷ τὸν ὄχλον ἐπικεῖσθαι αὐτῷ καὶ ἀκούειν τὸν λόγον τοῦ θεοῦ]) | καὶ αὐτὸς ἦν ἑστὼς (παρὰ τὴν λίμνην Γεννησαρέτ), | [2]καὶ εἶδεν δύο πλοῖα ἑστῶτα (παρὰ τὴν λίμνην), | οἱ δὲ ἁλιεῖς [(ἀπ᾽ αὐτῶν) ἀποβάντες] ἔπλυνον τὰ δίκτυα. | [3][ἐμβὰς δὲ (εἰς ἓν τῶν πλοίων), <ὃ ἦν Σίμωνος>], ἠρώτησεν αὐτὸν [(ἀπὸ τῆς γῆς) ἐπαναγαγεῖν ὀλίγον], | [καθίσας δὲ (ἐκ τοῦ πλοίου)] ἐδίδασκεν τοὺς ὄχλους. | [4]ὡς δὲ ἐπαύσατο λαλῶν, εἶπεν (πρὸς τὸν Σίμωνα)· | Ἐπανάγαγε (εἰς τὸ βάθος) | καὶ χαλάσατε τὰ δίκτυα ὑμῶν (εἰς ἄγραν). | [5]καὶ [ἀποκριθεὶς] Σίμων εἶπεν· | Ἐπιστάτα, [(δι᾽ ὅλης νυκτὸς) κοπιάσαντες] οὐδὲν ἐλάβομεν, | (ἐπὶ δὲ τῷ ῥήματί σου) χαλάσω τὰ δίκτυα. | [6]καὶ [τοῦτο ποιήσαντες] συνέκλεισαν πλῆθος ἰχθύων πολύ, | διερρήσσετο δὲ τὰ δίκτυα αὐτῶν. | [7]καὶ κατένευσαν τοῖς μετόχοις (ἐν τῷ ἑτέρῳ πλοίῳ) [τοῦ <ἐλθόντας> συλλαβέσθαι αὐτοῖς]· | καὶ ἦλθον, | καὶ ἔπλησαν ἀμφότερα τὰ πλοῖα | ὥστε βυθίζεσθαι αὐτά. | [8][ἰδὼν] δὲ Σίμων Πέτρος προσέπεσεν τοῖς γόνασιν Ἰησοῦ [λέγων]· | Ἔξελθε (ἀπ᾽ ἐμοῦ), | ὅτι ἀνὴρ ἁμαρτωλός εἰμι, κύριε· | [9]θάμβος γὰρ περιέσχεν αὐτὸν καὶ πάντας τοὺς (σὺν αὐτῷ) (ἐπὶ τῇ ἄγρᾳ τῶν ἰχθύων [ὧν συνέλαβον]), [10]<ὁμοίως δὲ καὶ Ἰάκωβον καὶ

58. 3 pl. act. Aor. ind. < πίμπλημι, I fill
59. acc. pl. neut. < ἀμφότεροι, αι, α, both
60. Pres pass. inf. < βυθίζω, I sink
61. nom. sg. masc. act. Aor. ptc. < ὁράω, I see
62. 3 sg. act. Aor. ind. < προσπίπτω, I fall down before
63. dat. pl. neut. < γόνυ, ατος, τό, knee
64. 2 sg. act. Aor. impv. < ἐξέρχομαι, I go away
65. nom. sg. neut. < θάμβος, ους, τό, amazement, awe. This word can also be masculine, θάμβος, ου, ὁ. Either form of the word fits in this sentence.
66. 3 sg. act. Aor. ind. < περιέχω, I come upon, seize
67. 3 pl. act. Aor. ind. < συλλαμβάνω, I catch (see BDAG, συλλαμβάνω 2, 955)
68. adv., ὁμοίως, likewise, also
69. nom. pl. masc. < κοινωνός, οῦ, ὁ/ἡ, companion, partner
70. 2 sg. mid. Pres. impv. < φοβέομαι, I fear
71. 2 sg. mid. Fut. ind. < εἰμί, I am
72. nom. sg. masc. act. Pres. ptc. < ζωγρέω, I capture alive. Here with ἔσῃ for a periphrastic future.
73. nom. pl. masc. act. Aor. ptc. < κατάγω, I bring down; "bring the boats to land (fr. the 'high' seas)" (BDAG 516)
74. nom. pl. masc. act. Aor. ptc. < ἀφίημι, I leave

Ἰωάννην υἱοὺς Ζεβεδαίου, [οἳ ἦσαν κοινωνοὶ τῷ Σίμωνι]>. | καὶ εἶπεν (πρὸς τὸν Σίμωνα· ὁ Ἰησοῦς· | Μὴ φοβοῦ· | (ἀπὸ τοῦ νῦν) ἀνθρώπους ἔσῃ ζωγρῶν. | ¹¹καὶ [καταγαγόντες τὰ πλοῖα (ἐπὶ τὴν γῆν)] [ἀφέντες πάντα] ἠκολούθησαν αὐτῷ.

Sentence Map

1 Ἐγένετο δὲ
      ἐν τῷ τὸν ὄχλον ἐπικεῖσθαι αὐτῷ
                      καὶ ἀκούειν τὸν λόγον τοῦ θεοῦ
      καὶ αὐτὸς ἦν ἑστὼς
                      παρὰ τὴν λίμνην Γεννησαρὲτ

2 καὶ εἶδεν δύο πλοῖα ἑστῶτα
                      παρὰ τὴν λίμνην,
      οἱ δὲ ἁλιεῖς . . . ἔπλυνον τὰ δίκτυα.
                      . . . ἀποβάντες
                          ἀπ᾽ αὐτῶν

3   ⌐ ἐμβὰς δὲ
          εἰς ἓν τῶν πλοίων,
            └ ὃ ἦν Σίμωνος,
      ἠρώτησεν αὐτὸν
          . . . ἐπαναγαγεῖν ὀλίγον,
                  ἀπὸ τῆς γῆς

      ⌐ καθίσας δὲ
        ⌐ ἐκ τοῦ πλοίου
      ἐδίδασκεν τοὺς ὄχλους.

4   ὡς δὲ ἐπαύσατο λαλῶν,
      εἶπεν
          πρὸς τὸν Σίμωνα
          Ἐπανάγαγε
              εἰς τὸ βάθος
          καὶ χαλάσατε τὰ δίκτυα ὑμῶν
              εἰς ἄγραν.

5   ⌐ ἀποκριθεὶς
      καὶ . . . Σίμων εἶπεν·
              Ἐπιστάτα, . . .¹ . . .² οὐδὲν ἐλάβομεν,
                          ²κοπιάσαντες
                              ¹δι᾽ ὅλης νυκτὸς

[καὶ . . . Σίμων εἶπεν·]
⌐ ἐπὶ δὲ τῷ ῥήματί σου
χαλάσω τὰ δίκτυα.

6   ⌐ καὶ τοῦτο ποιήσαντες
συνέκλεισαν πλῆθος ἰχθύων πολύ,
διερρήσσετο δὲ τὰ δίκτυα αὐτῶν.

7 καὶ κατένευσαν τοῖς μετόχοις
                    ἐν τῷ ἑτέρῳ πλοίῳ
        τοῦ . . . συλλαβέσθαι αὐτοῖς
                    ἐλθόντας
καὶ ἦλθον
καὶ ἔπλησαν ἀμφότερα τὰ πλοῖα
        ὥστε βυθίζεσθαι αὐτά.

8   ⌐ ἰδὼν δὲ
Σίμων Πέτρος προσέπεσεν τοῖς γόνασιν Ἰησοῦ
            λέγων
                Ἔξελθε
                    ἀπ᾽ ἐμοῦ,
                ὅτι ἀνὴρ ἁμαρτωλός εἰμι, κύριε·

9 θάμβος γὰρ περιέσχεν αὐτὸν καὶ πάντας τοὺς σὺν αὐτῷ
                ἐπὶ τῇ ἄγρᾳ τῶν ἰχθύων
                        ὧν συνέλαβον,

10 ὁμοίως δὲ καὶ   Ἰάκωβον   ⌐
                καὶ Ἰωάννην   ⌐
                υἱοὺς Ζεβεδαίου, ⌐
                        οἳ ἦσαν κοινωνοὶ τῷ Σίμωνι.

    καὶ εἶπεν . . . ὁ Ἰησοῦς·
        πρὸς τὸν Σίμωνα
        Μὴ φοβοῦ·
                ⌐ ἀπὸ τοῦ νῦν
        ἀνθρώπους ἔσῃ ζωγρῶν.

11   ⌐ καὶ καταγαγόντες τὰ πλοῖα
                ἐπὶ τὴν γῆν
            ⌐ ἀφέντες πάντα
        ἠκολούθησαν αὐτῷ.

Guided Tour of the Passage

Notes for this passage include additional comments on a few of the discourse features and more extensive examples of attention to verbal aspect and *Aktionsart*.[75]

5:1. ἐγένετο δέ ("and/now it happened") is frequently used to introduce a sentence in the LXX and occurs 37 times in Luke and Acts.[76] This expression moves a narrative along by providing a point of transition to a new scene.[77] It often has an infinitive for a subject, but here the independent clause at the end of this verse is the "it" that happened.

The prepositional phrase with ἐν plus two infinitives sets the scene. Both infinitives are present tense-form and thus imperfective in aspect, here with the *Aktionsart* of progression. Ἐπικεῖσθαι is from the lemma ἐπίκειμαι, which in this context is a middle for positive interaction.[78] In such constructions the infinitive is the object of the preposition, and the accusative is that with reference to which the action takes place. In English we have to change the infinitive to a finite verb and the accusative to a subject: "while the crowd was pressing around him and listening." Αὐτῷ is a dative complement. Λόγον has a genitive modifier.

In the second clause, αὐτός expresses a bit of emphasis; Jesus is the focus of the scene. Γεννησαρέτ is indeclinable, so this is probably a genitive, "lake of Gennesaret," but could be apposition, "by the lake, Gennesaret."

5:2. Καί signals that the scene is still being set, providing further description of Jesus. The verb has a double accusative of object and complement, with a participle serving as the complement.[79]

75. For resources for discourse features, see chap. 4, note 27. For verbal topics, see app. 5.

76. Similarly, καὶ ἐγένετο is used in this way 22 times in Luke and very frequently in the LXX. These expressions, along with ἔσται, introduce sentences "in imitation of Hebrew idiom" (F. C. Conybeare and St. George Stock, *Grammar of Septuagint Greek with Selected Readings from the Septuagint according to the Text of Swete* [1905; repr., Peabody, MA: Hendrickson, 1988], 51). BDAG (4.f, 198) explains: "καὶ ἐγένετο (ἐγένετο δέ) periphrastic like וַיְהִי with וְ foll. to indicate the progress of the narrative."

77. Ἐγένετο δέ "is a device found in the LXX that Luke often uses to background information with respect to the following foreground events" (Stephen H. Levinsohn, *Discourse Features of New Testament Greek: A Coursebook on the Information Structure of New Testament Greek*, 2nd ed. [Dallas: SIL, 2000], 177).

78. See app. 5 regarding so-called deponents. Neva Miller lists ἐπίκειμαι under the category "state, condition" that occurs when "the subject is the center of gravity" since a primary sense is "lie upon" (Neva F. Miller, "Appendix 2: A Theory of Deponent Verbs," in *Analytical Lexicon of the Greek New Testament*, Timothy Friberg, Barbara Friberg, and Neva Miller, eds. [Grand Rapids: Baker Academic, 2000], 429). In this context, however, the verb means "to press around," and so it is an example of her category "positive interaction," which occurs when "verbs involve situations where two parties are involved and where the removal of one party would render the verb meaningless and no action possible" (ibid., 427).

79. See BDAG, εἶδον 1.b, 279. The participle could be attributive, but ὁράω "often takes a double accusative." Martin M. Culy, Mikeal C. Parsons, and Joshua J. Stigall, *Luke: A Handbook*

Δέ signals a development, with the subject now changing to the fisher-
men. The picture is developed with an adverbial participle and a verb in the
imperfect, here referring to an action in progress.

5:3. Our next sentence has two main clauses, each initiated by δέ and a
participle, either adverbial or indicating attendant circumstance. The first δέ
signals the change of subject back to Jesus. The object of the preposition εἰς
is modified by a genitive and a relative clause. Ἐπαναγαγεῖν gives the content
of the request, and it is modified by an adverbial accusative, ὀλίγον. The δέ
at the outset of the second half of the sentence points to the shift to teaching.
The aorists set the scene, and the imperfect ἐδίδασκεν zooms in on the action
as Jesus begins to teach them (an ingressive *Aktionsart*).

5:4. This sentence begins with δέ, moving the story along, as do the two
aorist indicatives. Ὡς serves as a temporal conjunction. The verb has a supplementary participle. Ὑμῶν modifies the direct object. The two imperatives are
in the aorist, with their common nuance of referring to specific things to be
done by specific people in a specific setting.[80]

5:5. We now hear Peter's response, and the καί may suggest the attention
is on the continuation from Jesus's promise to Peter's response. Ἀποκριθείς
is a "redundant quotative frame," which signals a response and highlights
the following saying.[81]

The direct discourse begins with a vocative, and the picture is expanded
with an adverbial participle. Σοῦ modifies the object of the preposition. The
use of δέ makes a slight break in this reported speech to highlight Peter's
obedient response.

5:6. Καί suggests a linking of the obedient response in verse 5 with its
results in verse 6. The verse begins with an adverbial participle and its aorist
main verb, which moves the story along. The direct object in the first clause
is modified by a genitive, ἰχθύων, and an adjective, πολύ. Δέ makes a slight
break to focus on the dramatic consequence. The imperfect, διερρήσσετο,
could be a simple ingressive *Aktionsart*, though perhaps this is an example of
a tendential *Aktionsart*, for something that almost happens.[82] Αὐτῶν modifies
the subject of the second clause.

The punctuation suggests the second clause is part of the same sentence,
but the δέ could suggest it initiates a new part of the story, going more closely
with the clauses in verse 7.

---

on the Greek Text, Baylor Handbook on the Greek New Testament (Waco: Baylor University
Press, 2010), 155.

80. Campbell, *Basics*, 92.

81. Steven E. Runge, *Discourse Grammar of the Greek New Testament: A Practical
Introduction for Teaching and Exegesis* (Peabody, MA: Hendrickson, 2010), 145.

82. See Wallace, 550.

5:7. The three clauses linked by καί describe a distinct section of the narrative. Κατένευσαν has a dative complement. The infinitive τοῦ . . . συλλαβέσθαι could signify purpose but more likely provides the content of what is being signaled. The infinitive is modified by a participle of attendant circumstance. The subordinate result clause with ὥστε has an infinitive, and its subject is in the accusative. Again, the aorists move the story along.

5:8. Δέ signals a new chunk as we now hear of Peter's response to the catch of fish. The first participle is adverbial or attendant circumstance. The main clause includes a dative complement with a genitive modifier, followed by a participle to signal direct discourse. Again we see an aorist imperative referring to a specific thing to be done by a specific person in a specific setting. The final clause includes a vocative placed at the end, which is an unusual position.[83]

5:9. Γάρ "does not advance the mainline of the discourse but rather introduces offline material that strengthens or supports what precedes."[84] The main clause has a compound direct object. The object of ἐπί has a genitive modifier. The relative pronoun should be in the accusative (οὕς) as the direct object of συνέλαβον, but here it has been attracted to the case of the antecedent, the genitive ἰχθύων.[85]

5:10. Since δέ initiates clauses, it assumes a repetition of θάμβος περιέσχον, now with James and John singled out from among the πάντας τοὺς σὺν αὐτῷ of verse 9. Ὁμοίως modifies the implied περιέσχον, as does καί, which is adjunctive ("also"). The two direct objects are modified by υἱούς in apposition. They are further described by a relative clause, which includes a predicate noun modified by a dative of association.

Since δέ is a development marker to chunk a discourse, it seems that verse 10a may be a little unit within the offline comment. Thus verses 9–10a explain Peter's response and add that the other disciples shared this amazement. The second half of this verse is a new sentence that moves back online with the development of the discourse. The focus returns to Peter, with καί connecting back to verse 8.

5:11. Our final sentence begins with two participles, which are either adverbial or attendant circumstance. Ἠκολούθησαν has a dative complement. We translate this verb as an active in English, but this seems to be an example of a θη form functioning like a middle.[86] Middles include an emphasis on the subject, and here the idea fits with Miller's category of positive interaction.[87]

---

83. BDF §474(6).
84. Runge, *Discourse Grammar*, 52.
85. For the attraction of the relative, see Funk, §670; Wallace, 338–39; Young, 76–77.
86. See app. 5.
87. Miller, "Theory," 427.

Bonus Coverage

5:4. ἐπανάγαγε, χαλάσατε. The shift from singular to plural in these two verbs focuses the attention on Simon.[88] Jesus is speaking to Simon as the one in charge. He is to put out into the deep, and he and his crew are supposed to let down their nets. This same shift occurs in verses 5 and 6: *We* have labored and taken nothing, but at your word *I* will let down the nets. When *they* had done this they enclosed a great multitude of fish. This focus on Simon continues throughout this narrative.

5:7, 10. μετόχοις, κοινωνοί. Both adjectives, when used as substantives, refer to partners, that is, those who partake of or share in something together. In nonbiblical texts both words can be used in a variety of contexts, including, frequently, passages referring to business partners. Of the 13 uses of μέτοχος[89] and 18 uses of κοινωνός[90] in biblical texts, they have this sense only in our passage. Elsewhere in the New Testament μέτοχος is found only in Hebrews, where it refers to sharing in spiritual realities (Heb. 1:9; 3:1, 14; 6:4; 12:8). Κοινωνός and its cognate words (κοινός, κοινωνέω, κοινωνία, κοινωνικός, συγκοινωνέω, συγκοινωνός)[91] are used frequently for sharing in Christ, the church, and spiritual realities. Perhaps there is a similar association in our passage as well. In verse 10 the focus is not on the fishing business, as it is in verse 7, but rather on sharing in Peter's experience of amazement at Jesus. So κοινωνός in verse 10 may add to the focus in this passage on the partnership centered on Jesus which Peter, James, and John share.

5:9. περιέσχεν. They had enclosed fish (συνέκλεισαν, v. 6), and now awe "surrounds" them.[92]

5:10. μὴ φοβοῦ. Both present imperatives and aorist subjunctives can be used for prohibitions. The imperfective aspect of the present and the perfective aspect of the aorist express the viewpoint of the speaker/writer. "With the aorist the speaker prohibits an activity in its totality (Don't do it). . . . With the present the speaker views the prohibition as a process or something that pertains to habitual activities (Don't be in the habit of doing it)."[93] In

---

88. Peter is referred to as Simon in this story since he is not given the name Peter until later (Luke 6:14). The name Simon Peter, used in verse 8, occurs in the Synoptics only here and in Matt. 16:16, though fifteen times in John.

89. It is used seven times in the LXX and six in the GNT.

90. Two of the seven occurrences in the LXX may refer to business partners (Sir. 41:19; 42:3), as may two of the eleven uses in the GNT (our passage and Philem. 17), but none clearly are such.

91. As listed by Barclay M. Newman, *A Concise Greek-English Dictionary of the New Testament*, rev. ed. (Stuttgart: Deutsche Bibelgesellschaft, 2010), 103, under κοινόω.

92. A basic meaning of περιέχω. See BDAG, περιέχω 1, 800.

93. Young, 140. So also Wallace, 717; and Douglas S. Huffman, *Verbal Aspect Theory and the Prohibitions in the Greek New Testament*, Studies in Biblical Greek 16 (New York: Peter Lang, 2014), who provides an extensive study of the topic.

particular contexts μὴ with a present imperative can have the sense of "stop doing something," in contrast to μὴ with the aorist subjunctive, which can mean "do not start doing something."[94] These constructions do not always have these nuances, but they are always worth considering since the pragmatics of the context can warrant this distinction. Here Jesus is not telling Peter not to be in the habit of fearing, but not to continue being afraid, that is, to stop being afraid.

ζωγρῶν. English translations use "catch" for this verb, but ζωγρέω means "to catch alive."[95] In the ancient world, to be captured alive often meant enslavement and/or torture.[96] Jesus is telling Peter, "He will no longer catch dead fish, in order to eat them; rather, he will catch living people, not to reduce them to servitude, after the fashion of prisoners, but to give them liberty and true life."[97] Actually, this capturing *is* for servitude, but it is a servanthood that is true life and freedom.

1 Peter 3:17–22

Text with Basic Reading Helps

[17]κρεῖττον[98] γὰρ ἀγαθοποιοῦντας,[99] εἰ θέλοι[100] τὸ θέλημα τοῦ θεοῦ, πάσχειν ἢ κακοποιοῦντας.[101] [18]ὅτι καὶ Χριστὸς ἅπαξ[102] περὶ ἁμαρτιῶν ἔπαθεν,[103] δίκαιος ὑπὲρ ἀδίκων,[104] ἵνα ὑμᾶς προσαγάγῃ[105] τῷ θεῷ θανατωθεὶς[106] μὲν σαρκὶ ζωοποιηθεὶς[107] δὲ πνεύματι· [19]ἐν ᾧ καὶ τοῖς ἐν φυλακῇ πνεύμασιν πορευθεὶς[108]

---

94. "Thus, if the conditions are right, the aorist prohibition may well have the force of 'Do not start.' This is an affected meaning or specific usage. But to call this the *essential* idea is not correct" (Wallace, 717, emphasis original). For examples, see ibid., 723–24.

95. Both *CGEL* and Abbott-Smith say the word is formed from ζωός, ή, όν, alive, and ἀγρεύω, catch; though note ἀγρέω, take, seize (LSJ 14). Compare ἄγρα, a catch, in verses 4 and 9.

96. Ceslas Spicq, *Theological Lexicon of the New Testament*, trans. and ed. James D. Ernest (Peabody, MA: Hendrickson, 1994), 2:162–63.

97. Spicq, *Lexicon*, 2:162. Obviously, fish are not dead when they are caught!

98. nom. sg. neut. < κρείττων, ον, gen. ονος, and κρείσσων, better; comparative of ἀγαθός, ή, όν, good

99. acc. pl. masc. act. Pres. ptc. < ἀγαθοποιέω, I do good, do what is right

100. 3 sg. act. Pres. opt. < θέλω, I will

101. acc. pl. masc. act. Pres. ptc. < κακοποιέω, I do evil, do what is wrong

102. adv., ἅπαξ, once for all

103. 3 sg. act. Aor. ind. < πάσχω, I suffer

104. gen. pl. masc. < ἄδικος, ον, unrighteous

105. 3 sg. act. Aor. subjn. < προσάγω, I bring to

106. nom. sg. masc. pass. Aor. ptc. < θανατόω, I put to death

107. nom. sg. masc. pass. Aor. ptc. < ζωοποιέω, I make alive

108. nom. sg. masc. pass. Aor. ptc. < πορεύομαι, I go

ἐκήρυξεν[109] [20]ἀπειθήσασίν[110] ποτε[111] ὅτε ἀπεξεδέχετο[112] ἡ τοῦ θεοῦ μακροθυμία[113] ἐν ἡμέραις Νῶε κατασκευαζομένης[114] κιβωτοῦ[115] εἰς ἣν ὀλίγοι, τοῦτ᾽ ἔστιν ὀκτὼ[116] ψυχαί, διεσώθησαν[117] δι᾽ ὕδατος. [21]ὃ καὶ ὑμᾶς ἀντίτυπον[118] νῦν σῴζει βάπτισμα,[119] οὐ σαρκὸς ἀπόθεσις[120] ῥύπου[121] ἀλλὰ συνειδήσεως ἀγαθῆς ἐπερώτημα[122] εἰς θεόν, δι᾽ ἀναστάσεως Ἰησοῦ Χριστοῦ, [22]ὅς ἐστιν ἐν δεξιᾷ θεοῦ πορευθεὶς εἰς οὐρανὸν ὑποταγέντων[123] αὐτῷ ἀγγέλων καὶ ἐξουσιῶν καὶ δυνάμεων.

Passage Scan

[17]κρεῖττον γὰρ [ἀγαθοποιοῦντας], [εἰ θέλοι τὸ θέλημα τοῦ θεοῦ], πάσχειν ἢ [κακοποιοῦντας]. | [18]ὅτι καὶ Χριστὸς ἅπαξ (περὶ ἁμαρτιῶν) ἔπαθεν, <δίκαιος (ὑπὲρ ἀδίκων)>, | ἵνα ὑμᾶς προσαγάγῃ τῷ θεῷ [θανατωθεὶς μὲν σαρκὶ] [ζωοποιηθεὶς δὲ πνεύματι]· | [19](ἐν ᾧ καὶ [τοῖς (ἐν φυλακῇ) πνεύμασιν πορευθεὶς] ἐκήρυξεν), [20]<ἀπειθήσασίν ποτε [ὅτε ἀπεξεδέχετο ἡ τοῦ θεοῦ μακροθυμία (ἐν ἡμέραις Νῶε)> <κατασκευαζομένης κιβωτοῦ> (εἰς ἣν ὀλίγοι, [τοῦτ᾽ ἔστιν ὀκτὼ ψυχαί], διεσώθησαν (δι᾽ ὕδατος). | [21]ὃ καὶ ὑμᾶς ἀντίτυπον νῦν σῴζει βάπτισμα, <οὐ σαρκὸς ἀπόθεσις ῥύπου> <ἀλλὰ συνειδήσεως ἀγαθῆς ἐπερώτημα (εἰς θεόν)>, (δι᾽ ἀναστάσεως Ἰησοῦ Χριστοῦ), [22][ὅς ἐστιν (ἐν δεξιᾷ [τοῦ] θεοῦ)] [πορευθεὶς (εἰς οὐρανὸν)] [ὑποταγέντων αὐτῷ ἀγγέλων καὶ ἐξουσιῶν καὶ δυνάμεων].

109. 3 sg. act. Aor. ind. < κηρύσσω, I preach
110. dat. pl. neut. act. Aor. ptc. < ἀπειθέω, I disobey
111. adv., ποτέ, at some time or other
112. 3 sg. mid. Impf. ind. < ἀπεκδέχομαι, I await eagerly
113. nom. sg. fem. < μακροθυμία, ας, ἡ, patience
114. gen. sg. fem. pass. Pres. ptc. < κατασκευάζω, I build
115. gen. sg. fem. < κιβωτός, οῦ, ἡ, boat, ark
116. ὀκτώ, indeclinable, eight
117. 3 pl. pass. Aor. ind. < διασῴζω, I bring safely through, save
118. nom./acc. sg. neut. < ἀντίτυπος, ον, corresponding to; copy, antitype, representation
119. nom. sg. neut. < βάπτισμα, ατος, τό, baptism
120. nom. sg. fem. < ἀπόθεσις, εως, ἡ, removal
121. gen. sg. masc. < ῥυπος, ου, ὁ, dirt
122. nom. sg. neut. < ἐπερώτημα, ατος, τό, appeal; promise
123. gen. pl. masc. pass. Aor. ptc. < ὑποτάσσω, I subject, subordinate

Sentence Map

17 κρεῖττον γὰρ   [   ] . . .[1] . . .[2]πάσχειν . . .[3]
                             [1]ἀγαθοποιοῦντας,
                          [2]εἰ θέλοι τὸ θέλημα τοῦ θεοῦ,
  [3]ἢ   [   ]   [πάσχειν]
                        κακοποιοῦντας.

18 ὅτι καὶ Χριστὸς ἅπαξ . . .   ἔπαθεν,
                             περὶ ἁμαρτιῶν
       δίκαιος   [ἔπαθεν]
                           ὑπὲρ ἀδίκων,

  ἵνα ὑμᾶς προσαγάγῃ τῷ θεῷ
          θανατωθεὶς μὲν σαρκὶ
          ζωοποιηθεὶς δὲ πνεύματι
          ⌐ or ⌐

19 |< or ἐν ᾧ καὶ τοῖς . . .[3] πνεύμασιν [or . . .[1]] . . .[2] ἐκήρυξεν
                          [3]ἐν φυλακῇ
                                    [2]πορευθεὶς
                                    [[1]τοῖς . . .[3] πνεύμασιν
                                            [3]ἐν φυλακῇ]

20   ἀπειθήσασίν ποτε

                 ὅτε ἀπεξεδέχετο ἡ τοῦ θεοῦ μακροθυμία
                     ἐν ἡμέραις Νῶε
                     κατασκευαζομένης κιβωτοῦ

  εἰς ἣν   ὀλίγοι, . . .[1]   διεσώθησαν
         [1]τοῦτ' ἔστιν ὀκτὼ ψυχαί,   δι' ὕδατος.

21   ὃ καὶ ὑμᾶς . . .[1] νῦν   σῴζει . . .[2]
        |<or [1]ἀντίτυπον   or >|
        [2]βάπτισμα,
        οὐ σαρκὸς ἀπόθεσις ῥύπου
        ἀλλὰ συνειδήσεως ἀγαθῆς ἐπερώτημα
                        εἰς θεόν,

                δι' ἀναστάσεως Ἰησοῦ Χριστοῦ,

22   ὅς ἐστιν

> [ὅς ἐστιν]
>> ἐν δεξιᾷ θεοῦ
>> πορευθεὶς
>>> εἰς οὐρανὸν
>> ὑποταγέντων αὐτῷ ἀγγέλων καὶ ἐξουσιῶν καὶ δυνάμεων.

Guided Tour of the Passage

3:17. Our passage comes in the midst of a section focused on how Christians should respond to evil and suffering. Γάρ signals either an explanation or the grounds for the response to suffering outlined in verses 8–16. Πάσχειν is the subject, and the verb ἐστίν is elided. Πάσχειν is modified by an adverbial participle and a conditional clause. Θεοῦ modifies the subject of the conditional clause.

Κρεῖττον begins a comparison that is completed by ἤ, implying a new clause with an elided verb. Κακοποιοῦντας modifies an implied repetition of the infinitive.

3:18. The general point made in verse 17 is now supplemented by a much more specific cause (ὅτι) for the Christian response to evil and suffering: the example of Christ. Everything in verses 18–22 is flowing from this first clause, as the map depicts.

The verb in the first clause is modified by the adjunctive use of καί, "also," and ἅπαξ. Δίκαιος is in apposition to Χριστός with an implied repetition of the verb. Two adverbial particles modify προσαγάγῃ. They are connected to each other through a μέν . . . δέ construction, which "point to the two things set over against each other."[124]

3:19. The object of the preposition ἐν is a relative clause. Καί is adjunctive, "also," and the verb is modified by an adverbial participle. Πνεύμασιν could be the indirect object of ἐκήρυξεν or a dative of destination with πορευθείς.[125] Ἐν ᾧ is easy to read, but there are three major options for the antecedent of the relative pronoun. (1) It could refer to πνεύματι, in which case ἐν could signal either sphere or agency depending on whether πνεύματι refers to the spiritual sphere or to the Holy Spirit. Alternatively, (2) the antecedent could be ζῳοποιηθεὶς πνεύματι as the circumstance that enabled the preaching, or (3) ᾧ could be a reference back to verse 18 in general, "in which circumstances" he preached.

---

124. Funk, §635.2.
125. Thus this dative may either be an item on the main line of the clause or under another element. This kind of alternative can be represented on a map, as in the one above, but it can get cluttered. In such cases, you can map the option you think is most likely correct and then add a footnote mentioning the alternative.

3:20. The dative participle has an adverbial modifier and is in agreement with πνεύμασιν.[126] Θεοῦ modifies μακροθυμία. A genitive absolute provides additional detail for the scene being described. The subject of the genitive absolute, κιβωτοῦ, is further developed by a prepositional phrase with a relative clause for its object. The subject is modified by a parenthetical statement, τοῦτ' ἔστιν ὀκτὼ ψυχαί.

3:21. The new sentence continues with yet another relative clause, this one referring back to ὕδατος. The relative pronoun serves as the subject of the verb σῴζει. This verb has two adverbs, νῦν and καί, the second of which is either adjunctive ("also") or ascensive ("even," "indeed").

The function of ἀντίτυπον is unclear, as noted on the map. It may serve as (1) an accusative of manner modifying σῴζει; (2) a nominative in apposition to ὅ and the three other appositives that follow, so water is the antitype; or (3) a collective singular in the accusative in apposition to ὑμᾶς, so the persons addressed (ὑμᾶς) correspond to the ὀλίγοι.

Βάπτισμα is in apposition to ὅ, which refers to ὕδατος. The core terms in the οὐ . . . ἀλλά construction, ἀπόθεσις and ἐπερώτημα, are also in apposition to βάπτισμα, and each has a genitive modifier. Διά modifies σῴζει, despite being separated by the long string of appositives.

3:22. The final section is a relative clause focusing on Jesus. The picture is developed by an adverbial participle and a genitive absolute with a compound subject composed of three genitive nouns.

Bonus Coverage

3:17. θέλοι. An optative is used in a conditional clause to signal that there is a remote possibility of the thing happening. Here θέλοι is matched a few verses earlier when Peter uses an optative to make a similar point: ἀλλ' εἰ καὶ πάσχοιτε διὰ δικαιοσύνην, μακάριοι, "But even if you should suffer because of righteousness, [you are/will be/would be] blessed" (1 Pet. 3:14).[127] These optatives suggest such suffering is a possibility but not yet on the horizon. A few verses later Peter says, Ἀγαπητοί, μὴ ξενίζεσθε τῇ ἐν ὑμῖν πυρώσει πρὸς πειρασμὸν ὑμῖν γινομένῃ ὡς ξένου ὑμῖν συμβαίνοντος (1 Pet. 4:12). This verse can be taken two different ways.

---

126. Since πνεύμασιν has an article and ἀπειθήσασιν does not, the participle is in predicate position. Accordingly some translations take the participle adverbially ("after they were disobedient long ago," NET; "because they formerly did not obey," ESV), though most translate it as adjectival, assuming the article has been left out.

127. Neither of these verses contains a complete condition of remote possibility, since the apodosis (the "then" clause) would also have an optative. An optative could be supplied for the elided verb in verse 14 (represented by the translation "would be"), but the optative is not clearly present. Indeed, there are no complete examples of this form of condition in the GNT. See Wallace, 484; Young, 227; Funk, §859.

Beloved, do not be surprised at the fiery trial when it comes upon you to test you, as though something strange were happening to you. (ESV)

Dear friends, do not be surprised at the fiery ordeal that has come on you to test you, as though something strange were happening to you. (NIV)

Does this verse indicate that the trials have now arrived (NIV), or that they are still in the future (ESV)?[128] Suffering is a theme throughout this letter (beginning with 1 Pet. 1:6–7). Clearly the recipients are already experiencing trials in the form of slander and social marginalization (1 Pet. 2:12, 15; 3:9, 14, 16). If the "fiery trial" is something more intense, then a shift from the remote possibility to trials that have now come (taking the NIV interpretation of 4:12) could suggest that news has arrived while Peter is writing; what seemed a remote possibility has already begun. But even in this context Peter refers explicitly only to insults (4:14), so perhaps "fiery trial" is not a more severe form of adversity. In that case either the ESV or NIV interpretation fits the context and chapter 4 continues the perspective of chapter 3.[129]

3:18. σαρκί, πνεύματι. There is much discussion of the meaning of these two terms and the nuance of the datives. One major option is that the words refer to two aspects of Christ's person, his flesh and spirit. If so, σάρξ would refer to his physical existence, while πνεῦμα might refer to "that which animates or gives life to the body" and thus here to "that part of Christ which, in contrast to σάρξ, did not pass away in death, but survived as an individual entity after death."[130] Alternatively, πνεῦμα could refer to "a part of human personality. . . . When used with σάρξ, the flesh, it denotes the immaterial part. . . . *Flesh and spirit* = the whole personality, in its outer and inner aspects."[131] Perhaps this latter meaning is more likely in this passage since Peter says this πνεῦμα is made alive after Christ's death, not that it "survived." In either case, the datives could signal sphere or reference.

Another major option is that these terms refer to two spheres of existence, the realm of the σάρξ, characterized by sin and weakness, and the realm of the πνεῦμα, characterized by the life and the power of the Spirit. Karen Jobes notes that "the majority of recent commentators understand the contrasting phrases 'put to death in flesh' but 'made alive in spirit' to refer either to two spheres of Christ's existence (the earthly sphere versus the eschatological) or to two modes of his personal existence (in human form before his death

128. ESV takes γινομένη as adverbial, and NIV takes it as attributive.
129. The form of prohibition could point in this direction as well if μὴ ξενίζεσθε has the sense "stop being surprised." See the discussion above on μὴ φοβοῦ in Luke 5:10.
130. BDAG, πνεῦμα 2, 832–33.
131. BDAG, πνεῦμα 3, 833 (italics original).

and in glorified form after his resurrection)."[132] Here also the datives could signal sphere or reference.

Yet another interpretation takes σάρξ as referring to the physical, and πνεύματι to the Spirit. In this case σαρκί would be sphere or reference, but πνεύματι would be instrument or agency.[133]

Just in these two words, the Greek in this passage touches on major issues in Christology, pneumatology, soteriology, and anthropology!

3:21. συνειδήσεως ἀγαθῆς ἐπερώτημα. The word ἐπερώτημα has often been translated as "appeal," but there is no good evidence for this meaning. BDAG gives "appeal" but provides no examples of this meaning and refers to LSJ for the option "pledge." Now in *CGEL* Danker does not mention "appeal" at all, but says ἐπερώτημα is "a rare word perh. best understood in the sense of *pledge*."[134]

Συνείδησις can mean either "consciousness"[135] or "moral consciousness, conscience."[136] These senses are related, since the conscience works on the basis of a consciousness of the difference between right and wrong. It is usually thought that συνείδησις refers here to moral consciousness, but perhaps the focus instead is on being conscious of God. Similarly, when Peter says earlier συνείδησιν ἔχοντες ἀγαθήν, he may mean not "having a good conscience" (so ESV) but rather "having your consciousness focused on God." It is precisely having such a consciousness of God that enables one to respond appropriately to attacks. Peter refers to a similar theme earlier in the same sentence: κύριον δὲ τὸν Χριστὸν ἁγιάσατε ἐν ταῖς καρδίαις ὑμῶν (3:15), "But set Christ apart as Lord in your hearts" (NET). This hallowing of Christ in one's heart, like the hallowing of the Father's Name (Matt. 6:9; Luke 11:2), is the prerequisite for doing God's will. Our passage may point to consciousness of God as the fundamental disposition that grounds and is the source of true obedience.

Baptism here is usually understood to mean an appeal to God for a good conscience, or a pledge to maintain a good conscience, taking συνειδήσεως as an objective genitive. But if συνείδησις is "consciousness," the subjective genitive would represent baptism as a pledge to God enacted by a sound mindfulness of God, while the objective genitive would say baptism is a pledge to God to maintain a sound mindfulness of God. The objective is more likely,

---

132. Karen H. Jobes, *1 Peter*, Baker Exegetical Commentary on the New Testament (Grand Rapids: Baker Academic, 2005), 242.

133. Instrument is impersonal and agency is personal. The "distinct personality and deity of the Spirit" are not "foreign to the NT," but these truths are developing within the New Testament (Wallace, 166). "It should be noted that, in all probability, *none* of the examples involving πνεύματι in the NT should be classified as agency" (ibid., emphasis original).

134. *CGEL* 139 (bold and italics original).

135. BDAG, συνείδησις 1, 967.

136. BDAG, συνείδησις 2, 967.

given the contrast with removal of bodily dirt (σαρκὸς ἀπόθεσις ῥύπου) in the μέν . . . δέ construction, suggesting the focus is on the effects of baptism, not its source. This interpretation of συνείδησις shifts the focus from simple morality to what today might be called spirituality, which itself grounds and enables a pattern of life pleasing to God.

SENTENCE MAPPING

As noted in chapter 4, I have tried to describe this technique clearly, but the material is dense. Students usually find an oral presentation easier to follow, so I have provided videos that walk through the main points of this technique (see the website for this book).

The sentence map is a valuable tool for studying a text carefully. It is useful in exegesis and meditation but can also help sort out particularly difficult sentences while one is reading. Producing a sentence map forces you to think through a passage in detail, and the resulting map represents your understanding of how the language of the text is put together to communicate its message. Just as geographical maps vary in the level of detail provided, so sentence maps can differ in the amount of information they provide. A basic-level map shows the relation between independent and dependent clauses. An intermediate-level map adds information about prepositional phrases and the words they modify. An advanced map offers deeper analysis of the structures within clauses and phrases. I will focus on mapping sentences, but the same techniques can be used to map larger sections, even whole documents.

The Three Levels of Sentence Mapping

Level	What Is Shown
1	clauses
2	clauses and prepositional phrases
3	clauses, prepositional phrases, and smaller constructions

You can use labels to note the particular information that various words contribute to the overall meaning of the sentence and how clauses and sentences relate to one another. You may not want to label every clause, especially when its meaning is obvious, but labels can be helpful for preserving the fruit of your analysis of constructions that are difficult or unusual. In appendix 2, I list some commonly used labels and their meanings.

The approach to sentence mapping offered here works equally well in English or in Greek. To make it easier to see the principles, I will begin with instructions for mapping texts in English.

Sentence Maps in English

Obtain a copy of your passage from one of the Bible software programs (e.g., BibleWorks, Logos, or Accordance) or from one of the many websites that offer copies of the Bible (e.g., biblehub.com).[1] Copy the passage into a new document in your word processing program. For a video of these procedures, see the website for this book.

Level 1 Sentence Maps in English

1. Divide the sentences in the passage into clauses. A clause is a cluster of words with a verb at its center. Make use of punctuation, conjunctions, and verbs to help recognize clauses.

- Periods and question marks always indicate a break between clauses. Commas can do so as well but often do not.
- Locating verbs helps identify clauses, since a clause is centered on a verb.
- Place each clause on its own line.

2. Line up coordinate clauses and indent subordinate clauses.

- Coordinate clauses are parallel to each other, while a subordinate clause is dependent on another clause.
- For a rough guide to identifying clauses, note the conjunctions used:
  Coordinate clauses begin with conjunctions such as "and, but, for, or, nor, so, yet."
  Subordinate clauses begin with conjunctions such as "after, although, as, as if, because, before, even if, even though, for, if, in order to,

1. The verses I have selected for this section on mapping in English come from the ESV (Matt. 13:53; Luke 16:13; John 1:1; 11:39; Eph. 5:17; 6:10–13).

      since, that, though, unless, until, whatever, when, whenever, whether, while, who, whoever."

- Some conjunctions, such as "for," can introduce either a coordinate or a subordinate clause.
- Some clauses do not have a conjunction, so the meaning of the clause is all we have to go on to determine its function in the flow of thought.
- Coordinate clauses are lined up flush with each other, using tabs so the alignment is exact. It is best to set tab stops at 0.25 inch or smaller.
- Subordinate clauses are indented under the verb in the clause being modified.

Examples of Coordinate-Clause Alignment

John 1:1

    The Word was with God
    and the Word was God.

This combination of two independent clauses is known as a compound sentence.

Ephesians 5:17

    Do not be foolish,
    but understand what the will of the Lord is.

Examples of Subordinate-Clause Alignment

John 11:39

    Lord, by this time there will be an odor,
                          for he has been dead four days.

Matthew 13:53

          ⌐ When Jesus had finished these parables,
    he went away from there.

Here the subordinate clause comes before the main clause in the original sentence, so it can be indented above the main clause, and the ⌐ symbol is used to indicate the connection.[2]

---

2. The Times New Roman font, which is usually included with Microsoft Word for Windows, has an extensive set of symbols. The ones I use in mapping are ⌐ — ⌐ ⌐ ⌐ , which will be illustrated when we come to maps in Greek. On the website for this book, you will find a document containing the symbols I use for mapping. I suggest that you copy this page to your computer, and then when you begin a map, copy these symbols from that document to the top of the page where you are working. This will allow you to copy and paste the symbols as needed.

Luke 16:13

No servant can serve two masters,
     for either he will hate the one
             and love the other,
       or he will   be devoted to the one
             and despise the other.

In this verse the sentence combines coordinate and subordinate clauses. This combination of independent and dependent clauses is known as a complex sentence.

3. Label the function of each clause. Labels represent your understanding of how each clause contributes to the message of the sentence.

The Word was with God [*assertion*]
and the Word was God. [*addition*]

Do not be foolish,   [*exhortation*]
but understand what the will of the Lord is. [*contrast*]

Lord, by this time there will be an odor,   [*assertion*]
       for he has been dead four days. [*cause*]

   ⌐ When Jesus had finished these parables, [*time*]
he went away from there.   [*action*]

No servant can serve two masters,   [*assertion*]
    for   [*grounds*]
      either he will   hate the one   [*alternative*]
          and love the other, [*addition*]
      or he will   be devoted to the one [*alternative*]
          and despise the other. [*addition*]

If you want to access the symbols directly instead of using the set provided on the website for this book, you should look online for help if needed, since the procedures for accessing these symbols vary between different operating systems and word processing programs. Another method is to use the alt codes associated with each Unicode character. Again, if you need help, check on the web. I usually use a slightly smaller font for these symbols than for the surrounding text (e.g., 10 point for the symbols, if the text is in 12 point). If you use a font other than Times New Roman for the Greek, I recommend that you still use Times New Roman for the symbols, since many fonts either lack these symbols or do not display them correctly. Macros are useful for quickly shifting between fonts that you use frequently. For a video demonstrating these procedures, see the website for this book.

In this last example, notice that when a clause has two conjunctions that signal two different functions (here "for" and "either"), both functions are labeled. In this case it seems clearest to separate them on different lines, but in other situations it might be clearer to keep them on the same line, in which case two labels would be given for that line, separated by a period. Here is what that approach would look like for this verse:

No servant can serve two masters,   [*assertion*]
    for either he will hate the one   [*grounds. alternative*]
            and love the other, [*addition*]
     or he will be devoted to the one [*alternative*]
           and despise the other. [*addition*]

4. Use alignment and indention to show the relationships between the sentences in the passage.

- Apply these same principles to show the relations between the sentences themselves in order to trace the larger flow of the passage.
- Insert a blank line between sentences.
- If an item has to be moved, mark its original spot with ellipsis points (. . .).

  If more than one item is moved, include a superscript number after the ellipsis points (. . .[1]) and also before the item moved ([1]*item moved*).[3]

  Add numbers any time you think they are needed to ensure clarity.

Ephesians 6:10–13

Finally, be strong in the Lord and in the strength of his might.

Put on the whole armor of God,
 that you may be able to stand against the schemes of the devil.
 For we do not wrestle against flesh and blood,
         but against the rulers,
         against the authorities,

      against the cosmic powers over this present darkness,
      against the spiritual forces of evil in the heavenly places.

---

3. Placing numbers after the ellipsis points and before the text moved allows you to include footnotes without confusion, since a superscript number after text will signal a footnote.

[For we do not wrestle   against flesh and blood,]

      Therefore take up the whole armor of God,
             that you may be able   to withstand in the evil day,
                                  ┌¹having done all,
         and . . .¹   to stand firm.

        5. Label the function of each sentence.

Finally, be strong in the Lord and in the strength of his might.   *[exhortation]*

Put on the whole armor of God,   *[exhortation]*
  that you may be able to stand against the schemes of the devil.   *[purpose]*
  For we do not wrestle   against flesh and blood,   *[basis]*
                  but against the rulers,   *[contrast]*
                  against the authorities,   *[series]*
    ┌─────────────┘
      against the cosmic powers over this present darkness,   *[series]*
      against the spiritual forces of evil in the heavenly places.   *[series]*

      Therefore take up the whole armor of God,   *[inference]*
           that you may be able to withstand in the evil day, *[purpose]*
                     ┌¹having done all, *[circumstance]*
        and . . .¹   to stand firm. *[addition]*

Level 2 Sentence Maps in English

    1. Within the level 1 map, separate out the prepositional phrases and indent them under the word they modify. You can put them over the word if the prepositional phrase comes first in the original sentence.

Level 1
    Lord, by this time there will be an odor,
                  for he has been dead four days.

Level 2
              ┌¹by this time
    Lord, . . .¹ there will be an odor,
               for he has been dead four days.

Level 1
    Put on the whole armor of God,
        that you may be able to stand against the schemes of the devil.

Level 2
    Put on the whole armor
                of God,
    that you may be able to stand
                    against the schemes
                        of the devil.

2. Each prepositional phrase can be labeled.

┌¹by this time	[*measure*]
Lord, . . .¹ there will be an odor,	[*statement*]
for he has been dead four days.	[*explanation*]
Put on the whole armor	[*exhortation*]
of God,	[*possession*]
that you may be able to stand	[*purpose*]
against the schemes	[*disadvantage*]
of the devil.	[*source*]

Level 3 Sentence Maps in English

1. Determine which items in a clause are part of the core of the clause. The basic elements of a clause are the subject, verb, direct object, and indirect object. Not all of these items are present in each clause.

2. Leave the core elements on their line and in their original order. Move other items in the clause to show what they modify within the core clause.

- The four core items are placed on a line, along with any conjunctions, articles, and negative adverbs (i.e., "not") present in the clause.
- Other items in a clause are arranged above or below this baseline of the clause.

Level 1
    Lord, by this time there will be an odor,
                    for he has been dead four days.

Level 3
                ┌¹by . . . time
                    this
Lord, . . .¹ there will be an odor,
            for he has been dead . . . days.
                      four

The prepositional phrase is moved above its line, and its original place is marked with ellipsis points. "This" modifies "time," and "four" modifies "days," so they are put under the words they modify and their original locations marked. It is sometimes unclear whether an item should go above or below its original line, and sometimes both are options. So this example could be done:

```
Lord, . . . there will be an odor,
                  by . . . time
                       this
           for he has been dead . . . days.
                                     four
```

In this second version, the prepositional phrase is still connected to the verb it modifies. The ellipsis points on the first line mean that the item on the second line came from there. Note that the "by" and the "for" are not aligned with one another even though they both modify the same verb. This difference in alignment helps signal that they function differently, one as a prepositional phrase and the other as initiating another whole clause.

Level 1

```
    ⌐ When Jesus had finished these parables,
he went away from there.
```

Level 3

```
    ⌐ When Jesus had finished . . . parables,
he went away                             these
    from there.
```

"These" is an adjective modifying "parables" and thus is put under the word it modifies. "From there" is a prepositional phrase modifying the verb. In this case, there is enough space between "he went away" and "these" to allow them to be on the same line without confusion. Often this will not be the case, and one of them must be put on the next line down. For example:

```
    ⌐ When Jesus had finished . . . parables
                                     these
he went away
    from there.
```

There is flexibility within these general guidelines. Compare the following two examples.

Example 1

Put on the . . .[1] armor

               [1]whole

           of God,

Example 2

against the . . .[1] forces   . . .[2] . . .[3]

            [1]spiritual

         [2]of evil

       [3]in the . . . places.

                     heavenly

In the first example, I numbered "whole" to clarify where it came from, even though ellipsis points already indicate this and point to the next line by default. Since "of God" comes next in the sentence after "armor," no ellipsis points are needed, though they could be included to help clarify.

The second example illustrates this point, since "of evil" comes right after "forces" and thus does not need a number, and "in the heavenly places" follows next and also does not need a number, but adding the numbers may help clarify the original order because of the placement of "spiritual." Since "spiritual" comes before "forces" in the original text, it could have been put on the line above "forces." I have put it beneath in order to keep all the modifiers of "forces" together.

In the following sentence map of Eph. 6:10–13, the phrase "the whole armor of God" appears twice and with differing arrangements to illustrate the two sentence mapping approaches presented thus far.

Detailed Sentence Map for Ephesians 6:10–13

. . . be strong

    Finally,

   in the Lord

   and in the strength

             of . . . might.

                his

Put on the . . .[1] armor

              [1]whole

          of God,

  that you may be able to stand

                against the schemes

                     of the devil.

[Put on the . . . armor]
   For[4] we do not wrestle   against   flesh
                                       and blood,
               but against the rulers,
               against the authorities,
               against the . . . powers
                           cosmic
                     over . . .[1] . . .[2] darkness,
                             [1]this
                         [2]present
          against the . . .[1] forces
                    [1]spiritual
               of evil
               in the . . . places.
                    heavenly

   Therefore take up the . . .[1] armor . . .[2]
                 [1]whole
                 [2]of God,
        that you   may be able   to withstand
                           in the . . . day,
                           evil
                    ┌[1]having done all,
        and . . .[1]   to stand
                      firm.

3. Label the items that are not part of the clause's core. In a thorough sentence map every item would have a label. Many items would simply be labeled "adjective" or "adverb," though even these could be more deeply analyzed. Indeed, even articles ("a" and "the") can be analyzed, and sometimes they can be theologically significant, though this requires work in the original language.

Sentence Maps in Greek

Obtain a copy of your passage from one of the Bible software programs (e.g., BibleWorks, Logos, or Accordance) or from a site on the web.[5] Copy the pas-

---

4. "For" is indented under "Put," but "Put" is so short the indention may not be clear.
5. The Tyndale House (Cambridge) website is one place you can download a copy of the GNT. See http://www.tyndale.cam.ac.uk/index.php?page=UnicodeBibles. There are a number of free Greek fonts on the web, but the Unicode fonts that come standard on computers usually contain all the Greek characters. For help with Unicode fonts, see http://www.tyndale.cam.ac.uk/fonts.

sage you want to map into a new document in your word processing program. For a video of these procedures, see the website for this book.

Level 1 Sentence Map in Greek

1. Divide the sentences of the passage into clauses. This first step is the same as in English maps, though Greek sentences often contain more clauses than in modern English. When you are first getting started with this form of analysis it helps to make use of punctuation, conjunctions, and verbs. In Greek, finite verbs are the heart of a clause, but occasionally infinitives and participles can serve in this way as well, as we will see.

I will use John 3:16–18 as a sample passage. Before proceeding, you need to read through the passage so you are familiar with it in Greek. Use the notes in appendix 3 to facilitate reading through these verses and understanding their grammar.

[16]Οὕτως γὰρ ἠγάπησεν ὁ θεὸς τὸν κόσμον ὥστε τὸν υἱὸν τὸν μονογενῆ ἔδωκεν, ἵνα πᾶς ὁ πιστεύων εἰς αὐτὸν μὴ ἀπόληται ἀλλ᾽ ἔχῃ ζωὴν αἰώνιον. [17]οὐ γὰρ ἀπέστειλεν ὁ θεὸς τὸν υἱὸν εἰς τὸν κόσμον ἵνα κρίνῃ τὸν κόσμον, ἀλλ᾽ ἵνα σωθῇ ὁ κόσμος δι᾽ αὐτοῦ. [18]ὁ πιστεύων εἰς αὐτὸν οὐ κρίνεται· ὁ δὲ μὴ πιστεύων ἤδη κέκριται, ὅτι μὴ πεπίστευκεν εἰς τὸ ὄνομα τοῦ μονογενοῦς υἱοῦ τοῦ θεοῦ.

When first learning to recognize clauses, some people find it helpful to go through the passage and put a box around each conjunction, a circle around each punctuation mark, a single line under each infinitive and participle, and a double line under each finite verb. These marks help the clauses stand out. In the final map you do not need to retain punctuation, but it is usually helpful to retain raised dots, question marks, and periods. Dividing this passage into clauses, we get the following:

16 Οὕτως γὰρ ἠγάπησεν ὁ θεὸς τὸν κόσμον
    ὥστε τὸν υἱὸν τὸν μονογενῆ ἔδωκεν,
    ἵνα πᾶς ὁ πιστεύων εἰς αὐτὸν μὴ ἀπόληται
    ἀλλ᾽ ἔχῃ ζωὴν αἰώνιον.
17 οὐ γὰρ ἀπέστειλεν ὁ θεὸς τὸν υἱὸν εἰς τὸν κόσμον
    ἵνα κρίνῃ τὸν κόσμον,
    ἀλλ᾽ ἵνα σωθῇ ὁ κόσμος δι᾽ αὐτοῦ.
18 ὁ πιστεύων εἰς αὐτὸν οὐ κρίνεται·
    ὁ δὲ μὴ πιστεύων ἤδη κέκριται,
    ὅτι μὴ πεπίστευκεν εἰς τὸ ὄνομα τοῦ μονογενοῦς υἱοῦ τοῦ θεοῦ.

Notice that all but one of the clauses have a conjunction, most of them have punctuation at the end, and each of them has one finite verb. The third clause in verse 17 has two conjunctions, which we will deal with later; for now, we will work with just the first conjunction in that line, ἀλλά.

2. Determine which clauses are coordinate and which are subordinate. As you consider how the clauses relate to one another in the passage's flow of thought, check to see which are coordinate with one another (i.e., parallel) and which are subordinate to another clause (i.e., dependent on it). As we saw in English mapping, conjunctions provide a rough guide. The main coordinate conjunctions are δέ, καί, ἀλλά, πλήν, and ἤ. The major types of subordinate clauses and the conjunctions that typically introduce them are as follows:

- Temporal (ὅτε, ἐπεί, ἕως, πρίν, ὡς)
- Local (οὗ, ὅθεν, ὅπου)
- Purpose (ἵνα, ὡς, ὅπως)
- Result (ὥστε, ἵνα)
- Causal (ὅτι, ἐπεί)
- Comparative (ὡς, ὥσπερ, καθώς)
- Concessive (καίπερ)
- Conditional (εἰ, ἐάν, εἰ μή)
- Direct discourse and Indirect Discourse (ὅτι)

The coordinate and subordinate clauses are labeled in our sample passage below. In the first line, γάρ indicates that our whole passage is linked to what precedes it in John 3. Since γάρ can introduce either an independent or dependent clause (compare "for" in English), we would need to study the flow of thought in the larger context to determine how it is used here.

16 Οὕτως γὰρ ἠγάπησεν ὁ θεὸς τὸν κόσμον	
ὥστε τὸν υἱὸν τὸν μονογενῆ ἔδωκεν,	[*subordinate*]
ἵνα πᾶς ὁ πιστεύων εἰς αὐτὸν μὴ ἀπόληται	[*subordinate*]
ἀλλ' ἔχῃ ζωὴν αἰώνιον.	[*coordinate*]
17 οὐ γὰρ ἀπέστειλεν ὁ θεὸς τὸν υἱὸν εἰς τὸν κόσμον	[*subordinate*]
ἵνα κρίνῃ τὸν κόσμον,	[*subordinate*]
ἀλλ' ἵνα σωθῇ ὁ κόσμος δι' αὐτοῦ.	[*coordinate*]
18 ὁ πιστεύων εἰς αὐτὸν οὐ κρίνεται·	[*subordinate*]
ὁ δὲ μὴ πιστεύων ἤδη κέκριται,	[*coordinate*]
ὅτι μὴ πεπίστευκεν εἰς τὸ ὄνομα τοῦ μονογενοῦς υἱοῦ τοῦ θεοῦ.	[*subordinate*]

3. Line up coordinate clauses flush with each other using quarter-inch (0.25 in.) tab settings or smaller. Since subordinate clauses modify a whole clause, they are placed under or over the verb of the clause they modify. Below is a selection of examples of this principle.

ὅτε ἐτέλεσεν ὁ Ἰησοῦς τοὺς λόγους τούτους, μετῆρεν ἀπὸ τῆς Γαλιλαίας
when Jesus finished these sayings, he went away from Galilee (Matt. 19:1 ESV)

⌐ ὅτε ἐτέλεσεν ὁ Ἰησοῦς τοὺς λόγους τούτους
μετῆρεν ἀπὸ τῆς Γαλιλαίας

Here the subordinate clause comes before the main clause in the text, so it is indented over the main clause, and the ⌐ symbol helps show it is modifying the main clause that comes next. Even though the ὅτε clause comes first in the text, it can be placed under the main clause if that seems clearer. Its original place is marked by ellipsis points, as in English sentence maps.

. . . μετῆρεν ἀπὸ τῆς Γαλιλαίας
    ὅτε ἐτέλεσεν ὁ Ἰησοῦς τοὺς λόγους τούτους

οἶδα ὅτι σπέρμα Ἀβραάμ ἐστε
I know that you are descendants of Abraham (John 8:37)

οἶδα
    ὅτι σπέρμα Ἀβραάμ ἐστε

This is an example of indirect discourse. Recall that "indirect discourse" is not just for speech but also for thinking, feeling, perceiving, and so forth.

ὡμολόγησεν ὅτι Ἐγὼ οὐκ εἰμὶ ὁ Χριστός
he confessed, "I am not the Christ" (John 1:20)

ὡμολόγησεν
    ὅτι Ἐγὼ οὐκ εἰμὶ ὁ Χριστός

Here we see an example of ὅτι introducing direct discourse, as indicated by the shift to the first person in the quote. *He* confessed, "*I* . . ."

Participles

Most participles should be given their own line. This principle is clear for adverbial participles (also known as circumstantial participles), since they are the equivalent of subordinate clauses, but even adjectival participles have verbal qualities and should have their own line as well. However, when a participle serves as a subject, direct object, or indirect object, it should remain on the same line as the verb, since it serves as part of the core of the clause.

Examples of Adjectival Participles

ὁ λύχνος ὁ καιόμενος καὶ φαίνων
the burning and shining lamp (John 5:35)

ὁ λύχνος
   ὁ καιόμενος
    καὶ φαίνων

These two participles join together to modify the noun λύχνος. The fact that the participles share the article means they are closely bound together, but compound constructions like this are broken down in a sentence map as shown. Since they are coordinate, they are tabbed to line up equally, along with the coordinating conjunction καί.

Κορνήλιος, . . . εὐσεβὴς καὶ φοβούμενος τὸν θεόν
Cornelius, . . . a religious man and one who feared God (Acts 10:1–2)

Κορνήλιος   εὐσεβὴς
           καὶ φοβούμενος τὸν θεόν

Here the adjective εὐσεβής is coordinate with an adjectival participle, this time without an article before the participle. This participle is serving as an adjective modifying Κορνήλιος, but it still has its verbal qualities and here has a direct object, τὸν θεόν. In constructions like this one, a direct object stays on the same line as its verb, just as it does in main clauses. In a level 3 map, the adjective εὐσεβής would be placed under the noun in modifies, but in a level 1 map, only a participle serving as an adjective is moved.

Examples of Adverbial Participles

An adverbial participle is lined up under the verb it modifies, usually near the beginning of the verb in order to save space. Such participles can have many different nuances,[6] but the same layout is used whatever the nuance.

ὁ δὲ ἀποκριθεὶς εἶπεν Γέγραπται· οὐκ ἐπ' ἄρτῳ μόνῳ ζήσεται ὁ ἄνθρωπος
and he answered and said, "It is written, 'A person will not live by bread alone'" (Matt. 4:4)

---

6. See Wallace, 621–46; Young, 152–57.

ὁ δὲ . . . εἶπεν
      ἀποκριθεὶς
      Γέγραπται
           οὐκ ἐπ᾽ ἄρτῳ μόνῳ ζήσεται ὁ ἄνθρωπος

Here we see indirect discourse within direct discourse. I have kept δέ with ὁ because ὁ δέ is usually a signal for a shift of speakers/agents in a narrative, with the article functioning as a pronoun ("and he . . ."). Ἀποκριθείς is an adverbial participle, so it is given its own line, and its original place is marked with ellipsis points (. . .). Γέγραπται is the main verb in the direct discourse, with the other indirect discourse clause (the quote from Scripture) subordinated under it.

ταῦτα τὰ ῥήματα ἐλάλησεν ἐν τῷ γαζοφυλακίῳ διδάσκων ἐν τῷ ἱερῷ
he spoke these words in the treasury while teaching in the temple (John 8:20)

ταῦτα τὰ ῥήματα ἐλάλησεν ἐν τῷ γαζοφυλακίῳ
          διδάσκων ἐν τῷ ἱερῷ

The adverbial participle is placed under the verb in the clause it modifies.

καὶ πάντες ἐφοβοῦντο αὐτόν, μὴ πιστεύοντες ὅτι ἐστὶν μαθητής
and all were fearing him, since they did not believe he was a disciple (Acts 9:26)

καὶ πάντες ἐφοβοῦντο αὐτόν
      μὴ πιστεύοντες
          ὅτι ἐστὶν μαθητής

The adverbial participle, with its negative adverb, is under the verb. It is placed near the beginning of the verb and so away from the right margin. The participle has another clause modifying it, a ὅτι clause for indirect discourse, that is, the content of what they did not believe. This ὅτι clause is indented under the verb.

ἦλθεν ὁ υἱὸς τοῦ ἀνθρώπου ἐσθίων καὶ πίνων
the Son of Man came eating and drinking (Matt. 11:19)

ἦλθεν ὁ υἱὸς τοῦ ἀνθρώπου
    ἐσθίων
    καὶ πίνων

Both participles are put under the verb and are given their own line.

Level 1 Map of John 3:16–18

In the following level 1 sentence map for John 3:16–18, note that it shows not only the relation between clauses within sentences but also the relation between sentences within this passage. In this map we see an example of what to do when material would go off the right side of the page. Use the symbol ⌐⌐ from the set of symbols in the Times New Roman font to move back to the left. This symbol is made from three separate symbols: ⌐—⌐ . To change the length, simply copy and paste the middle symbol as needed.

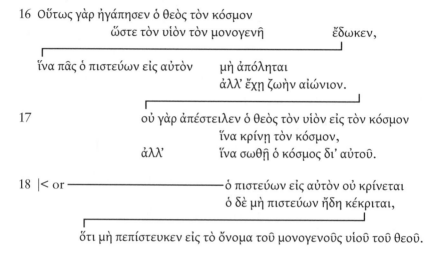

I have shifted ἔδωκεν to the right in order to show that the material in verses 17 and 18 is dependent on it; the οὐ in verse 17 needs a line of sight, as it were, to ἔδωκεν. If only the ἵνα clause in verse 16 were dependent on ἔδωκεν, this shift would not be necessary. Since verse 18 does not begin with a conjunction, its place in the flow of thought is more difficult to determine. It seems to be an explanation of verse 17, but it also seems to be related to verse 16. I will discuss this analysis more when we look at level 3 maps below.

Level 2 Sentence Map in Greek

A level 1 map provides an analysis of the main lines of thought in a passage. To deepen the analysis a bit, paying attention to the prepositional phrases is a good next step, since much meaning is conveyed by prepositional phrases.[7] Prepositional phrases are indented under the word they modify,

---

7. See M. J. Harris, *Prepositions and Theology in the Greek New Testament* (Grand Rapids: Zondervan, 2012).

and their original place is marked by an ellipsis. However, if the prepositional phrase comes at the end of its clause, the map simply continues on the next line, and an ellipsis is not needed. Also, if a prepositional phrase is used as a subject, direct object, or indirect object, it is kept on the line with the verb.

Below are two common forms the prepositional phrase can take when modifying a noun.

οἱ ἱερεῖς ἐν τῷ ἱερῷ, the priests in the temple (Matt. 12:5)

οἱ ἱερεῖς
    ἐν τῷ ἱερῷ

The prepositional phrase is placed under the word it modifies.

τοὺς προφήτας τοὺς πρὸ ὑμῶν, the prophets before you (Matt. 5:12)

τοὺς προφήτας
    τοὺς πρὸ ὑμῶν

A prepositional phrase can be in attributive position (that is, with an article before it). In a level 2 map, an adjective is left on the same line as the noun it modifies, but it is best to move a prepositional phrase when it functions as an adjective since the prepositional phrase can often be complex, making the core line of the clause a bit cluttered.

When the prepositional phrase modifies a verb, it is simply indented under the verb.

παρ᾽ αὐτῷ ἔμειναν, they stayed with him (John 1:39)

. . . ἔμειναν
    παρ᾽ αὐτῷ

The prepositional phrase is moved under the verb it modifies, and its original location is marked by ellipsis points.

Level 2 Map of John 3:16–18

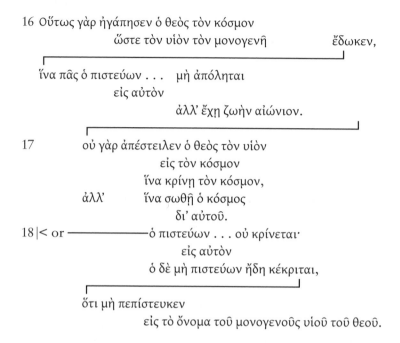

16 Οὕτως γὰρ ἠγάπησεν ὁ θεὸς τὸν κόσμον
        ὥστε τὸν υἱὸν τὸν μονογενῆ   ἔδωκεν,

ἵνα πᾶς ὁ πιστεύων . . . μὴ ἀπόληται
      εἰς αὐτὸν
            ἀλλ' ἔχῃ ζωὴν αἰώνιον.

17   οὐ γὰρ ἀπέστειλεν ὁ θεὸς τὸν υἱὸν
          εἰς τὸν κόσμον
          ἵνα κρίνῃ τὸν κόσμον,
   ἀλλ'   ἵνα σωθῇ ὁ κόσμος
          δι' αὐτοῦ.
18 |< or ———————ὁ πιστεύων . . . οὐ κρίνεται·
          εἰς αὐτὸν
      ὁ δὲ μὴ πιστεύων ἤδη κέκριται,

ὅτι μὴ πεπίστευκεν
      εἰς τὸ ὄνομα τοῦ μονογενοῦς υἱοῦ τοῦ θεοῦ.

Level 3 Sentence Map in Greek

Once the clauses and prepositional phrases are in order, the words in each clause that are not part of the core elements (i.e., subject, verb, direct object, indirect object) or a core part of a prepositional phrase are arranged to convey their function in the clause. Usually they are placed under the words they modify.

A. *Indention.* I will begin by listing the main principles of indention. Many of these principles have been used in level 1 and level 2 maps, but for convenience, I will repeat them here and add a few more details. In the abstract, these principles can appear more difficult and complex than they really are, so read them over without trying to work out all the details the first time through. Study the examples carefully to see these principles in action, and then return to this list for reference as needed.

Summary of Principles

1. Coordinate clauses and phrases are lined up flush with each other using tabs.

2. Subordinate clauses are indented under the verb of the clause they modify. If the verb in the main clause has more than one word, as in periphrastics

in Greek (e.g., ἦν διδάσκων) or tense and modal auxiliaries in English (e.g., "might have come"), the subordinate clause can be put under any part of the verb of the main clause.

3. When an item within a clause is in apposition to another item, it is lined up flush with the word or construction to which it is in apposition.

4. Vocatives are lined up in apposition to the subject, whether stated or embedded in the verb.

5. Most modifiers are placed under the word they modify and indented a bit.

6. Adverbial participles and prepositional phrases modifying verbs are placed under the verb in the clause they modify and indented slightly.

7. When two or more items modify the same word, the ones higher up the page are indented farther to the right than the modifiers below them. This allows each modifier to have a line of sight, as it were, to the word modified. Modifiers are lined up flush only if they are in apposition to one another.

8. When words or phrases must be moved out of order, their original place is marked by an ellipsis. If more than one item in a clause must be moved, each ellipsis and its corresponding moved item should be numbered (e.g., . . .[1] and [1]*item moved*; . . .[2] and [2]*item moved*). Note that the superscript number *follows* the ellipsis but *precedes* the item that has been moved, as described above regarding level 1 maps in English.

9. Use the symbols ⌐ and ¬ from Times New Roman when needed to clarify which item is being modified.

10. When it is not clear which item is being modified, place the modifier under one of the options and indicate the other possible placement with a straight horizontal line (|), an angle bracket, and "or" (|< or; or >|) to point to the alternative.

11. Sometimes a large number of modifiers under items on the main line can get cluttered. Spreading out the items on the main line provides space so the lines of modification under the main line are clearer.

12. It is often helpful to have a blank line between sentences, and sometimes also between sections of a sentence that are separated by a raised dot.

13. You do not need to retain punctuation in a map, but it is usually helpful to retain raised dots, question marks, and periods.

14. When material is in danger of going off the right side of the page, use the symbol ⌐⌐ (⌐—⌐) from Times New Roman to move back to the left.

15. Postpositive conjunctions may be left in place or moved to the beginning of the clause.

B. *Modification of the subject, direct object, and indirect object.* In chapter 4 we saw how the subject, direct object, and indirect object of a clause can be expanded by means of various modifiers. Below are those same examples as they would be mapped, along with a few additional ones.

Adjective

ὁ λόγος ὁ σός, your word (John 17:17)

ὁ λόγος
  ὁ σός

The adjective modifies the noun and so is placed under the noun and indented.

τὴν δόξαν τὴν παρὰ τοῦ μόνου θεοῦ
the glory from the only God (John 5:44)

τὴν δόξαν
    τὴν παρὰ τοῦ . . . θεοῦ
        μόνου

This prepositional phrase in attributive position illustrates the same principle, since the object of the preposition (τοῦ θεοῦ) is itself modified by the adjective μόνου, which is indented under the word it modifies.

Adverb

ἡ δὲ ἄνω Ἰερουσαλήμ, the Jerusalem which is above (Gal. 4:26)

ἡ δὲ . . . Ἰερουσαλήμ
    ἄνω

This adverb modifies the noun and so is placed under the noun as in the previous example.

Noun

Nominative (= Apposition)

Ἐγὼ Ἰωάννης, ὁ ἀδελφὸς ὑμῶν, I John, your brother (Rev. 1:9)

Ἐγὼ Ἰωάννης
    ὁ ἀδελφὸς
        ὑμῶν

Since the noun ὁ ἀδελφός is in apposition to Ἰωάννης, it is placed under it and lined up with it (using tabs to get the exact alignment). Actually, here Ἰωάννης is also in apposition to ἐγώ, so both nouns could be lined up directly under ἐγώ:

Ἐγὼ
Ἰωάννης
ὁ ἀδελφὸς
   ὑμῶν

Notice that the genitive ὑμῶν modifies ἀδελφός and so is placed under that noun and indented. This genitive is an example of how to handle genitives, which is the next category we consider.

Genitive

τὴν μάχαιραν αὐτοῦ, his sword (Matt. 26:51)

τὴν μάχαιραν
   αὐτοῦ

The genitive is placed under the word it modifies.

Dative

οἱ δὲ σοὶ μαθηταί, but your disciples (Mark 2:18)

οἱ δὲ . . . μαθηταί
   σοὶ

Since this dative modifies a noun, it is placed under it and indented, as in the examples above.

οἱ πτωχοὶ τῷ πνεύματι, the poor in spirit (Matt. 5:3)

οἱ πτωχοὶ
   τῷ πνεύματι

This pattern is the same as that of the previous example.

Accusative

Ἀνδρέαν τὸν ἀδελφὸν Σίμωνος, Andrew the brother of Simon (Mark 1:16)

Ἀνδρέαν
τὸν ἀδελφὸν
   Σίμωνος

The main use of the accusative to modify a noun is in apposition, so the accusative is lined up flush with the noun it modifies.

ἀνέπεσαν οὖν οἱ ἄνδρες τὸν ἀριθμὸν ὡς πεντακισχίλιοι
So the men sat down, in number about five thousand (John 6:10)

ἀνέπεσαν οὖν οἱ ἄνδρες . . .¹ . . .²
              ὡς πεντακισχίλιοι
                τὸν ἀριθμὸν

Here the adjective πεντακισχίλιοι is modifying οἱ ἄνδρες and is itself being modified by τὸν ἀριθμόν, an accusative of respect.

Prepositional Phrase

Πάτερ ἡμῶν ὁ ἐν τοῖς οὐρανοῖς, Our Father in heaven (Matt. 6:9)

Πάτερ ἡμῶν
  ὁ ἐν τοῖς οὐρανοῖς

It is common for a prepositional phrase to be substantivized by an article and function as a noun or, as here, an adjective.

Participle

The participle can function like a noun or like an adjective modifying another substantive. If a participle has an article, then it will certainly function as a noun or adjective, but it may have this function even if it does not have an article. Such participles are mapped just like nouns and adjectives.

καὶ ὁ πατήρ σου ὁ βλέπων ἐν τῷ κρυπτῷ ἀποδώσει σοι
And your Father who sees in secret will reward you. (Matt. 6:6)

καὶ ὁ πατήρ
    σου
    ὁ βλέπων . . . ἀποδώσει σοι
      ἐν τῷ κρυπτῷ

Infinitive

The most common way an infinitive modifies a noun (or pronoun or adjective) is the epexegetic use to explain or clarify.[8]

8. See Wallace, 607; Young, 175.

ἔδωκεν αὐτοῖς ἐξουσίαν τέκνα θεοῦ γενέσθαι
he gave them power to become children of God (John 1:12)

ἔδωκεν αὐτοῖς ἐξουσίαν
        τέκνα . . . γενέσθαι
        θεοῦ

The epexegetic infinitive explains what sort of ἐξουσία is in view, so it is placed under the noun it modifies and indented. Because the infinitive is a verbal noun, it can have its own object. The infinitive in this example is an equative verb, so it has a predicate noun, τέκνα, which in turn has a genitive modifier, θεοῦ, beneath it. An ellipsis stands where θεοῦ originally appeared in the sentence.

ἐπλήσθη ὁ χρόνος τοῦ τεκεῖν αὐτήν
the time for her to give birth arrived (Luke 1:57)

ἐπλήσθη ὁ χρόνος
      τοῦ τεκεῖν
      αὐτήν

This challenging example illustrates several principles of sentence mapping. The articular infinitive is under the noun it is modifying. This infinitive is like a verbal noun, something like "the giving birth." Αὐτήν is under this verbal noun because it is an accusative of respect, that is, it indicates that with respect to which something is stated. Very woodenly: "the time of the giving birth with respect to her." In an idiomatic English translation, the infinitive can be rendered as a finite verb and the accusative as its subject. If we were mapping according to the English sense rather than according to Greek grammar, we could leave the accusative on the same line as the verb:[9]

ἐπλήσθη ὁ χρόνος
      τοῦ τεκεῖν αὐτήν

Clause

Relative Clause

τὸ ὕδωρ ὃ δώσω αὐτῷ, the water which I will give him/her (John 4:14)

τὸ ὕδωρ
    ὃ δώσω αὐτῷ

---

9. As you develop fluency, you learn to pick up the meaning of the Greek constuctions without changing them into English idiom.

A relative clause is indented under the word it modifies.

A Normally Adverbial Clause

ἔρχεται ὥρα ὅτε ... προσκυνήσετε τῷ πατρί
the hour is coming when you will worship the Father (John 4:21)

ἔρχεται ὥρα
      ὅτε προσκυνήσετε τῷ πατρί

Since this ὅτε clause modifies the noun ὥρα, it is indented under it.
The only other item is τῷ πατρί, which is kept on the same line as the verb
since this verb takes a dative for its direct object; and thus this dative is part
of the core elements of the clause.

    C. *Expansion of the verb*. The verb can be expanded by means of a prepo-
sitional phrase, as in level 2 maps, and by the following items.

Verb Chains

Periphrastic participles, complementary participles, and supplementary
infinitives are kept on the main line along with their finite verb.

Periphrastic Construction

ἦν ... διδάσκων αὐτούς, he was teaching them (Matt. 7:29)

τῇ γὰρ χάριτί ἐστε σεσωσμένοι, by grace you have been saved (Eph. 2:8)

        ┌ ²τῇ ...¹ χάριτί
¹γὰρ ...² ἐστε σεσωσμένοι

Here the verb is modified by a dative. Since the dative comes before the verb
in the sentence, it can be indented above the verb. It can be placed over either
the finite verb or the participle since they function together as the verb of this
clause. Postpositive conjunctions like γὰρ can be left in place or moved to the
beginning of the clause if that seems clearer.

Complementary Participle

ἐπαύσατο λαλῶν, he finished speaking (Luke 5:4)

Supplementary Infinitive

ὑμεῖς οὐ δύνασθε ἐλθεῖν, you are not able to come (John 8:21)

Noun

Genitive

ἠγοράσθητε ... τιμῆς, you were bought for a price (1 Cor. 6:20)

ἠγοράσθητε
 τιμῆς

Dative

τῇ τρίτῃ ἡμέρᾳ ἐγερθήσεται, on the third day he will be raised (Matt. 17:23)

. . . ἐγερθήσεται
  τῇ . . . ἡμέρᾳ
   τρίτῃ

Since τῇ τρίτῃ ἡμέρᾳ is moved out of order, its place is marked by ellipsis points. Since τρίτῃ modifies ἡμέρᾳ, it is moved under the noun, and its original place is marked by ellipsis points.

Accusative

δωρεὰν ἐλάβετε, you received freely (Matt. 10:8)

. . . ἐλάβετε
 δωρεὰν

This is an accusative of manner.[10]

Adjective

Μικρὸν καὶ οὐ θεωρεῖτέ με
in a little while you will no longer see me (John 16:19)

. . . καὶ οὐ θεωρεῖτέ με
  Μικρὸν

The negative adverb οὐ is kept with its verb, as is the direct object, με. The adjective μικρόν is put under the verb since it functions as an adverbial accusative, also known as an accusative of manner.[11] Its original location is marked by ellipsis points.

Adverb

ἤδη κέκριται, he has already been judged (John 3:18)

. . . κέκριται
 ἤδη

10. See Wallace, 200–201; Young, 19–20.
11. BDAG, μικρός 1.d.β, 651.

The adverb is moved under the verb it modifies, and its original location is marked by ellipsis points.

Prepositional Phrase

παρ' αὐτῷ ἔμειναν, they stayed with him (John 1:39)

. . . ἔμειναν
    παρ' αὐτῷ

The prepositional phrase is moved under the verb and its original position is marked by ellipsis points.

ἐξετάσατε ἀκριβῶς περὶ τοῦ παιδίου, search carefully for the child (Matt. 2:8)

ἐξετάσατε
    ἀκριβῶς
    περὶ τοῦ παιδίου

Both the adverb and prepositional phrase modify the verb and are placed under it, indented so that each has "sight" of the verb. Since these modifiers follow in order in the original sentence, there is no need for ellipsis points.

Participle

Here are the examples of adverbial participles given above but now in a level 3 map.

καὶ νηστεύσας ἡμέρας τεσσεράκοντα καὶ νύκτας τεσσεράκοντα, ὕστερον ἐπείνασεν
having fasted forty days and forty nights, afterward he was hungry (Matt. 4:2)

    ⌐ καὶ νηστεύσας
           ἡμέρας τεσσεράκοντα καὶ νύκτας τεσσεράκοντα,
. . . ἐπείνασεν
    ὕστερον

The adverbial participle comes first in the sentence, so it can be placed over the main verb. The accusative modifiers are placed under the participle. The main verb has an adverbial modifier, which is placed under the verb.

ὁ δὲ ἀποκριθεὶς εἶπεν· Γέγραπται· Οὐκ ἐπ' ἄρτῳ μόνῳ ζήσεται ὁ ἄνθρωπος
and he answered and said, "It is written, 'A person will not live by bread alone'" (Matt. 4:4)

ὁ δὲ . . . εἶπεν
  ἀποκριθεὶς
  Γέγραπται
   Οὐκ . . . ζήσεται ὁ ἄνθρωπος
    ἐπ᾽ ἄρτῳ
     μόνῳ

The changes for a level 3 map come in the last clause, where the object of the preposition (ἄρτῳ) has an adjectival modifier. This modifier is indented under it.

ταῦτα τὰ ῥήματα ἐλάλησεν ἐν τῷ γαζοφυλακίῳ, διδάσκων ἐν τῷ ἱερῷ, he spoke these words in the treasury while teaching in the temple (John 8:20)

. . .¹ τὰ ῥήματα ἐλάλησεν
  ¹ταῦτα   ἐν τῷ γαζοφυλακίῳ
       διδάσκων
       ἐν τῷ ἱερῷ

The changes from the level 1 map given earlier are the positions of adjective ταῦτα and of the two prepositional phrases (which would also have been moved for a level 2 map, of course). Since there are two items on the second line independent of each other, I added a number for clarification.

καὶ πάντες ἐφοβοῦντο αὐτόν, μὴ πιστεύοντες ὅτι ἐστὶν μαθητής
and all were fearing him, since they did not believe he was a disciple (Acts 9:26)

καὶ πάντες ἐφοβοῦντο αὐτόν
  μὴ πιστεύοντες
   ὅτι ἐστὶν μαθητής

The level 3 map of this verse is the same as the level 1.

ἦλθεν ὁ υἱὸς τοῦ ἀνθρώπου ἐσθίων καὶ πίνων
the Son of Man came eating and drinking (Matt. 11:19)

ἦλθεν ὁ υἱὸς
  τοῦ ἀνθρώπου
 ἐσθίων
 καὶ πίνων

For a level 3 map, the genitive is moved under the word it modifies.

Infinitive

The infinitive can modify a verb in diverse ways. Here are examples of some common ways and how each would be represented in a sentence map.

οὐ δύναται ἰδεῖν τὴν βασιλείαν τοῦ θεοῦ
one is not able to see the kingdom of God (John 3:3)

οὐ δύναται ἰδεῖν τὴν βασιλείαν
                         τοῦ θεοῦ

A complementary infinitive is used with a main verb that is incomplete in itself; that is, the idea "be able" cannot be pictured without more content added. Since a complementary infinitive works to complete the meaning of the main verb, it is kept on the same line as the main verb and placed after it. In this case the infinitive itself has a direct object, τὴν βασιλείαν, which remains with the infinitive. The genitive is placed under the word it modifies.

ἦλθες ἀπολέσαι ἡμᾶς; Did you come to destroy us? (Mark 1:24)

ἦλθες
    ἀπολέσαι ἡμᾶς;

An adverbial infinitive (here signaling purpose) is placed under the main verb, along with its direct object.

Ἄνθρωποι δύο ἀνέβησαν εἰς τὸ ἱερὸν προσεύξασθαι
two men went up to the temple to pray (Luke 18:10)

Ἄνθρωποι . . .¹ ἀνέβησαν
    ¹δύο   εἰς τὸ ἱερὸν
                   προσεύξασθαι

Δύο modifies ἄνθρωποι and so is placed under it, with ellipsis points marking its original position and a number included because there are two items on the second line. Both the prepositional phrase and the infinitive modify the verb and are placed under it. Notice that the infinitive is less indented than the prepositional phrase in order to represent that these two items modify the same word independently.

λέγω γὰρ Χριστὸν διάκονον γεγενῆσθαι περιτομῆς
for I say that Christ has become a servant of the circumcision (Rom. 15:8)

    λέγω γὰρ
        Χριστὸν διάκονον γεγενῆσθαι
            περιτομῆς

A postpositive conjunction like γάρ or δέ could be moved to the beginning of the clause if you want, but it seems clear enough in its normal spot. Sometimes a postpositive can be several words from the beginning of the clause, or it may be in some other construction in which it might be best to move it for clarity. This infinitive, γεγενῆσθαι, follows a verb of speech, so it indicates indirect discourse and provides the content. The content clause is subordinated under the main verb, just as in the more common form of indirect discourse using ὅτι. In this case the infinitive, γεγενῆσθαι, is an equative verb, with Χριστόν as the subject and διάκονον as a predicate noun. The genitive is placed under the word it modifies, διάκονον.

The use of the infinitive in a prepositional phrase that modifies a verb is very common. Here are a couple of examples.

Καὶ μετὰ τὸ παραδοθῆναι τὸν Ἰωάννην ἦλθεν ὁ Ἰησοῦς
and after John was taken into custody Jesus came (Mark 1:14)

    ⌐ Καὶ μετὰ τὸ παραδοθῆναι
           τὸν Ἰωάννην
ἦλθεν ὁ Ἰησοῦς

This sentence has a modifier (the prepositional phrase) before the main subject and verb, so it can be placed above the main clause. The ⌐ symbol is not necessary but adds clarity. This infinitive functions like a verbal noun with an accusative of respect, something like "the taking into custody with respect to John" (see the discussion of Luke 1:57 above). In Greek this is simply a prepositional phrase that has a nominal infinitive for its object.

ἐνδύσασθε τὴν πανοπλίαν τοῦ θεοῦ πρὸς τὸ δύνασθαι ὑμᾶς στῆναι
put on the whole armor of God so that you may be able to stand (Eph. 6:11)

ἐνδύσασθε τὴν πανοπλίαν
           τοῦ θεοῦ
   πρὸς τὸ δύνασθαι . . . στῆναι
       ὑμᾶς

The subject and verb are clear, and τοῦ θεοῦ is moved under the noun it modifies. The prepositional phrase is moved under the verb. The main verb within the prepositional phrase is δύνασθαι, with στῆναι added as its complement and the accusative of respect, ὑμᾶς, modifying it. As noted above on Luke 1:57, the accusative of respect could be on the same line as the infinitive in such constructions.

D. *Additional constructions.*

Apposition

An appositive is added to a noun for "clarification, description, or identification of who or what is mentioned."[12]

ὅταν ὁ Χριστὸς φανερωθῇ, ἡ ζωὴ ὑμῶν, τότε καὶ ὑμεῖς σὺν αὐτῷ φανερωθήσεσθε ἐν δόξῃ.

When Christ, your life, appears, then you yourselves also will appear with him in glory. (Col. 3:4)

```
  ┌ ὅταν      ὁ Χριστὸς φανερωθῇ
  │               ἡ ζωὴ
  │                  ὑμῶν
...¹ ...² ὑμεῖς ...³ φανερωθήσεσθε
                  ¹τότε
                  ²καὶ
                  ³σὺν αὐτῷ
                  ἐν δόξῃ
```

This is another example of a subordinate clause that comes first in the sentence, so the whole clause can be put above the main clause. Ἡ ζωή is in apposition to ὁ Χριστός and so is lined up flush with it. The main verb has four modifiers, three of which are relocated. Καί here is used as the adverb "also," not the conjunction, so it modifies the verb and is placed under it. These modifiers are "back indented" so that each of them can, as it were, "see" the verb being modified. That is, each modifies the verb independently, so each should be directly under the verb and not lined up flush with one another. Lining up flush is reserved for coordinate clauses and apposition.

Vocative

Σὺ κατ᾽ ἀρχάς, κύριε, τὴν γῆν ἐθεμελίωσας
and you, Lord, established the earth in the beginning (Heb. 1:10)

```
Σὺ ...¹ ...² τὴν γῆν ἐθεμελίωσας
²κύριε            ¹κατ᾽ ἀρχάς
```

12. Wallace, 48; cf. Young, 12.

From this illustration you see that the vocative is placed in apposition to the subject.

ὁ δὲ Ἰησοῦς . . . εἶπεν· Θάρσει, θύγατερ· ἡ πίστις σου σέσωκέν σε.
And Jesus said, "Take heart, daughter! Your faith has saved you." (Matt. 9:22)

ὁ δὲ Ἰησοῦς εἶπεν
                    Θάρσει
                    θύγατερ·

                    ἡ πίστις . . . σέσωκέν σε
                        σου

The vocative is placed in apposition to the subject, which here is embedded in the verb. Because the subject is not explicitly given, the vocative is lined up with the verb. The direct discourse here contains one sentence in two major parts, separated by the raised dot. Putting an extra line between the two parts makes the map clearer.

Multiple Modifiers of a Common Item

Καὶ παράγων παρὰ τὴν θάλασσαν τῆς Γαλιλαίας εἶδεν Σίμωνα καὶ Ἀνδρέαν τὸν ἀδελφὸν Σίμωνος ἀμφιβάλλοντας ἐν τῇ θαλάσσῃ
passing alongside the Sea of Galilee, he saw Simon and Andrew the brother of Simon casting a net into the sea (Mark 1:16)

              Γ¹παράγων
                        παρὰ τὴν θάλασσαν
                                    τῆς Γαλιλαίας
Καὶ . . .¹ εἶδεν   Σίμωνα   ꓶ
              καὶ   Ἀνδρέαν   ꓶ
                        τὸν ἀδελφὸν
                                    Σίμωνος
                                    ἀμφιβάλλοντας
                                        ἐν τῇ θαλάσσῃ

The participle ἀμφιβάλλοντας modifies both nouns. Using the ꓶ symbol is an easy and clear way to signal this construction.

Uncertainty about a Modifier

Sometimes it is unclear which item is being modified. As noted earlier, you can indicate alternatives with "|< or," or "or >|," depending on whether the alternative site is to the right or left of where you place the modifier. For example, the ESV and the NIV differ in how they interpret what the prepositional phrases in Eph. 1:3 are modifying.

> Εὐλογητὸς ὁ θεὸς καὶ πατὴρ τοῦ κυρίου ἡμῶν Ἰησοῦ Χριστοῦ, ὁ εὐλογήσας ἡμᾶς ἐν πάσῃ εὐλογίᾳ πνευματικῇ ἐν τοῖς ἐπουρανίοις ἐν Χριστῷ,

> Blessed be the God and Father of our Lord Jesus Christ, who has blessed us in Christ with every spiritual blessing in the heavenly places. (ESV)

> Praise be to the God and Father of our Lord Jesus Christ, who has blessed us in the heavenly realms with every spiritual blessing in Christ. (NIV)

If we map this verse, we see that there are even more options in the Greek.

```
Εὐλογητὸς    ὁ θεὸς
             καὶ πατὴρ
                  τοῦ κυρίου
                        ἡμῶν
                  Ἰησοῦ Χριστοῦ,
             ὁ εὐλογήσας ἡμᾶς
                  ἐν . . .¹ εὐλογίᾳ . . .²
                             ¹πάσῃ
                             ²πνευματικῇ
             |< or        ἐν τοῖς ἐπουρανίοις
             |< or    |< or      ἐν Χριστῷ,
```

Thus, "in the heavenlies" (ἐν τοῖς ἐπουρανίοις) may be telling us where every blessing is located or where God is blessing. Similarly, "in Christ" (ἐν Χριστῷ) may tell us where God is blessing or where the blessing is located, either directly or by associating Christ with the heavenlies. Mapping helps us see such alternatives and provides a convenient way to explore the options and record our findings.

Three Sentence Map Principles Illustrated by John 3:16–18

I will give each clause in its original form and as a map, with comments. Then I will put the clauses together in a sentence map in its full form.

1. John 3:16–18 Clause by Clause

¹⁶Οὕτως γὰρ ἠγάπησεν ὁ θεὸς τὸν κόσμον

```
16 . . . γὰρ ἠγάπησεν ὁ θεὸς τὸν κόσμον
         οὕτως
```

The core elements are subject, verb, direct object. The only other items are the postpositive conjunction and the adverb. Postpostive conjunctions may be moved to the beginning of the clause, if it helps clarify the map. It is not necessary here, however; the conjunction already stands first because the adverb has been placed under the verb and its original location marked with an ellipsis.

ὥστε τὸν υἱὸν τὸν μονογενῆ ἔδωκεν,

ὥστε τὸν υἱὸν . . . ἔδωκεν
              τὸν μονογενῆ

The core elements are verb and direct object. The direct object has an adjective modifier.

ἵνα πᾶς ὁ πιστεύων εἰς αὐτὸν μὴ ἀπόληται

ἵνα . . .¹ ὁ πιστεύων . . .² μὴ ἀπόληται
          ¹πᾶς
          ²εἰς αὐτὸν

The core elements are subject and verb, along with the negative adverb. The subject is an articular adjectival participle that has two modifiers. We know that the adjective, πᾶς, modifies the participle, because they agree in gender, number, and case. The prepositional phrase also modifies it. Ellipses mark the two original locations.

ἀλλ᾽ ἔχῃ ζωὴν αἰώνιον.

ἀλλ᾽ ἔχῃ ζωὴν
          αἰώνιον.

The core elements are verb and direct object. The adjective is placed under the noun it modifies. The ἀλλά connects this second subjunctive to the ἵνα, making this a compound ἵνα clause. When we put the two clauses together in the full map, we will align them to show the μή . . . ἀλλά pattern.

¹⁷οὐ γὰρ ἀπέστειλεν ὁ θεὸς τὸν υἱὸν εἰς τὸν κόσμον

17 οὐ γὰρ ἀπέστειλεν ὁ θεὸς τὸν υἱὸν
                    εἰς τὸν κόσμον

The core elements are subject, verb, and direct object; with them is a negative adverb. The prepositional phrase is under the verb it modifies. The postpositive conjunction could be moved, but it seems clear enough in its original spot.

ἵνα κρίνῃ τὸν κόσμον,

ἵνα κρίνῃ τὸν κόσμον,

With only core elements (verb and direct object) the original order is the same as the map.

ἀλλ᾽ ἵνα σωθῇ ὁ κόσμος δι᾽ αὐτοῦ.

ἀλλ᾽ ἵνα σωθῇ ὁ κόσμος
     δι᾽ αὐτοῦ.

The core elements of this ἵνα clause are subject and verb. The prepositional phrase is put under the verb it modifies. This section begins with two conjunctions. The first one, ἀλλά, is a coordinate conjunction linking the two ἵνα clauses. The ἀλλά is assuming the same main clause that the first ἵνα clause modified. When I put these clauses together in the full map, I will align them to show the οὐ . . . ἀλλά pattern, like the μή . . . ἀλλά pattern just above.

¹⁸ὁ πιστεύων εἰς αὐτὸν οὐ κρίνεται

18 ὁ πιστεύων . . . οὐ κρίνεται
     εἰς αὐτὸν

The core elements are subject and verb, and with them a negative adverb. The prepositional phrase is put under the verb it modifies. As we saw in verse 16, the articular attributive participle serves as the subject. Note that there is no conjunction to tell us how this thought is connected with what went before. I will discuss this verse further below.

ὁ δὲ μὴ πιστεύων ἤδη κέκριται,

ὁ δὲ μὴ πιστεύων . . . κέκριται
     ἤδη

The core elements are subject and verb. A negative adverb modifies the articular attributive participle serving as the subject. Δέ is a coordinate conjunction, postpositive. The only other item here is an adverb, which is placed under the verb it modifies.

ὅτι μὴ πεπίστευκεν εἰς τὸ ὄνομα τοῦ μονογενοῦς υἱοῦ τοῦ θεοῦ.

ὅτι μὴ πεπίστευκεν
       εἰς τὸ ὄνομα
            τοῦ . . .¹ υἱοῦ
                 ¹μονογενοῦς
             τοῦ θεοῦ.

The only core element is the verb, and with it the negative adverb. The prepositional phrase is placed under the verb it modifies. The object of the preposition, τὸ ὄνομα, has a genitive modifier, which is placed under it. This genitive modifier, υἱοῦ, has an adjective modifier of its own and a genitive modifier, both of which are placed under it. For clarity I have numbered the word that was relocated, but this is not really necessary, since the ellipsis naturally points to the first word of the next line.

2. The Full Level 3 Sentence Map for John 3:16–18

Now adding the coordination and subordination of the clauses, we can see the full sentence map.

16 . . . γὰρ ἠγάπησεν ὁ θεὸς τὸν κόσμον
            οὕτως
      ὥστε τὸν υἱὸν . . .   ἔδωκεν
           τὸν μονογενῆ
                ἵνα . . .¹ ὁ πιστεύων . . .²   μὴ ἀπόληται
                           ¹πᾶς
                        ²εἰς αὐτὸν
                            ἀλλ' ἔχῃ ζωὴν
                                αἰώνιον.

17
                οὐ γὰρ ἀπέστειλεν ὁ θεὸς τὸν υἱὸν
                    εἰς τὸν κόσμον
                    ἵνα κρίνῃ τὸν κόσμον
       ἀλλ'   ἵνα ὁ κόσμος σωθῇ
                       δι' αὐτοῦ.

18 |< or —————————————————— ὁ πιστεύων . . . οὐ κρίνεται
                               εἰς αὐτὸν
                         ὁ δὲ μὴ πιστεύων κέκριται
                                  ἤδη

            ὅτι μὴ πεπίστευκεν
                 εἰς τὸ ὄνομα
                     τοῦ . . .¹ υἱοῦ
                         ¹μονογενοῦς
                     τοῦ θεοῦ.

3. The Full Level 3 Sentence Map for John 3:16–18 with Analysis

Labels can be used to describe the function of the elements of a sentence.[13] I have put the labels for clauses in boldface, since the clauses usually represent the main lines of thought in a text, and I have indented the labels for the other two levels of analysis, and illustrated below:

clause
    prepositional phrase
      other modifier

The indention of the labels does not mirror the flow of thought in the passage but reflects only the level of analysis.

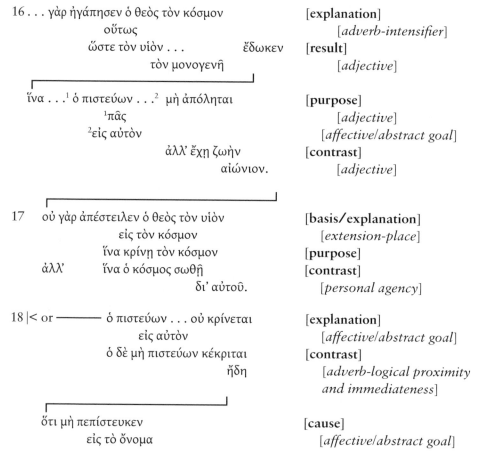

16 . . . γὰρ ἠγάπησεν ὁ θεὸς τὸν κόσμον   **[explanation]**
        οὕτως   *[adverb-intensifier]*
        ὥστε τὸν υἱὸν . . .   ἔδωκεν   **[result]**
            τὸν μονογενῆ   *[adjective]*

ἵνα . . .¹ ὁ πιστεύων . . .² μὴ ἀπόληται   **[purpose]**
        ¹πᾶς   *[adjective]*
      ²εἰς αὐτὸν   *[affective/abstract goal]*
            ἀλλ' ἔχῃ ζωὴν   **[contrast]**
               αἰώνιον.   *[adjective]*

17   οὐ γὰρ ἀπέστειλεν ὁ θεὸς τὸν υἱὸν   **[basis/explanation]**
          εἰς τὸν κόσμον   *[extension-place]*
          ἵνα κρίνῃ τὸν κόσμον   **[purpose]**
ἀλλ'   ἵνα ὁ κόσμος σωθῇ   **[contrast]**
              δι' αὐτοῦ.   *[personal agency]*

18 |< or ——— ὁ πιστεύων . . . οὐ κρίνεται   **[explanation]**
          εἰς αὐτὸν   *[affective/abstract goal]*
          ὁ δὲ μὴ πιστεύων κέκριται   **[contrast]**
             ἤδη   *[adverb-logical proximity and immediateness]*

ὅτι μὴ πεπίστευκεν   **[cause]**
    εἰς τὸ ὄνομα   *[affective/abstract goal]*

13. This analysis can be done on any of the three levels of maps. It is best to display this final form of the map with landscape orientation (i.e., the long edge of the paper positioned horizontally) with narrow margins to provide more room for the labels.

[εἰς τὸ ὄνομα]
    τοῦ . . .¹ υἱοῦ   [*possession*]
            ¹μονογενοῦς   [*adjective*]
        τοῦ θεοῦ.   [*relationship*]

These labels represent the fruit of reflection and exegesis. Thus, this map could be the basis for a discussion of the reasoning that went into each label and its significance for understanding this passage. The following notes on a few of the issues in this passage illustrate this point.

- I interpret γάρ (v. 16) as indicating that we are being given an explanation of why God makes eternal life possible, as just stated in verse 15. This analysis relies in part on larger discourse features. There is a parallel section of explanation later in the chapter (3:31–36), suggesting both 3:16–21 and 3:31–36 are comments by John, the Gospel writer.[14]
- Οὕτως (v. 16) could mean "in this way," referring back to something just said or ahead to something about to be said. But neither of these options seems to do justice to the result clause that follows (ὥστε), so I am taking it as signaling intensity.[15]
- Several times εἰς is labeled "affective/abstract goal." This label is based on BDAG[16] and illustrates my point in appendix 2 that the list offered there is not exhaustive.
- Since verse 18 lacks a conjunction, we are left to figure out its place in the map from its content. It connects two themes within the passage.

First theme: On the larger level, it forms a pattern with verses 16–17.

A Corporate (v. 16a)
  B Individual (v. 16b)
A′ Corporate (v. 17)
  B′ Individual (v. 18)

---

14. See my commentary on John for further discussion: *John*, IVP New Testament Commentary Series (Downers Grove, IL: InterVarsity, 1999), 91–92, 98.

15. BDAG thinks this verse illustrates οὕτως meaning "in this way," "as follows" (οὕτως 2, 742) and cites BDF §391.2. But BDF substitutes ὅτι for ὥστε and comes to "ingenious but bizarre conclusions" (Wallace, 480n86). Robert H. Gundry and Russell W. Howell have a very helpful article on this passage, arguing that οὕτως refers back to what precedes. But they seem to reverse the prominence between γάρ and ὥστε. See "The Sense and Syntax of John 3:14–17 with Special Reference to the Use of Οὕτως . . . Ὥστε in John 3:16," *Novum Testamentum* 41, no. 1 (1999): 24–38. So I go with οὕτως meaning "so intensely" (BDAG, οὕτως 3, 742), in parallel with its use in 1 John 4:11, as noted in BDAG.

16. BDAG, εἰς 4.c.β, 290.

Second theme: It also develops the theme of believing on the individual level in verse 16b in connection with the theme of condemning on the corporate level in verse 17.

So in the map I have indented verse 18 under the ἵνα clauses in verse 17 to signal its relation to the immediate context, and I have put an alternative on the left margin to signal its place in the larger pattern.

Conclusion

Sentence mapping is a way of sorting out difficult passages as you are reading, but its main place is in detailed exegesis and reflective meditation. In addition to using labels, you can add more extensive comments and reflections through footnotes in a digital copy or through handwritten notes on a paper copy. Indeed, at times I have used sentence maps as sermon outlines, with appropriate expository and homiletical notes added. Sentence mapping is a skill well worth learning.

LABELS FOR SENTENCE MAPS

When reading rapidly, you do not stop to analyze the text, but when reading more carefully, you do sort out the details. The most detailed form of analysis I have covered is the sentence map. This exercise is especially helpful for exegesis and, to some extent, for meditation. As you sort out the flow of thought in a sentence and passage, you can summarize your analysis by using the labels in this appendix. Many of these labels refer to usages that are common or easy to understand, so there is no need to apply the label. Some of the labels describe very minute distinctions that can be difficult to assess. But in general the labels often can be useful to record your assessment of how particular words or constructions are functioning in a sentence or paragraph.

Sentence maps usually focus on paragraphs, and then further analysis is done for the relations between paragraphs in the larger discourse. The following list of labels provides most of the common types of information signaled by elements in a map and in larger discourses. While this list provides the options needed for most sentence maps and discourse analyses, it is not complete. Further help can be found in the lexicons (under the particular conjunctions and prepositions), in Greek grammars, and in the resources listed at the end of this appendix. Note that labels may be useful for more than one level of analysis; I have not repeated many of the labels between sections. So, for example, a label you need in order to identify a discourse function may appear in one of the other sections.[1]

---

1. The italic words in the examples are the portion that would receive the particular label in a sentence map. All translations are from the ESV.

Labels for Elements within Clauses

Addition—the connection of two or more items within a clause that are grammatically alike, such as two phrases or two nouns

For from him *and through him and to him* are all things. (Rom. 11:36)

Advantage/Benefaction—the person who is benefitted by some thing or action

Go to the sea and cast a hook and take the first fish that comes up, and when you open its mouth you will find a shekel. Take that and give it to them *for me* and *for yourself*. (Matt. 17:27)

Agent—the person who accomplishes something[2]

He was in the wilderness forty days, being tempted *by Satan*. (Mark 1:13)

Apposition—a noun or participle that explains or identifies the word it modifies

as it is written in Isaiah *the prophet* (Mark 1:2)

Assistance—the presence of something or someone who provides help

I worked harder than any of them, though it was not I, but the grace of God that is *with me*. (1 Cor. 15:10)

Association—one who is present with, is engaged in an activity with, or accompanies someone

And immediately he left the synagogue and entered the house of Simon and Andrew, *with James and John*. (Mark 1:29)

Attribute—a characteristic or quality of something[3]

And the Lord said, "Hear what *the unrighteous judge* says" [judge of unrighteousness, ὁ κριτὴς τῆς ἀδικίας]. (Luke 18:6)

---

2. Some use "agent" for both persons and impersonal forces. In this list "agent" is used for persons, and "means" and "instrument" are used for other options.
3. This is the normal function of an adjective, but a noun can also function in this way, esp. in the genitive case.

Authority—the object over which someone exercises authority or control

> And he will reign *over the house* of Jacob forever, and of his kingdom there will be no end. (Luke 1:33)

Basis—that which serves as a foundation for something happening

> But if he does not listen, take one or two others along with you, that every charge may be established *by the evidence* of two or three witnesses. (Matt. 18:16)

Cause—explains why a result or effect happened by identifying what initiated it[4]

> And when Jesus finished these sayings, the crowds were astonished *at his teaching*. (Matt. 7:28)

Cessation—an activity that comes to a conclusion or end

> Blessed are the dead who die in the Lord from now on. "Blessed indeed," says the Spirit, "that they may rest *from their labors*, for their deeds follow them!" (Rev. 14:13)

Circumstance—a condition under which something takes place

> Now *in putting everything in subjection to him*, he left nothing outside his control. (Heb. 2:8)

Comment—information about a unit in another clause to further describe it[5]

> But when he *who had set me apart before I was born, and who called me by his grace*, was pleased to reveal his Son to me, (Gal. 1:15–16a)

Content—that which fills something, either materially or immaterially[6]

> The other disciples came in the boat, dragging the net full *of fish*. (John 21:8)

---

4. See the note on "cause" in the section below, "Labels for Relations between Clauses."

5. In the example, we have a compound relative clause. Relative clauses will usually be "comment" and sometimes "identification." "Comment" is used when the person or thing is already known and is simply being described for some reason, whereas "identification" is used to clarify who or what is being referred to.

6. Note the different use of this label for clauses, though even within a clause the content can refer to communication: "Hear then the parable *of the sower*" (Matt. 13:18).

Correspondence—that which something is similar to or in agreement with

Therefore let those who suffer *according to God's will* entrust their souls to a faithful Creator while doing good. (1 Pet. 4:19)

Degree—a mark of the extent to which something is true[7]

For this light momentary affliction is preparing for us an eternal weight of glory *beyond all comparison*. (2 Cor. 4:17)

Description—a characteristic or significant detail about someone, something, or some event[8]

For he says, "In a favorable time I listened to you, and in a day *of salvation* I have helped you." (2 Cor. 6:2)

Destination/Goal—the place, result, or achievement toward which something is directed[9]

For it was fitting that he, for whom and by whom all things exist, in bringing many sons *to glory*, should make the founder of their salvation perfect through suffering. (Heb. 2:10)

Disadvantage—the person who is adversely affected by some thing or action

You witness *against yourselves*. (Matt. 23:31)

Distribution—members of a group of people or things viewed as spread out through time or space

And every day, in the temple and *from house to house*, they did not cease teaching and preaching that the Christ is Jesus. (Acts 5:42)

7. The label "measure" is used for answers to the question "How much?" that are in terms of space, time, or quantity of people or things. "Degree" is used for less tangible realities. "Extent" is for how far or for how long something goes on.
8. "Description" is a very general label, because all adjectives describe. But the label is useful for some constructions, such as a prepositional phrase in English representing a genitive noun in Greek.
9. Both of these terms are used for this idea. You may choose which to use consistently, or use "destination" for spatial direction and "goal" for nonphysical realities.

Exchange—a person or thing that is replaced by another person or thing

Looking to Jesus, the founder and perfecter of our faith, who *for the joy that was set before him* endured the cross (Heb. 12:2)

Experiencer—one who experiences something done by someone else

Men of Israel, take care what you are about to do *with these men.* (Acts 5:35)

Explanation—that which explains or interprets something by giving a reason for it[10]

For it was Herod who had sent and seized John and bound him in prison *for the sake of Herodias.* (Mark 6:17)

Extension—the space, object, or route through which someone or something moves

he decided to return *through Macedonia* (Acts 20:3)

Goal—the vocation, use, or end for something or someone

Even in Thessalonica you sent me help *for my needs* once and again. (Phil. 4:16)

Guarantor—one called upon to guarantee the carrying out of an oath

And the high priest said to him, "I adjure you *by the living God*, tell us if you are the Christ, the Son of God." (Matt. 26:63)

Identification—information that helps distinguish or identify a unit in another clause[11]

And Joseph also went up . . . to the city of David, *which is called Bethlehem.* (Luke 2:4)

Instrument—something concrete by which something is done[12]

[She] wiped his feet *with her hair.* (John 11:2)

---

10. See the note on "cause" in the section below, "Labels for Relations between Clauses."

11. Identification occurs when the thing is being singled out in order to be identified. A "comment" is a description of a person or thing that is already known. Most relative clauses are "comment" or, less frequently, "identification."

12. See "means" for a nonconcrete entity by which something is done.

Location—a physical place where something exists or happens[13]

> that you may eat and drink *at my table* in my kingdom and sit *on thrones* judging the twelve tribes of Israel (Luke 22:30)

Manner—the emotion or attitude describing how something is accomplished

> Each one must give as he has decided in his heart, not *reluctantly* or *under compulsion*, for God loves a cheerful giver. (2 Cor. 9:7)

Material—that from which something is made

> No one sews a piece *of unshrunk cloth* on an old garment. (Mark 2:21)

Means—that by which something is done, referring to something nonphysical[14]

> For we hold that one is justified *by faith*. (Rom. 3:28)

Measure—the indication of how far, how much, or how many[15]

> Do you think that I cannot appeal to my Father, and he will at once send me *more than twelve* legions of angels? (Matt. 26:53)

Object—the equivalent of a direct object, found especially with the Greek objective genitive

> but the blasphemy *against the Spirit* will not be forgiven (Matt. 12:31)[16]

Partitive—the whole, of which the word being described is a part

> Now some *of the scribes* were sitting there. (Mark 2:6)[17]

---

13. For location in a nonphysical sense, see "sphere." Some do not make this distinction since the semantic concept is the same in both cases. See, e.g., Wallace, 153nn38, 39. In the example above, "in my kingdom" would be "sphere." "Table" and "thrones" are concrete things, so "location" works, even though they are used figuratively. Alternatively, Young (48) has dative of space, within which he has literal and metaphorical uses. See also the label "position."

14. "Means" can also be a clause relationship when a clause gives an action that is the means of something being done. See "instrument" for a concrete entity by which something is done.

15. This label is similar to "degree." See the note on that label.

16. This is equivalent to "but blaspheming the Spirit shall not be forgiven."

17. Here "the scribes" is the whole group, of which "some" is a part.

Position—the relative location of a person or thing

He who comes *after me* ranks before me. (John 1:15)[18]

Possession—the one who owns the thing described[19]

the strap of *whose* sandals I am not worthy to stoop down and untie (Mark 1:7)

Price—the cost of something

Are not two sparrows sold *for a penny*? (Matt. 10:29)

Producer—the person or thing that produces something[20]

eager to maintain the unity *of the Spirit* in the bond of peace (Eph. 4:3)

Product—that which is produced by someone or something

May the God *of hope* fill you with all joy and peace in believing. (Rom. 15:13)

Purpose—the intended result or outcome of an action

You know that after two days the Passover is coming, and the Son of Man is to be delivered up *to be crucified* [εἰς τὸ σταυρωθῆναι]. (Matt. 26:2)

Reason—The label can be used in a variety of ways, including for cause, explanation, and grounds. It is best to use one of these more precise labels if possible. *See* "cause."

Recipient—the person(s) who receives something, esp. in titles and salutations[21]

Paul and Timothy, servants of Christ Jesus, *To all the saints in Christ Jesus* who are at Philippi, with the overseers and deacons (Phil. 1:1)

---

18. Alternatively, "after me" here could refer to time. See BDAG, ὀπίσω 2.b, 716.
19. Grammarians differ over whether this term should be restricted to ownership of property or should include "ideas, names, abstract qualities, or parts of a person" (Young, 81).
20. The Greek genitive can have this nuance, as in the example above. This use is a more specific idea than the related idea of "source."
21. Wallace (148) notes that this is similar to an indirect object.

Reference—that with respect to which something is true or accurate, or what the verb is about

For Moses writes *about the righteousness that is based on the law*, that the person who does the commandments shall live by them. (Rom. 10:5)

Relationship—an expression indicating a family relationship, including within the church among believers

Then the mother *of the sons of Zebedee* came up to him with her sons. (Matt. 20:20)[22]

Responsibility—the one who is responsible for an action or state

so that *on you* may come all the righteous blood shed on earth (Matt. 23:35)

Result—the outcome of some action

This illness does not lead *to death* [πρὸς θάνατον]. It is for the glory of God, so that the Son of God may be glorified through it. (John 11:4)

Separation—removal or dissociation from something

I do not ask that you take them *out of the world*, but that you keep them *from the evil one*. (John 17:15)

Source—that from which something derives or depends

And you show that you are a letter *from Christ* delivered by us. (2 Cor. 3:3)

Specific/Specification—added detail to clarify or further identify something[23]

but God, being rich *in mercy*, because of the great love with which he loved us (Eph. 2:4)

Sphere—a nonphysical location where something exists or happens[24]

Blessed are the pure *in heart*. (Matt. 5:8)

22. Both "of the sons" and "of Zebedee" are expressions of relationship.
23. This use is close to "reference."
24. For physical location, see the discussion above on "location."

Status—statement of rank or position

> A disciple is not *above his teacher*, nor a servant *above his master*. (Matt. 10:24)

Subject—the equivalent of a grammatical subject[25]

> Do you suppose, O man—you who judge those who practice such things and yet do them yourself—that you will escape the judgment *of God*? (Rom. 2:3)

Time—indication of when something happens[26]

> This man came to Jesus *by night* and said to him, "Rabbi, we know that you are a teacher come from God." (John 3:2)

Value—an indication of the worth or importance of something

> *Above all*, keep loving one another earnestly, since love covers a multitude of sins. (1 Pet. 4:8)

Viewpoint—the person whose point of view is the focus of the statement

> For it is not the hearers of the law who are righteous *before God*, but the doers of the law who will be justified. (Rom. 2:13)

Labels for Relations between Clauses

The following relations illustrate one clause joined to another clause equally ("and," "or" relations) as well as one clause supporting another clause by providing argumentation, orientation, or clarification.[27]

Alternative—opposing possibilities, with one of them being denied ("*x* or *y*")

> "Whom do you want me to release for you: Barabbas, *or Jesus who is called Christ*?" (Matt. 27:17)

---

25. This is found esp. with the Greek subjective genitive.

26. Further labels could be used for more specific time references (before, during, after, beginning, ending) and the nuance of the cases when used with words for time (genitive: time during which; dative: time at which; accusative: length of time). A couple of these nuances are represented in this list of labels, but in most cases a general label for "time" seems sufficient.

27. See Peter Cotterell and Max Turner, *Linguistics and Biblical Interpretation* (Downers Grove, IL: InterVarsity, 1989), 205–17.

Amplification—restatement that gives extra information[28]

a devout man, *who feared God* (Acts 10:2)

Cause—explains why a result or effect happened by giving its cause[29]

We love *because he first loved us.* (1 John 4:19)[30]

Comparison—makes an item clearer by stating what it is like

Just as Moses lifted up the serpent in the wilderness, so must the Son of Man be lifted up. (John 3:14)

Concession—an affirmation despite the information in the other unit

though he was rich, yet for your sake he became poor (2 Cor. 8:9)

Conclusion/Inference—that which follows from what has just been said (the supporting information *precedes* what is being supported; cf. "Grounds")[31]

Therefore, since we have been justified by faith, *we have peace with God.* (Rom. 5:1)[32]

Condition—provides the condition that, if fulfilled, leads to the consequence related in the other unit[33]

If anyone would come after me, let him deny himself. (Mark 8:34)

28. Contrast "equivalence."

29. "Cause" should be distinguished from "grounds" and "conclusion." When a writer appears to be developing an argument, label it "grounds" or "conclusion" (depending on whether the supporting material precedes or follows that which is being supported); when he or she is citing a sequence of events in a cause-and-effect relationship, use the label "cause." The label "reason" is ambiguous since it is sometimes used for cause, explanation, and grounds.

30. Determining whether a unit gives the cause or the means can be confusing at times. The example from 1 John seems clear, but the example from Romans below, under "means," could be analyzed as giving the cause rather than the means.

31. Both of these terms are used for this relation, so I list them both. In a map, however, you should pick one and use it consistently throughout.

32. This subordinate clause would be "cause." Within this subordinate clause "by faith" would be "means."

33. Conditions implicitly include other argumentation relations as well. E.g., Mark 8:34, "If anyone wishes to come after me, let him deny himself," implies means (it is *by* denying oneself that a person will enter into discipleship). "If you have been raised with Christ, seek the things above" (Col. 3:1) contains a condition but also implies the grounds for the exhortation. Sometimes the meaning of a unit will not be exactly what its form leads you to expect. You should label according to the grammar, but at times add a second label to catch any further significance.

Content—that which another unit indicates is/was said, thought, felt, meant, seen, etc.[34]

And these know *that you have sent me.* (John 17:25)

Continuation—a conjunction (often omitted in English translations) such as καί, δέ, γάρ, or οὖν simply signaling that the story or discussion is moving along to the next point

In those days ['Εν δὲ ταῖς ἡμέραις ἐκείναις] John the Baptist came, preaching in the wilderness of Judea. (Matt. 3:1)

Contrast—a difference between two statements with neither being denied ("*x*, but also *y*")

For many are called, *but few are chosen.* (Matt. 22:14)

Direct Discourse—a content clause, with a verb of speech, giving the words spoken

And then will I declare to them, [ὅτι] "*I never knew you; depart from me, you workers of lawlessness.*" (Matt. 7:23)[35]

Equivalence—essentially the same thought, restated in other words for emphasis

Let the children come to me, *and do not hinder them.* (Luke 18:16)

Exception—an exception to what is said in another unit

For nothing is hidden *except to be made manifest*; nor is anything secret *except to come to light.* (Mark 4:22)

Explanation—explains or interprets the meaning of another unit

I wrote to you in my letter not to associate with sexually immoral people—*not at all meaning the sexually immoral of this world.* (1 Cor. 5:9–10)

---

34. "Content" is a general label that can be used for all direct and indirect discourse.
35. This example has both a ὅτι used for direct discourse and pronouns that signal direct discourse. If it were indirect discourse, it would say "I never knew *them*," and the ὅτι would be translated "that."

Extent—indicates the length of time or distance something goes on[36]

> We must work the works of him who sent me *while it is day*; night is coming, when no one can work. (John 9:4)

General/Specific—a general point is further developed through a more specific idea

> Now this I say *and testify in the Lord*. (Eph. 4:17)

Grounds—the basis or evidence for what has just been said (the supporting information *follows* what is being supported; cf. "Conclusion/Inference")[37]

> For these people are not drunk . . . *since it is only the third hour of the day.* (Acts 2:15)

Illustration—an analogy or example to support an assertion that is being argued[38]

> *We put bits into the mouths of horses. . . . Look at the ships also . . . guided by a very small rudder. . . .* So also the tongue (James 3:3–5)

Indirect Command—a report of a command, giving the content of an exhortation

> And he commanded us *to preach* to the people. (Acts 10:42)

Indirect Discourse—usually any form of reported content[39]
Indirect Question—a report of a question

> And the high priest said to him, "I adjure you by the living God, tell us *if you are the Christ, the Son of God.*" (Matt. 26:63)[40]

---

36. This label for *how long* or *how far* is different from "measure," which is for *how much*, and also "degree," which is for less tangible realities. See the note on "degree."

37. This is not a direct cause-effect relation (for which, see "cause").

38. In general a comparison is used for clarification, while an illustration has an argumentative force.

39. See the labels "indirect command," "indirect question," "indirect statement," and "content."

40. In English, indirect questions often are introduced by "whether."

Indirect Statement—report of a statement

Therefore I testify to you this day *that I am innocent of the blood of all.* (Acts 20:26)

Inference—*see* "Conclusion"

Location—the place where something happens

So he came again to Cana in Galilee, *where he had made the water wine.* (John 4:46)[41]

Manner—the emotion or attitude describing how something is accomplished[42]

For this I toil, *struggling with all his energy* (Col. 1:29)

Means—the action by which something is accomplished or achieved[43]

And, *having been set free from sin*, [you] have become slaves of righteousness. (Rom. 6:18)[44]

Negative-Positive—one alternative is denied and the other is affirmed ("not *x*, but *y*")

For I did not receive it from any man . . . but I received it through a revelation from Jesus Christ. (Gal. 1:12)

Orienter—the general context for a statement in narrative[45]

saying, "Give me this power also" (Acts 8:19)

---

41. In form this is "location," but it could also be labeled "identification" since it serves to identify Cana in Galilee.

42. "Manner" is often confused with "means." In this example, "struggling" is the manner and "with all his energy" would be "means" in the sense of nonconcrete instrument (see the section above, "Labels for Elements within Clauses"), not "means" for an action, which is discussed in the next entry.

43. "Means" is also used within clauses when the nonconcrete instrument of an action is given (see the section above, "Labels for Elements within Clauses").

44. Determining whether a unit gives the cause or the means can be confusing at times. This example from Romans could be analyzed as giving the cause rather than the means.

45. This relation is very common since it covers the introduction to both direct and indirect discourse. Whenever the content of what is said, thought, felt, meant, perceived, etc., is given, the introduction will be an orienter, though other relations may also be involved.

Progression—a series that implies movement toward a climax

> *and* those whom he predestined[46] *he also called, and* those whom he called *he also justified, and* those whom he justified *he also glorified.* (Rom. 8:30)

Purpose—the intended result of what is stated in another unit[47]

> But God chose what is foolish in the world *to shame the wise.* (1 Cor. 1:27)

Reason—a general term that can mean cause, explanation, or grounds, so it is best to use one of these more precise terms if possible[48]

Result—the consequence or outcome that occurs due to what is stated in another unit

> Where does this man intend to go *that we will not find him?* (John 7:35)

Resumptive—resuming a narrative or flow of thought that had been interrupted

> *Now [δέ] John wore a garment of camel's hair and a leather belt around his waist,* and his food was locusts and wild honey. (Matt. 3:4)[49]

Sequential—two events happen, one after the other

> They stripped him of the purple cloak *and put his own clothes on him.* (Mark 15:20)

Series—a list of two or more clauses

> Love bears all things, *believes all things* (1 Cor. 13:7)

Simultaneous—two events are happening at the same time

> He healed many . . . *and cast out many demons.* (Mark 1:34)

---

46. In a sentence map, these relative clauses could be indented under "those" in each clause, or they could be placed on their own line to bring out the rhetorical force. In either placement they would be labeled "identification."

47. The difference between purpose and result is clear, since purpose includes conscious intention. But it is often difficult to know which a given statement represents, and Wallace (473–74) thinks that sometimes both are included. See also BDAG, ἵνα 3, 477.

48. See footnote on "cause."

49. The previous verse is Matthew's parenthetical comment linking John the Baptist to Isa. 40, and now he picks up the story again.

Time—the time before, during, or after which something takes place[50]

> *That evening at sundown* they brought to him all who were sick. (Mark 1:32)

Transition—a clause that initiates a change to a new thought or some new element in a story (e.g., new development, character, event)

> *Now* [δέ] *Simon's mother-in-law lay ill with a fever*, and immediately they told him about her. (Mark 1:30)

Labels for Discourse Functions

The labels in this section can apply to clauses and to larger units.[51] Virtually any clause could be identified with one of the following labels. They are especially useful for those clauses that are not otherwise labeled with the options in sections I and II. Some of these labels function more exclusively on the level of the larger discourse (see, e.g., "conclusion," "introduction," and the passage given below for "problem/resolution").

Assertion—a statement

> God is love. (1 John 4:8)

Conclusion—a summary or final decisive statement that brings a section to an end

> This was now the second sign that Jesus did when he had come from Judea to Galilee. (John 4:54)

Desire—a wish or hope

> I hope to see you in passing as I go to Spain. (Rom. 15:24)

Event/Action—recounting something that happened

> While I was with them, I kept them in your name, which you have given me. (John 17:12)

---

50. "Time" is used for *when* something takes place, in distinction to "extent" (how long something goes on) and "measure" (how much time is spent).

51. For basic coverage of discourse features similar to those in this section and the next of this appendix, see William D. Mounce, *Greek for the Rest of Us* (Grand Rapids: Zondervan, 2003), 136–37; and J. Scott Duvall and J. Daniel Hays, *Grasping God's Word*, 3rd ed. (Grand Rapids: Zondervan, 2012), chap. 4. For greater detail, see the resources listed above in chap. 4, note 27.

Exclamation—a sharp or sudden utterance

My Lord and my God! (John 20:28)

Exhortation—a command or word of encouragement

I appeal to you therefore . . . to present your bodies as a living sacrifice. (Rom. 12:1)

Introduction—opening material that introduces a larger section

And he told them a parable to the effect that they ought always to pray and not lose heart. (Luke 18:1)

Problem/Resolution—stating a problem followed by its resolution

And you, who once were alienated and hostile in mind, doing evil deeds, he has now reconciled in his body of flesh by his death. (Col. 1:21–22)

Promise—a declaration of what one will do or refrain from doing

He who loves me will be loved by my Father, and I will love him and manifest myself to him. (John 14:21)

Question/Answer—conversation exchanges of question and answer

Simon Peter said to him, "Lord, where are you going?" Jesus answered him, "Where I am going you cannot follow me now, but you will follow afterward." (John 13:36)

Request—a petition for something or help of some sort

Holy Father, keep them in your name, which you have given me. (John 17:11)

Rhetorical question—a question that is not seeking information but rather is used to draw out information from the listener or to convey new information

Look, for three years now I have come seeking fruit on this fig tree, and I find none. Cut it down. Why should it use up the ground? (Luke 13:7)

Statement/Response—conversational exchanges of statement and response

> [Simon said] "Give me this power. . . ." But Peter said to him,[52] "May your silver perish with you." (Acts 8:19–20)

Warning—statement prior to danger

> I warn you, as I warned you before, that those who do such things will not inherit the kingdom of God. (Gal. 5:21)

Labels for Larger Discourse Patterns

Along with labeling items within clauses, sentences, and paragraphs, you can also label the relations between paragraphs for analysis on the larger discourse level. Indeed, an entire document can be represented in a sentence map with several layers of labels to represent the micro and macro levels of the text. Many of the labels given in earlier sections of this appendix can apply also on this larger discourse level.

Chiasm—series of items with the second half of the series in reverse order from the first half: ABB'A' or ABCB'A'[53]

> A The Sabbath
>   B was made for man,
>   B' not man
> A' for the Sabbath. (Mark 2:27)

> A So if you are offering your gift at the altar
>   B and there remember that your brother has something against you,
>   C leave your gift there before the altar and go.
>   B' First be reconciled to your brother,
> A' and then come and offer your gift. (Matt. 5:23–24)

---

52. This first clause is "contrast."

53. See Nils W. Lund, *Chiasmus in the New Testament: A Study in the Form and Function of Chiastic Structures* (1942; repr., Peabody, MA: Hendrickson, 1992). Chiasms may be short, like these examples, or lengthy. In his commentary on 2 Corinthians, Fredrick Long highlights Paul's frequent use of chiasm in a single document and offers helpful analysis. See Fredrick J. Long, *II Corinthians: A Handbook on the Greek Text*, Baylor Handbook on the Greek New Testament (Waco: Baylor University Press, 2015), xxiii.

Inclusio—similar material at the beginning and end of a section that brackets the section

> Do not think that I have come to abolish the Law or the Prophets; I have not come to abolish them but to fulfill them.
> So whatever you wish that others would do to you, do also to them, for this is the Law and the Prophets. (Matt. 5:17; 7:12)

Resources Consulted for Labels

The following works were used in compiling this list of labels. For full information, see the bibliography.

Abbott-Smith
BDAG
Beekman, John, and John Callow. *Translating*, esp. 267–312.
Cotterell, Peter, and Max Turner. *Linguistics*, esp. 205–17.
Duvall, J. Scott, and J. Daniel Hays. *Grasping*, esp. chaps. 3–5.
Fee, Gordon D. *Exegesis*, esp. 71–78.
Fields, Lee M. *Hebrew*, esp. 77–84, 90–91.
Guthrie, George H., and J. Scott Duvall. *Exegesis*, esp. 27–53.
Harris, Murray J. "Prepositions and Theology."
———. *Prepositions and Theology*.
Huffman, Douglas S. *Guide*.
Klein, William W., Craig L. Blomberg, and Robert L. Hubbard Jr. *Interpretation*, esp. 205–14, 225–41.
Levinsohn, Stephen H. *Discourse Features*.
Louw, Johannes P., and Eugene A. Nida. *Greek-English Lexicon*.
Mounce, William D. *A Graded Reader*, esp. xv–xxiii.
———. *Greek for the Rest of Us*, esp. 136–41.
Osborne, Grant R. *Spiral*, esp. chaps. 1, 4.
Runge, Steven E. *Discourse Grammar*.
Wallace, Daniel B. *Grammar*.
Young, Richard A. *Intermediate*.

READER'S NOTES
FOR JOHN 3:16–18

These notes are provided to make it easier for you to sort out John 3:16–18 in preparation for using this passage in appendix 1 to illustrate sentence mapping in Greek.

John 3:16

οὕτως—adv., so.

γάρ—conj., for.

ἠγάπησεν—3 sg. act. Aor. ind. < ἀγαπάω, I love.

ὁ θεός—nom. sg. masc. < θεός, God. Subject.

τὸν κόσμον—acc. sg. masc. < κόσμος, world. Direct object.

ὥστε—conj., so that, with the result that.

τὸν υἱόν—acc. sg. masc. < υἱός, son. Direct object.

τὸν μονογενῆ—acc. sg. masc. < μονογενής, ές, only. Modifies τὸν υἱόν.

ἔδωκεν—3 sg. act. Aor. ind. < δίδωμι, I give.

ἵνα—conj., that, in order that.

πᾶς—nom. sg. masc. < πᾶς, πᾶσα, πᾶν, all. Modifies ὁ πιστεύων.

ὁ πιστεύων—nom. sg. masc. act. Pres. ptc. < πιστεύω, I believe. Attributive ptc.: noun. Subject.

εἰς—prep., w. acc., in, into.

αὐτόν—acc. sg. masc. < αὐτός, ή, ό, he, she, it. Object of the preposition.

μή—neg. adv., no, not.

ἀπόληται—3 sg. mid. Aor. subjn. < ἀπόλλυμι, I destroy/ruin.

ἀλλ' < ἀλλά—conj., but.

ἔχῃ—3 sg. act. Pres. subjn. < ἔχω, I have.

ζωήν—acc. sg. fem. < ζωή, life. Direct object.

αἰώνιον—acc. sg. fem. < αἰώνιος, ον, eternal, everlasting. Modifies ζωήν.

John 3:17

οὐ—neg. adv., no, not.

γάρ—conj., for.

ἀπέστειλεν—3 sg. act. Aor. ind. < ἀποστέλλω, I send.

ὁ θεός—nom. sg. masc. < θεός, God. Subject.

τὸν υἱόν—acc. sg. masc. < υἱός, son. Direct object.

εἰς—prep., w. acc., in, into.

τὸν κόσμον—acc. sg. masc. < κόσμος, world. Object of the preposition.

ἵνα—conj., that, in order that.

κρίνῃ—3 sg. act. Pres. subjn. < κρίνω, I judge, condemn.

τὸν κόσμον—acc. sg. masc. < κόσμος, world. Direct object.

ἀλλ' < ἀλλά—conj., but.

ἵνα—conj., that, in order that.

σωθῇ—3 sg. pass. Aor. subjn. < σῴζω, I save.

ὁ κόσμος—nom. sg. masc. < κόσμος, world. Subject.

δι' < διά—prep., w. gen., through.

αὐτοῦ—gen. sg. masc. < αὐτός, -ή, -ό, he, she, it. Object of the preposition.

John 3:18

ὁ πιστεύων—nom. sg. masc. act. Pres. ptc. < πιστεύω, I believe. Attributive
    ptc.: noun. Subject.

εἰς—prep., w. acc., in, into.

αὐτόν—acc. sg. masc. < αὐτός, -ή, -ό, he, she, it. Object of the preposition.

οὐ—neg. adv., no, not.

κρίνεται—3 sg. pass. Pres. ind. < κρίνω, I judge, condemn.

δέ—conj., and; but.

μή—neg. adv., no, not.

ὁ πιστεύων—nom. sg. masc. act. Pres. ptc. < πιστεύω, I believe. Attributive
　　ptc.: noun. Subject.

ἤδη—adv., already.

κέκριται—3 sg. pass. Pf. ind. < κρίνω, I judge, condemn.

ὅτι—conj., because.

μή—neg. adv., no, not.

πεπίστευκεν—3 sg. act. Pf. ind. < πιστεύω, I believe.

εἰς—prep., w. acc., in, into.

τὸ ὄνομα—acc. sg. neut. < ὄνομα, name. Object of the preposition.

μονογενοῦς—gen. sg. masc. < μονογενής, ές, only. Modifies τοῦ υἱοῦ.

τοῦ υἱοῦ—gen. sg. masc. < υἱός, son. Possession.

τοῦ θεοῦ—gen. sg. masc. < θεός, God. Relationship.

CORE PATTERNS
FOR GREEK MORPHOLOGY

⸻

This appendix contains all the core material discussed in chapter 3. Knowing this material will enable you to parse most of the forms you will see as you read the GNT. The website for this book has a downloadable and printable PDF containing all this information on a single page.

General Material

Square of Stops

- labials   π, β, φ   + σ =   ψ
- velars   κ, γ, χ   + σ =   ξ
- dentals   τ, δ, θ, ζ   + σ =   ς

Vowel Contraction

- α   <   α + ε
- ει   <   ε + ε
- η   <   ε + α
- οι   <   ο + ει
- ου   <   ε + ο, ο + ε, or ο + ο
- ω   <   any vowel + ο or ω (except as above)

Nominal System

Sg.	Definite Article			Endings		
	Masc.	Fem.	Neut.	Masc.	Fem.	Neut.
Nom.	ὁ [ος]	ἡ [α]	τό [ον]	ος	η/α	ον
Gen.	τοῦ	τῆς	τοῦ	ου	ης/ας	ου
Dat.	τῷ	τῇ	τῷ	ῳ	ῃ/ᾳ	ῳ
Acc.	τόν	τήν	τό [ον]	ον	ην/αν	ον
Voc.	[ε]			ε		
Pl.						
Nom.	οἱ	αἱ	τά	οι	αι	α
Gen.	τῶν	τῶν	τῶν	ων	ων	ων
Dat.	τοῖς	ταῖς	τοῖς	οις	αις	οις
Acc.	τούς	τάς	τά	ους	ας	α

Sg.	Indefinite Pronoun		Endings	
	Masc./Fem.	Neut.	Masc./Fem.	Neut.
Nom.	τις [–]	τι [–]	ς, –	–
Gen.	τινος	τινος	ος	ος
Dat.	τινι	τινι	ι	ι
Acc.	τινα [ν]	τι [–]	α, ν	–
Pl.				
Nom.	τινες	τινα	ες	α
Gen.	τινων	τινων	ων	ων
Dat.	τισι(ν)	τισι(ν)	σι(ν)	σι(ν)
Acc.	τινας [ες]	τινα	ας, ες	α

πᾶς, πᾶσα, πᾶν

Sg.	Masc.	Fem.	Neut.
Nom.	πᾶς	πᾶσα	πᾶν
Gen.	παντός	πάσης	παντός
Dat.	παντί	πάσῃ	παντί
Acc.	πάντα	πᾶσαν	πᾶν
Pl.			
Nom.	πάντες	πᾶσαι	πάντα
Gen.	πάντων	πασῶν	πάντων
Dat.	πᾶσι(ν)	πάσαις	πᾶσι(ν)
Acc.	πάντας	πάσας	πάντα

Personal Pronouns

	First Person		Second Person	
	Sg.	Pl.	Sg.	Pl.
Nom.	ἐγώ	ἡμεῖς	σύ	ὑμεῖς
Gen.	ἐμοῦ, μου	ἡμῶν	σοῦ, σου	ὑμῶν
Dat.	ἐμοί, μοι	ἡμῖν	σοί, σοι	ὑμῖν
Acc.	ἐμέ, με	ἡμᾶς	σέ, σε	ὑμᾶς

Verbal System

Principal Part	Tense-Form	Augment or Reduplication	Stem	Tense-Form Sign	Variable Vowel	Endings
1st	Pres. A/M/P		λυ		ο ε	Primary
	Impf. A/M/P	ε	λυ		ο ε	Secondary
2nd	Fut. A/M		λυ	σ	ο ε	Primary
	Liq. Fut. A/M		λ/μ/ν/ρ	ε(σ)	ο ε	Primary
3rd	1 Aor. A/M	ε	λυ	σα/ε		Secondary
	2 Aor. A/M	ε	?		ο ε	Secondary
	Liq. Aor. A/M	ε	λ/μ/ν/ρ	α/ε		Secondary
	κ Aor. A/M	ε	stem	κα/ε		Secondary
4th	1 Pf. Act.	λε	λυ	κα/ε		Primary
	2 Pf. Act.	λε	λυ	α/ε		Primary
	Plpf. Act.	(ε)λε	λυ	κει		Secondary
5th	Pf. M/P	λε	λυ			Primary
	Plpf. M/P	(ε)λε	λυ			Secondary
	Fut. Pf. M/P	λε	λυ	σ	ο ε	Primary
6th	Aor. Pass.	ε	λυ	θη		Secondary
	2 Aor. Pass.	ε	λυ	η		Secondary
	Fut. Pass.		λυ	θησ	ο ε	Primary
	2 Fut. Pass.		λυ	ησ	ο ε	Primary

- Variable vowels: ο before μ and ν; ε elsewhere (though in the present and future indicative the ε variable vowel is ει in the singular).
- Zero endings: α = 1 singular; ε = 3 singular indicative or 2 singular imperative.
- Moveable ν occurs only after ε and ι, so ον is always an ending.

Primary Personal Endings

	Act.	Mid./Pass.
1 Sg.	ω, μι, –	μαι
2 Sg.	ς	σαι (= ῃ)
3 Sg.	–(ν), σι(ν)	ται
1 Pl.	μεν	μεθα
2 Pl.	τε	σθε
3 Pl.	ουσι(ν), ασι(ν)	νται

Secondary Personal Endings

	Act.	Mid./Pass.
1 Sg.	ν, –	μην
2 Sg.	ς	σο (= ου)
3 Sg.	–(ν)	το
1 Pl.	μεν	μεθα
2 Pl.	τε	σθε
3 Pl.	ν, σαν	ντο

Mood Indicators

Subjunctive	ω and η variable vowel
Optative	ι before the ending
Participle	ντ, οτ, μεν
Infinitive	endings
Imperative	endings

Imperative Endings

	Act.	Mid./Pass.
2 Sg.	ε, σον	σο, ου, σαι, θι, τι
3 Sg.	τω	σθω
2 Pl.	τε	σθε
3 Pl.	τωσαν	σθωσαν

Infinitive Endings

εν [ειν]   ι [σαι]   ναι   σθαι

Participle Box

	Masc.	Fem.	Neut.	Stem Formative		Stem Formative
Pres./2 Aor. Act.	ων	ουσα	ον	οντ	Mid./Pass.	ομεν
1 Aor. Act.	σας	σασα	σαν	σαντ	Mid.	σαμεν
Aor. Pass.	θεις	θεισα	θεν	θεντ		
Perf. Act.	κως	κυια	κος	κοτ	Mid./Pass.	μεν

Forms of εἰμί

Present Indicative of εἰμί

	Sg.	Pl.
1	εἰμί	ἐσμέν
2	εἶ	ἐστέ
3	ἐστίν	εἰσί(ν)

Future Indicative of εἰμί

	Sg.	Pl.
1	ἔσομαι	ἐσόμεθα
2	ἔσῃ	ἔσεσθε
3	ἔσται	ἔσονται

Imperfect Indicative of εἰμί

	Sg.	Pl.
1	ἤμην	ἦμεν, ἤμεθα
2	ἦς, ἦσθα	ἦτε
3	ἦν	ἦσαν

Present Imperative of εἰμί

2 Sg.	ἴσθι
3 Sg.	ἔστω
2 Pl.	ἔστε
3 Pl.	ἔστωσαν

Present Infinitive of εἰμί

εἶναι

GREEK VERBS

TWO CURRENT TOPICS

Recent developments in the study of the Greek verb have produced insights that are very significant for exegesis and also fruitful for meditation. Two topics in particular have received a lot of attention recently: (1) verbal aspect and *Aktionsart*, and (2) verbal voice, especially the deponent verbs. This book is not meant to be a grammar, but since some who are using it have been away from Greek for a while, I want to at least introduce these topics. I hope that this discussion, along with notes to this material in some of my comments on passages in this book, will whet your appetite to learn more about these topics.[1]

Verbal Aspect and *Aktionsart*

Verb tense in English is largely related to time, and Greek verb tense was generally viewed the same way until the 1800s. Now, however, scholars agree that the tense of Greek verbs does not primarily signal time. For example, a verb in the present tense in Greek does not necessarily express an action that occurs in present time. Since tense is related to time in English,[2] some scholars

---

1. While this book was in production, publication was announced of Constantine R. Campbell, *Advances in the Study of Greek: New Insights for Reading the New Testament* (Grand Rapids: Zondervan, 2015). It looks like this book will include helpful material on the topics in this appendix as well as a number of other issues in Greek.

2. Indeed "tense" comes from a Latin word for time, *tempus*.

prefer a different label, such as "tense-form," when referring to Greek verb tense. That is the term I use in this book.

What, then, is the relation between Greek tense-forms and time? All agree that, outside the indicative, the tense-form does not have reference to time. Most scholars think time plays at least a secondary role in the Greek indicative, but some say that not even the indicative includes reference to time. For these scholars, tense-form has no relation to time, and time is indicated by other signals in a text.[3] Other scholars, however, say that the view that there is no time reference in the indicative does not do justice to the function of the augment in the indicative and is not borne out in how indicative verbs actually function.[4]

If the tense-form is not primarily signaling time, what does it "grammaticalize"?[5] Throughout the twentieth century, the tense-form of a Greek verb was understood as referring more to the type of action (*Aktionsart* in German; pl. *Aktionsarten*) than the time of action. Each tense-form was seen to have several *Aktionsarten*, some examples being "progressive present," "customary present," "iterative imperfect," "conative imperfect," "ingressive aorist," "gnomic aorist," "extensive perfect," and so on.[6]

The idea that such nuances are inherent in the tense-forms is being called into question. The view now is that a verb's tense-form essentially expresses "aspect," that is, the point of view of the speaker or writer, rather than a statement about the nature of the event itself.[7] The aspect associated with

3. Porter is the main proponent of the view that the verb in itself is timeless. For example, Stanley E. Porter, *Verbal Aspect in the Greek of the New Testament, with Reference to Tense and Mood* (New York: Peter Lang, 1989), 107–8; Stanley E. Porter, *Idioms of the Greek New Testament*, Biblical Languages: Greek 2 (Sheffield: JSOT Press, 1992), 25–26. Rodney Decker's doctoral dissertation tested Porter's view, and Decker believes his case study in Mark's Gospel confirms Porter's claim. See Rodney J. Decker, *Temporal Deixis of the Greek Verb in the Gospel of Mark with Reference to Verbal Aspect*, Studies in Biblical Greek 10 (New York: Peter Lang, 2001), 29–52, 149–55.

4. For a clear and concise statement, see the notes posted by Peter J. Gentry, "Aspect and the Greek Verb," section 4. Available online (see bibliography). See also T. V. Evans, *Verbal Syntax in the Greek Pentateuch: Natural Greek Usage and Hebrew Interference* (Oxford: Oxford University Press, 2001), 40–50; Daryl D. Schmidt, "Verbal Aspect in Greek: Two Approaches," in *Biblical Greek Language and Linguistics: Open Questions in Current Research*, ed. Stanley E. Porter and D. A. Carson, Journal for the Study of the New Testament Supplement Series 80 (Sheffield: Sheffield Academic Press, 1993), 70–71; and more extensively the series of blog posts by Steve Runge, "On Porter, Prominence, and Discourse." Available online (see bibliography). For Porter's response regarding time and aspect, see Stanley E. Porter, *Linguistic Analysis of the Greek New Testament: Studies in Tools, Methods, and Practice* (Grand Rapids: Baker Academic, 2015), chap. 10.

5. Some use this term for what the author/speaker is conveying by the grammatical form of a word.

6. Most grammars list several categories for each tense-form. See, e.g., Wallace, 513–86; and Young, 105–30.

7. Formerly, "aspect" and *Aktionsart* were used interchangeably, but now "aspect" is used to refer to how the speaker/author views the action, and *Aktionsart* is used to refer to the kind of action itself.

the aorist is "perfective," that is, a simple perspective in which the author/speaker views the event/action as a whole. Some add the idea that this aspect views the event from the outside, at a distance.[8] The present and the imperfect tense-forms have an "imperfective" aspect, which views the action as a process. Some scholars add that the present includes the idea of nearness or proximity, while the imperfect has the idea of remoteness.[9]

An example often cited is Paul's statement, "death reigned from Adam to Moses" (Rom. 5:14). Here the prepositional phrases tell us that this action lasted a long period of time, but Paul's use of an aorist (ἐβασίλευσεν) indicates he is viewing this lengthy reign as a whole. If Paul had used a present or an imperfect tense-form ("death was reigning from Adam to Moses") he would have been viewing the action according to the second aspect, from an internal perspective while it was in progress, within the bounds indicated by the prepositional phrase.

Some scholars say there are only these two aspects, while others add a third aspect, the stative, associated with the perfect and pluperfect tense-forms. This aspect views the verb as presenting a state of affairs, usually the result of action in the past.[10] Thus, Paul says, "I have fought [ἠγώνισμαι, pf. ind.] the good fight; I have finished [τετέλεκα, pf. ind.] the race" (2 Tim. 4:7).

Those who say there are only two aspects agree that the perfect is frequently stative, but they say this is due to other signals,[11] rather than the aspect of the tense-form itself.[12] Note that Campbell, who takes the perfect tense-form as

---

8. See Buist M. Fanning, *Verbal Aspect in New Testament Greek* (Oxford: Clarendon, 1990), 27–28; Porter, *Idioms*, 23–24. Campbell helpfully emphasizes that remoteness and proximity are used metaphorically. "When an aorist is used, it does not mean that the action occurred far away in a geographical sense, just because it encodes the spatial value of remoteness. . . . An action may be *portrayed* as remote without physically being distant. An action may be portrayed as proximate without physically being near" (Constantine R. Campbell, *Basics of Verbal Aspect in Biblical Greek* [Grand Rapids: Zondervan, 2008], 129–30, emphasis original). Such spatial nuances take the place of temporal ones for Porter, Decker, and Campbell.

9. For example, Campbell, *Basics*, 41–42.

10. It is debated whether or not the perfect includes a reference to the past. Porter (*Idioms*, 40), for example, rejects it as part of the aspect of the perfect. He notes, however, "While there may be reference to a previous act that results in a state or condition, this is a matter of lexis [the meaning of the lexeme] in context" (Porter, *Aspect*, 259). Fanning says the perfect indicative includes "an internal tense-feature of *anteriority*" (Fanning, *Aspect*, 290, emphasis original), a point that he develops further on 290–98. Porter has responded to the views of Fanning and Campbell on the perfect in chap. 12 of his *Linguistic Analysis*.

11. These signals are referred to as the verb's pragmatics, which will be discussed below.

12. Among those who reject stative as an aspect, some take the aspect of the perfect as perfective (e.g., Fanning, *Aspect*, 119–20; he uses the term "summary") and others as imperfective (e.g., Campbell, *Basics*, 50–51; Constantine R. Campbell, *Verbal Aspect, the Indicative Mood, and Narrative: Soundings in the Greek of the New Testament*, Studies in Biblical Greek 13 [New York: Peter Lang, 2007], 184–95; Evans, *Verbal Syntax*, 30–32). Evans (*Verbal Syntax*, 31) illustrates this view: "So ἀκηκόατε [a perfect tense-form] 'you are in hearing state' expresses the event in process. Perfective force is absent."

imperfective rather than stative,[13] states, "It is worth noting, however, that despite the significant disagreements about the semantic nature of the Greek perfect, Porter, Fanning, and I come to similar conclusions about its use in context."[14]

Along with this disagreement over the number of aspects, there is also no agreement on what to call each of these aspects. The following list summarizes some of the main terms you will see and the viewpoint usually associated with each aspect.

1. Perfective (external, aoristic, holistic, simple): aorist tense-form; viewed as a whole
2. Imperfective (progressive, internal): present and imperfect tense-forms; viewed as a process
3. Stative (perfective, perfect): perfect and pluperfect tense-forms; viewed as a state or condition (some add "resulting from prior action")

Note that the future tense-form is not included in this list. As K. L. McKay says, "The future is something of an anomaly in the ancient Greek verb system."[15] There is no agreement about the future tense-form and its aspect. Some say it is perfective, others imperfective, others that the future has no aspect, and yet others that the future is a fourth aspect.[16] There is also disagreement over whether the future includes a temporal nuance, setting it apart from the other tense-forms. According to McKay, "The future is used to express intention, and consequently simple futurity, and it is often difficult to distinguish between these."[17] Porter thinks the future expresses expectation.[18] Campbell thinks the future "refers to future time in its every usage and is therefore regarded as a genuine tense; that is, future temporal reference is a semantic feature of the verb alongside perfective aspect."[19] Fanning thinks the temporal element is primary: "The future must be taken as a non-aspectual

13. See *Basics*, chap. 5.

14. Constantine R. Campbell, *Colossians and Philemon: A Handbook on the Greek Text*, Baylor Handbook on the Greek New Testament (Waco: Baylor University Press, 2013), xxi–xxii. He explains, "Porter regards the perfect as always stative (due to its stative aspect), as does Fanning (due to the semantic encoding of stative *Aktionsart*). I regard the perfect as *normally* stative, but this is regarded as a key *function*, rather than a semantic, uncancelable quality of the perfect. Given that the perfect is often coupled with stative lexemes, its imperfective aspect works together with such lexemes to create a stative *Aktionsart*" (xxii, emphasis original). He cites his discussion of this topic in *Basics*, 106–7.

15. K. L. McKay, *A New Syntax of the Verb in New Testament Greek: An Aspectual Approach*, Studies in Biblical Greek 5 (New York: Peter Lang, 1994), 34.

16. That the future is a fourth aspect is a distinctive of McKay, *Syntax*, 27.

17. McKay, *Syntax*, 34.

18. Porter, *Aspect*, 427; Porter, *Idioms*, 44–45.

19. Campbell, *Basics*, 84.

tense-category, indicating occurrence *subsequent* to some reference-point. What is invariant about the future through all its forms is the temporal meaning of 'future occurrence,' which can have secondary nuances of intention, potential, command, and so forth as a consequence of this time-reference."[20] Thus, the relation of the future tense-form to both aspect and time is debated.

So, with the possible partial exception of the future, the use of a particular tense-form indicates how the author/speaker is viewing the action.[21] This essential nuance is sometimes referred to as the verb's semantics, that is, the meaning conveyed by the morphological form of the lexeme—what is hardwired into it and thus what that form brings to the sentence. Along with a verb's semantics is its pragmatics, that is, the further nuances conveyed through the meaning of the particular lexeme, its modifiers, and possible signals in the larger context of the sentence, paragraph, and discourse.

Constantine Campbell provides a helpful way to work with this approach in his *Basics of Verbal Aspect in Biblical Greek*. He discusses the major tense-forms of indicative and non-indicative verbs, illustrating how one should consider the contribution of several key elements related to each verb in a passage.

1. The semantics: What is the aspect of the tense-form?
2. The lexeme: Is the verb punctiliar, stative, transitive, etc.?[22]
3. The context: Are there references to time, duration, logic, etc.?

These three factors determine the verb's *Aktionsart*, which is thus its actual function, referred to by some as its *implicature*.[23]

Semantics + Lexeme + Context = *Aktionsart*

Thus the semantics is the aspect hardwired in the verb's tense-form, and the lexeme, context, and *Aktionsart* are the pragmatics. Decker refers to these four elements together as a verbal complex.[24]

So the various nuances of tense-forms listed in grammars are not types of aorists or other tense-forms but different *Aktionsarten*. Some scholars are adamant about doing away with labels like "constative aorist." But it seems better to use the terms as shorthand for our analysis of something being conveyed

---

20. Fanning, *Aspect*, 123 (emphasis original).

21. Some say the choice of aspect is rarely a conscious decision since this choice is "controlled to a significant extent by a verb's lexical semantics and the demands of linguistic context" (Evans, *Verbal Syntax*, 24). In other words, the patterns of the language limit one's options.

22. For a brief overview of some characteristics of lexemes, see Campbell, *Basics*, chap. 6.

23. Implicature "refers to the specific function of a form when in combination with certain pragmatic features" (Campbell, *Colossians*, xxiii).

24. Decker, *Temporal Deixis*, 27–28.

in a sentence, while recognizing that such terms do not refer to a particular kind of aorist, but rather its function in a particular context. As D. A. Carson puts it, "The only thing we must remember is that the label *constative aorist* is not meant to convey the results of morphological information, or even of semantic information borne exclusively by the aorist tense verb itself, but of semantic information borne by the aorist tense verb *in its relationship with the rest of this particular context.*"[25]

By way of illustration,[26] the *Aktionsart* "iterative" (actions that occur repeatedly) can occur with a present tense-form. Semantically, the aspect of a present tense-form is imperfective, and this can combine with lexeme and context in one of two ways. First, a lexeme that is punctiliar, such as πίπτω ("I fall"; a certain result has to be reached for falling to have taken place), signals iterative action if the context allows or requires it. In the following example πολλάκις ("often") requires it.

πολλάκις γὰρ πίπτει εἰς τὸ πῦρ καὶ πολλάκις εἰς τὸ ὕδωρ.
For he often falls into the fire and often into the water. (Matt. 17:15)[27]

The second way a present tense-form can signal an iterative *Aktionsart* is with a nonstative lexeme in a context that requires the idea of repeated action. Thus νηστεύω (I fast) is not a state but a dynamic action (that is, an action for which there is no result or limit that has to be reached for fasting to have happened), and in the following example δίς τοῦ σαββάτου (twice a week) signals the iterative *Aktionsart*.

νηστεύω δὶς τοῦ σαββάτου.
I fast twice a week. (Luke 18:12)

Compare this to a present tense-form (imperfective aspect) with a stative lexeme like γινώσκω ("I know"; we would not say "I am knowing," as if it were an activity) in a context that allows or creates stativity.[28]

ἐγώ εἰμι ὁ ποιμὴν ὁ καλός, καὶ γινώσκω τὰ ἐμὰ καὶ γινώσκουσί με τὰ ἐμά.
I am the good shepherd. I know my own and my own know me. (John 10:14)

These examples illustrate the role played by the lexical meaning of the verb. Different classifications of verbs have been proposed. Some prefer a simple

25. D. A. Carson, *Exegetical Fallacies*, 2nd ed. (Grand Rapids: Baker, 1996), 72 (emphasis original). So also Decker, *Temporal Deixis*, 27.

26. These first two examples are taken from Campbell, *Basics*, 65, simplified slightly.

27. All Scripture quotations in these examples are from the ESV.

28. Campbell uses this example in *Basics*, 64.

set of four categories: states and positions (stative types) and processes and actions (actional types).[29] Fanning has an elaborate list of eight categories:[30]

Fanning's Eight Categories of Verbal Action

Along with this role of the lexeme, these examples illustrate the influence of other items in the context.

Such analysis of the verb is important in exegesis and also very fruitful for meditation. An increasing number of resources are available for exploring verbal aspect. The present discussion among students of Biblical Greek began primarily with a series of stimulating articles by K. L. McKay in 1965, continued into the 1990s, and culminated in his book *A New Syntax of the Verb in New Testament Greek: An Aspectual Approach*.[31] Major studies by Stanley E. Porter (1989)[32] and Buist M. Fanning (1990)[33] have been the main focus of attention up to the present.[34] Among more recent major studies are two works by Constantine Campbell.[35] Both Porter[36] and Campbell[37] have also produced brief user-friendly introductions to the topic. Summaries of parts of the large, expensive books by Porter and Fanning are available,[38] and

29. Cited by Evans, *Verbal Syntax*, 25n47.

30. See Fanning, *Aspect*, chap. 3; and the brief survey and analysis in Kimmo Huovila, "Towards a Theory of Aspectual Nesting for New Testament Greek" (MA thesis, Department of General Linguistics, University of Helsinki, Spring 1999). Such analysis builds on the work of Zeno Vendler and Anthony Kenny (Fanning, *Aspect*, 127n1). Huovila (8–9) has a very brief but helpful introduction to Vendler's classification.

31. McKay, *Syntax*. On page xiii he lists his earlier articles, and he refers to them throughout the book.

32. Porter, *Aspect*.

33. Fanning, *Aspect*.

34. See esp. their comments on each other's work and the assessments of other scholars in Porter and Carson, *Open Questions*.

35. Campbell, *Indicative Mood*, and his *Verbal Aspect and Non-indicative Verbs: Further Soundings in the Greek of the New Testament*, Studies in Biblical Greek 15 (New York: Peter Lang, 2008).

36. Porter, *Idioms*, chap. 1.

37. Campbell, *Basics*. See also his helpful summary in *Colossians*, xxi–xxvii.

38. For Porter, see Rodney J. Decker, "The Poor Man's Porter" (which covers chaps. 1–5 of Porter's *Aspect*) and Decker's summary of Fanning (which covers chaps. 1–2 of Fanning's *Aspect*).

Porter[39] and Rodney J. Decker[40] include brief introductions to their views in their basic Greek textbooks. Monographs are appearing that apply the theory,[41] and commentaries are increasingly including analysis of verbal aspect.[42] Before tackling these major studies, you can start exploring this complex subject through the overview article by Andrew David Naselli[43] followed by that of Robert E. Picirilli,[44] with Campbell's *Basics of Verbal Aspect in Biblical Greek* then providing a user-friendly resource for applying verbal aspect theory. Such resources will enable you to benefit from these insights, even while scholars seek to further refine and clarify our understanding of verbal aspect and *Aktionsart*.[45]

Verbal Voice

Another point of discussion recently in the study of the Greek verb concerns verbs that lack an active form, traditionally called deponents. "Deponent" comes from the Latin *deponere*, "lay aside." "The term 'deponent' arose from the idea that these verbs had dropped the active voice."[46] The middle or passive forms of these verbs are understood to function as actives. The concept has

---

Major elements in Fanning's discussion in chap. 3 of *Aspect* ("The Effect of Inherent Meaning and Other Elements on Aspectual Function") are covered briefly in Huovila, "Aspectual Nesting," esp. 43–65. Huovila interacts also with Porter and McKay, among other scholars, offering his own proposals. These resources of Decker and Huovila are available online (see bibliography).

39. Stanley E. Porter, Jeffrey T. Reed, and Matthew Brook O'Donnell, *Fundamentals of New Testament Greek* (Grand Rapids: Eerdmans, 2010).

40. Rodney J. Decker, *Reading Koine Greek: An Introduction and Integrated Workbook* (Grand Rapids: Baker Academic, 2014).

41. See, e.g., Decker, *Temporal Deixis*; Evans, *Verbal Syntax*; David L. Mathewson, *Verbal Aspect in the Book of Revelation: The Function of Greek Verb Tenses in John's Apocalypse*, Linguistic Biblical Studies 4 (Leiden: Brill, 2010); Wally V. Cirafesi, *Verbal Aspect in Synoptic Parallels: On the Method and Meaning of Divergent Tense-Form Usage in the Synoptic Passion Narratives*, Linguistic Biblical Studies 7 (Leiden: Brill, 2013); and Douglas S. Huffman, *Verbal Aspect Theory and the Prohibitions in the Greek New Testament*, Studies in Biblical Greek 16 (New York: Peter Lang, 2014).

42. See esp. the volumes in the Baylor Handbook on the Greek New Testament. E.g., Campbell offers such analysis for every verb in his *Colossians*, and esp. thorough is Rodney J. Decker, *Mark: A Handbook on the Greek Text*, 2 vols. (Waco: Baylor University Press, 2014).

43. Andrew David Naselli, "A Brief Introduction to Verbal Aspect in New Testament Greek," *Detroit Baptist Seminary Journal* 12 (2007): 17–28. Available online (see bibliography).

44. Robert E. Picirilli, "The Meaning of the Tenses in New Testament Greek: Where Are We?," *Journal of the Evangelical Theological Society* 48 (2005): 533–55. Available online (see bibliography).

45. For an example of the continuing scholarly debate, see Porter's discussion of aspect in chaps. 10–12 and 15 of his *Linguistic Analysis*.

46. A. T. Robertson, *A Grammar of the Greek New Testament in the Light of Historical Research* (Nashville: Broadman, 1934), 333. Others suggest it is the middle or passive force that is laid aside (e.g., Wallace, 428).

been included in virtually all basic Greek courses, but it has also been called into question by some. Already in the 1930s, Robertson said this term "should not be used at all."[47] More recently the idea of verbal deponency has been challenged by a number of scholars.[48] One good reason is that ancient Greek grammarians did not understand verbs in this way. Rather, viewing such verbs as deponent seems to have arisen from scholars interpreting Greek using Latin categories.[49] A further influence for English speakers is the lack of a middle in English.[50] So a verb like ἔρχομαι gets translated "I go/come" as if it were an active form, and it is assumed that the Greeks viewed it this way as well.

It is being proposed that verbs that lack an active form should be interpreted as true middles. What would this mean? It is often taught that middles are reflexive (e.g., "I wash myself"). Very few middles have this sense, because in Koine Greek, as in English, the reflexive pronoun is usually used to convey this meaning.[51] Rather, the middle signals a more intense involvement of the subject in the action of the verb. The subject is the one for whom, on whom, toward whom, or in whose interest something is being done by the subject. Thus ἔρχομαι may need to be translated as an active in English, but a Greek would understand it as a middle, for it is one of the verbs that express "the notion of moving oneself in one direction or another."[52]

So the deponents are not a separate category; rather, these verbs that lack an active form are simply middles. When dealing with the details of a text in exegesis or meditation, it is worth considering how such a verb includes a

47. *Grammar*, 332.

48. Good introductions to this issue are provided by Jonathan T. Pennington in a paper delivered at the Society of Biblical Literature, "Is Deponency a Valid Category for Koine Greek?"; and Carl Conrad, "Propositions concerning Ancient Greek Voice" (both online; see bibliography). Conrad provides links to his other unpublished papers on this topic. See further the study across a number of languages by Suzanne Kemmer, *The Middle Voice*, Typological Studies in Language 23 (Amsterdam/Philadelphia: John Benjamins, 1993); and the following articles on Greek: Neva F. Miller, "Appendix 2: A Theory of Deponent Verbs," in *Analytical Lexicon of the Greek New Testament*, Timothy Friberg, Barbara Friberg, and Neva Miller, eds. (Grand Rapids: Baker Academic, 2000), 423–30; Jonathan T. Pennington, "Deponency in Koine Greek: The Grammatical Question and the Lexicographical Dilemma," *Trinity Journal* 24 (2003): 55–76; expanded in Jonathan T. Pennington, "Setting Aside 'Deponency': Rediscovering the Greek Middle Voice in New Testament Studies," in *The Linguist as Pedagogue: Trends in the Teaching and Linguistic Analysis of the Greek New Testament*, ed. Stanley E. Porter and Matthew Brook O'Donnell (Sheffield: Sheffield Phoenix, 2009), 181–203; and Bernard A. Taylor, "Deponency and Greek Lexicography," in *Biblical Greek Language and Lexicography: Essays in Honor of Frederick W. Danker*, ed. B. A. Taylor et al. (Grand Rapids: Eerdmans, 2004), 167–76.

49. See Taylor, "Deponency," 169–74; Pennington, "Deponency in Koine Greek," 62–64; and Pennington, "Setting Aside," 187–88.

50. Pennington, "Deponency in Koine Greek," 61–62; Pennington, "Setting Aside," 188–90.

51. "In most modern languages the middle is represented only by the use of the reflexive pronoun" (Robertson, *Grammar*, 333).

52. Miller, "Theory," 428.

middle sense, even if it is too subtle to convey in English. Kemmer has produced a list of types of verbs that are involved, and Neva Miller has produced a very helpful list of such verbs in the GNT.[53]

This approach is illustrated in Martin Culy's commentary on the Johannine Epistles.[54] He provides a brief introduction to this new approach[55] and then works with it for a number of the verbs in these documents. An example occurs in the first verse of 1 John. Ἐθεασάμεθα (from θεάομαι) is translated in English as an active (e.g., ESV "we looked upon"; NIV "we looked at"), which is fine as a translation. But Culy draws upon Miller's categories and comments, "The voice should probably be viewed as a true middle, indicating that the subject is 'the center of emphasis, the receiver of sensory perception.'"[56] We can take Culy's analysis further by noting how this emphasis on the subject in ἐθεασάμεθα corresponds to the same emphasis in the rest of the sentence, especially just before (ὃ ἑωράκαμεν τοῖς ὀφθαλμοῖς ἡμῶν, "what we have seen with our eyes") and just after (καὶ αἱ χεῖρες ἡμῶν ἐψηλάφησαν, "and our hands handled"). The emphasis on the subject in ἐθεασάμεθα in the middle corresponds to these other statements with their use of the first person pronoun ἡμῶν.

Another example of a verb with no active form occurs in 1 John 2:22:

τίς ἐστιν ὁ ψεύστης εἰ μὴ ὁ ἀρνούμενος ὅτι Ἰησοῦς οὐκ ἔστιν ὁ Χριστός;
Who is the liar but the one who denies that Jesus is the Christ?[57]

Here, regarding ἀρνούμενος (from ἀρνέομαι), Culy gives us another example of drawing on Miller's categories. "Miller . . . accounts for the use of the middle form with this verb by listing it as a verb that involves reciprocity, or more specifically, a situation 'where two parties are involved and where the removal of one party would render the verb meaningless and no action possible.'"[58]

A related issue involves verbs that have been known as "passive deponents" because they use a passive form and have no active form. This form of deponency is also being questioned. It has long been known that the passive is "a

---

53. Kemmer, *Middle*, 267–70; Miller, "Theory," 427–29. Conrad provides summaries of these two lists in "Propositions," section 8; and Pennington summarizes Miller's list in "Deponency in Koine Greek," 65–66; and "Setting Aside," 191.

54. Martin M. Culy, *I, II, III John: A Handbook on the Greek Text*, Baylor Handbook on the Greek New Testament (Waco: Baylor University Press, 2004).

55. Ibid., xx–xxii.

56. Ibid., 4.

57. My translation.

58. Ibid., 55.

later development,"[59] and some of the implications of this are being explored.[60] The passive, including the θη morpheme, is in the process of replacing middle forms in the Koine period.[61] Some aorists and futures with θη forms function as passives, and some have a middle sense.[62] Thus, a verb with θη should be viewed as a middle/passive, and the lexeme and context will indicate which way it is functioning. In the case of the so-called passive deponents, these verbs whose aorist tense-form is passive should be considered true middles.[63]

This understanding of voice explains Culy's suggestion regarding ἐφανερώθη in 1 John 3:8: "It would be possible . . . to view this and other cases of ἐφανερώθη in 1 John, where Jesus is the subject, as middle forms: 'the Son of God has revealed himself.'"[64]

I trust that these examples show the value of this analysis of verbal voice for exegesis and meditation. I encourage you to study this topic, beginning with the introductory articles by Pennington and Conrad.[65]

Conclusion

There is much more to these topics that I have not even touched on here. The discussion itself is still in the early stages, with new developments certain to come along.[66] This appendix is meant merely to introduce you to these significant discussions and provide resources for learning more.

59. Robertson, *Grammar*, 332; Pennington, "Setting Aside," 182.

60. See Conrad, "Propositions," sections 4–5; Pennington, "Deponency in Koine Greek," 68; Pennington, "Setting Aside," 195–96.

61. Robertson, *Grammar*, 333–34. He notes, "The passive forms maintain the field in modern Greek and appropriate the meaning of the middle. We see this tendency at work in the N. T. and the κοινή generally. . . . The result of this struggle between the middle and passive in the aorist and future was an increasing number of passive forms without the distinctive passive idea" (334). Conrad notes that the replacement of older middle-passive forms by θη/η forms is evident already in Classical Attic Greek ("Propositions," section 5).

62. Robertson, *Grammar*, 334.

63. Pennington, "Deponency in Koine Greek," 68.

64. Culy, *I, II, III John*, 76.

65. Pennington, "Is Deponency a Valid Category?"; Conrad, "Propositions"; and more generally, Carl Conrad, "Active, Middle, and Passive: Understanding Ancient Greek Voice." Available online (see bibliography).

66. In 2004 T. V. Evans listed four topics in verbal aspect in need of further research, and they remain so at this time. They include the need for studies that (1) span the history of Greek (a diachronic perspective), (2) explore the influence of personal style and language usage (idiolect) on choice of aspect, (3) focus on the effect of the lexical values of verbs, and (4) clarify how the perfect is to be understood. See T. V. Evans, "Future Directions for Aspect Studies in Ancient Greek," in Taylor, *Biblical Greek*, 202–6. Along with Campbell, *Advances*, see Steven E. Runge and Christopher J. Fresch, eds., *The Greek Verb Revisited: A Fresh Approach for Biblical Exegesis* (Bellingham, WA: Lexham, forthcoming).

BIBLIOGRAPHY

All URLs listed below were active when this book went to press.

Abbott-Smith, G. *A Manual Greek Lexicon of the New Testament*. 3rd ed. Edinburgh: T&T Clark, 1937. http://www.archive.org/details/cu31924021607464.

Aland, Barbara, Kurt Aland, Johannes Karavidopoulos, Carlo M. Martini, and Bruce M. Metzger, eds. *The Greek New Testament*. 4th rev. ed. Stuttgart: Deutsche Bibelgesellschaft, 1993.

———. *Novum Testamentum Graece*. 28th ed. Stuttgart: Deutsche Bibelgesellschaft, 2012.

Aland, Kurt, Barbara Aland, Johannes Karavidopoulos, Carlo M. Martini, and Bruce M. Metzger, eds. *Novum Testamentum Graece*. 27th ed. Stuttgart: Deutsche Bibelgesellschaft, 2001.

Alexander, T. Desmond, Brian S. Rosner, D. A. Carson, and Graeme Goldsworthy, eds. *New Dictionary of Biblical Theology: Exploring the Unity and Diversity of Scripture*. Downers Grove, IL: InterVarsity, 2000.

The Ante-Nicene Fathers. Edited by Alexander Roberts and James Donaldson. 10 vols. 1885–87. Reprint, Grand Rapids: Eerdmans, 1973.

Saint Augustine. *Confessions*. Translated by Henry Chadwick. Oxford: Oxford University Press, 1991.

Barclay, William. *New Testament Words*. Philadelphia: Westminster, 1964.

Barrett, C. K. *Acts*. 2 vols. International Critical Commentary. Edinburgh: T&T Clark, 1994, 1998.

Beekes, Robert, with Lucien van Beek. *Etymological Dictionary of Greek*. 2 vols. Leiden: Brill, 2010.

Beekman, John, and John Callow. *Translating the Word of God*. Grand Rapids: Zondervan, 1974.

Berding, Kenneth. *Sing and Learn New Testament Greek: The Easiest Way to Learn Greek Grammar*. Grand Rapids: Zondervan, 2008.

B-Greek: The Biblical Greek Forum. http://www.ibiblio.org/bgreek/forum/index.php.

Biblical Language Center. http://www.biblicallanguagecenter.com/.

Binz, Stephen J. *Conversing with God in Scripture: A Contemporary Approach to Lectio Divina*. Ijamsville, MD: The Word among Us Press, 2008.

Black, David Alan. *Learn to Read New Testament Greek*. 3rd ed. Nashville: B&H, 2009.

———. *Linguistics for Students of New Testament Greek: A Survey of Basic Concepts and Applications*. Grand Rapids: Baker, 1988.

———. *Using New Testament Greek in Ministry: A Practical Guide for Students and Pastors*. Grand Rapids: Baker, 1993.

Black, David Alan, with Katharine Barnwell and Stephen Levinsohn, eds. *Linguistics and New Testament Interpretation: Essays on Discourse Analysis*. Nashville: Broadman & Holman, 1992.

Blass, Friedrich, Albert Debrunner, and Robert W. Funk. *A Greek Grammar of the New Testament and Other Early Christian Literature*. Chicago: University of Chicago Press, 1961.

Bowne, Dale Russell. *Paradigms and Principal Parts for the Greek New Testament*. Lanham, MD: University Press of America, 1987.

Brenton, Lancelot C. L. *The Septuagint with Apocrypha: Greek and English*. London: Samuel Bagster and Sons, 1851.

Brown, A. Philip, II, Bryan W. Smith, Richard J. Goodrich, and Albert L. Lukaszewski, eds. *A Reader's Hebrew and Greek Bible*. Grand Rapids: Zondervan, 2010.

Burer, Michael H., and Jeffrey E. Miller, eds. *A New Reader's Lexicon of the Greek New Testament*. Grand Rapids: Kregel, 2008.

Campbell, Constantine R. *Advances in the Study of Greek: New Insights for Reading the New Testament*. Grand Rapids: Zondervan, 2015.

———. *Basics of Verbal Aspect in Biblical Greek*. Grand Rapids: Zondervan, 2008.

———. *Colossians and Philemon: A Handbook on the Greek Text*. Baylor Handbook on the Greek New Testament. Waco: Baylor University Press, 2013.

———. *Keep Your Greek: Strategies for Busy People*. Grand Rapids: Zondervan, 2010.

———. *Verbal Aspect and Non-indicative Verbs: Further Soundings in the Greek of the New Testament*. Studies in Biblical Greek 15. New York: Peter Lang, 2008.

———. *Verbal Aspect, the Indicative Mood, and Narrative: Soundings in the Greek of the New Testament*. Studies in Biblical Greek 13. New York: Peter Lang, 2007.

Carson, D. A. *Exegetical Fallacies*. 2nd ed. Grand Rapids: Baker, 1996.

Casey, Michael. *Sacred Readings: The Ancient Art of Lectio Divina*. Liguori, MO: Liguori Publications, 1995.

Cassian, John. *The Conferences*. Translated and edited by Boniface Ramsey. Ancient Christian Writers 57. New York: Paulist Press, 1997.

Chantraine, Pierre. *Dictionnaire Étymologique de la Langue Grecque: Histoire des Mots*. New ed. Paris: Klincksieck, 1999.

Cirafesi, Wally V. *Verbal Aspect in Synoptic Parallels: On the Method and Meaning of Divergent Tense-Form Usage in the Synoptic Passion Narratives.* Linguistic Biblical Studies 7. Leiden: Brill, 2013.

Colwell, E. C. "A Definite Rule for the Use of the Article in the Greek New Testament." *Journal of Biblical Literature* 52 (1933): 12–21. http://www.areopage.net/ColwellRule.pdf.

Conrad, Carl W. "Active, Middle, and Passive: Understanding Ancient Greek Voice." Accessed May 7, 2015. https://pages.wustl.edu/files/pages/imce/cwconrad/undancgrkvc.pdf.

———. "Propositions concerning Ancient Greek Voice." Last revised April 4, 2013. https://pages.wustl.edu/cwconrad/ancient-greek-voice.

Conybeare, F. C., and St. George Stock. *Grammar of Septuagint Greek with Selected Readings from the Septuagint according to the Text of Swete.* 1905. Reprint, Peabody, MA: Hendrickson, 1988.

Cotterell, Peter, and Max Turner. *Linguistics and Biblical Interpretation.* Downers Grove, IL: InterVarsity, 1989.

Culy, Martin M. *I, II, III John: A Handbook on the Greek Text.* Baylor Handbook on the Greek New Testament. Waco: Baylor University Press, 2004.

Culy, Martin M., Mikeal C. Parsons, and Joshua J. Stigall. *Luke: A Handbook on the Greek Text.* Baylor Handbook on the Greek New Testament. Waco: Baylor University Press, 2010.

Danker, Frederick William, rev. and ed. *Greek-English Lexicon of the New Testament and Other Early Christian Literature.* 3rd ed. Chicago: University of Chicago Press, 2000.

Danker, Frederick William, with Kathryn Krug. *The Concise Greek-English Lexicon of the New Testament.* Chicago: Chicago University Press, 2009.

Davies, W. D., and Dale C. Allison. *The Gospel according to Saint Matthew.* 3 vols. International Critical Commentary. Edinburgh: T&T Clark, 1988–97.

Decker, Rodney J. "LXX Vocabulary." NT Resources. http://ntresources.com/blog/documents/LXX_vocab.pdf.

———. *Mark: A Handbook on the Greek Text.* Baylor Handbook on the Greek New Testament. 2 vols. Waco: Baylor University Press, 2014.

———. "The Poor Man's Porter." NT Resources. http://www.ntresources.com/blog/documents/porter.pdf.

———. *Reading Koine Greek: An Introduction and Integrated Workbook.* Grand Rapids: Baker Academic, 2014.

———. "Summary of Fanning." NT Resources. http://www.ntresources.com/blog/wp-content/uploads/2014/05/FanningVA_smry.doc.

———. *Temporal Deixis of the Greek Verb in the Gospel of Mark with Reference to Verbal Aspect.* Studies in Biblical Greek 10. New York: Peter Lang, 2001.

Denniston, J. D. *The Greek Particles.* 2nd ed. Revised by K. J. Dover. London: Gerald Duckworth, 1950.

Deppe, Dean. *The Lexham Clausal Outlines of the Greek New Testament.* Bellingham, WA: Logos Bible Software, 2006.

Dooley, Robert A., and Stephen H. Levinsohn. *Analysing Discourse: A Manual of Basic Concepts*. Dallas: SIL International, 2001.

Duvall, J. Scott, and J. Daniel Hays. *Grasping God's Word: A Hands-On Approach to Reading, Interpreting, and Applying the Bible*. 3rd ed. Grand Rapids: Zondervan, 2012.

Duvall, J. Scott, and Verlyn D. Verbrugge, eds. *Devotions on the Greek New Testament: 52 Reflections to Inspire & Instruct*. Grand Rapids: Zondervan, 2012.

Easwaran, Eknath. *Passage Meditation: Bringing the Deep Wisdom of the Heart into Daily Life*. 3rd ed. Tomales, CA: Nilgiri, 2008. Related resources at http://www.easwaran.org/learning-how-to-meditate.html.

Evans, T. V. "Future Directions for Aspect Studies in Ancient Greek." In *Biblical Greek Language and Lexicography: Essays in Honor of Frederick W. Danker*, edited by Bernard A. Taylor et al., 202–6. Grand Rapids: Eerdmans, 2004.

———. *Verbal Syntax in the Greek Pentateuch: Natural Greek Usage and Hebrew Interference*. Oxford: Oxford University Press, 2001.

Fanning, Buist M. *Verbal Aspect in New Testament Greek*. Oxford: Clarendon, 1990.

Fee, Gordon D. *New Testament Exegesis: A Handbook for Students and Pastors*. 3rd ed. Louisville: Westminster/John Knox, 2002.

Ferguson, Everett. "Rule of Faith." In *Encyclopedia of Early Christianity*, edited by Everett Ferguson, 804–5. New York: Garland, 1990.

Fields, Lee M. *Hebrew for the Rest of Us*. Grand Rapids: Zondervan, 2008.

Frye, Northrop. *The Great Code: The Bible and Literature*. New York: Harcourt, Brace, Jovanovich, 1982.

Funk, Robert W. *A Beginning-Intermediate Grammar of Hellenistic Greek*. 3rd ed. Salem, OR: Polebridge, 2013.

Geannikis, Erikk, Andrew Romiti, and P. T. Wilford. *Greek Paradigm Handbook*. Newburyport, MA: Focus/Pullins, 2008.

Gentry, Peter J. "Aspect and the Greek Verb." NT Discourse. http://www.ntdiscourse.org/docs/Gentry-VerbalAspect.pdf.

Gillet, Lev. *The Jesus Prayer*. Rev. ed. Crestwood, NY: St. Vladimir's Seminary Press, 1987.

Goodrich, Richard J., and Albert L. Lukaszewski, eds. *A Reader's Greek New Testament*. 2nd ed. Grand Rapids: Zondervan, 2007.

Grabe, William. *Reading in a Second Language: Moving from Theory to Practice*. Cambridge Applied Linguistics Series. Cambridge: Cambridge University Press, 2009.

Graves, Michael. *The Inspiration and Interpretation of Scripture: What the Early Church Can Teach Us*. Grand Rapids: Eerdmans, 2014.

The Greek New Testament: SBL Edition. Atlanta: Society of Biblical Literature; Bellingham, WA: Logos Bible Software, 2010. Available online at http://sblgnt.com.

Gundry, Robert H., and Russell W. Howell. "The Sense and Syntax of John 3:14–17 with Special Reference to the Use of Οὕτως . . . Ὥστε in John 3:16." *Novum Testamentum* 41, no. 1 (1999): 24–38.

Guthrie, George. "Discourse Analysis." In *Interpreting the New Testament: Essays on Methods and Issues*, edited by David Alan Black and David S. Dockery, 253–71. Nashville: Broadman & Holman, 2001.

Guthrie, George H., and J. Scott Duvall. *Biblical Greek Exegesis*. Grand Rapids: Zondervan, 1998.

Hale, William Gardner. *Aims and Methods in Classical Study*. Boston: Ginn, 1888.

———. *The Art of Reading Latin: How to Teach It*. Boston: Ginn, 1887. http://www.perseus.tufts.edu/hopper/text?doc=Perseus%3atext%3a1999.04.0066.

———. "An Experiment in the Teaching of First and Second Year Latin." *Classical Journal* 1, no. 1 (Dec. 1905): 7–18. https://archive.org/details/jstor-3287568.

Hall, Christopher A. *Reading Scripture with the Church Fathers*. Downers Grove, IL: InterVarsity, 1998.

Harris, Murray J. *Prepositions and Theology in the Greek New Testament: An Essential Reference Resource for Exegesis*. Grand Rapids: Zondervan, 2012.

Harris, William. "The Sin of Transverbalizing . . . or Translating as you Read!" Latin Studies and Background Essays. http://community.middlebury.edu/~harris/Latin Background/transverbalizing.html.

Herbster, Richard G. "Integrating Biblical Language Study and Homiletical Preparation." DMin thesis, Trinity School for Ministry, 2013.

Holmes, Michael W., ed. and trans. *The Apostolic Fathers: Greek Texts and English Translations*. 3rd ed. Grand Rapids: Baker Academic, 2007.

Howard, Wilbert Francis. *Accidence and Word-Formation with an Appendix on Semitisms in the New Testament*. Vol. 2 of *A Grammar of New Testament Greek*, by James Hope Moulton, Wilbert Francis Howard, and Nigel Turner. Edinburgh: T&T Clark, 1919, 1920, 1929.

Hoyos, B. D. *Latin, How to Read It Fluently: A Practical Manual*. Amherst, MA: Classical Association of New England, 1997. www.canepress.org.

———. "The Ten Basic Reading Rules for Latin." Latinteach. http://www.latinteach.com/Site/ARTICLES/Entries/2008/10/15_Dexter_Hoyos_-_The_Ten_Basic_Rules_for_Reading_Latin_files/Reading%20%26Translating%20Rules.pdf.

Huffman, Douglas S. *The Handy Guide to New Testament Greek: Grammar, Syntax and Diagramming*. Grand Rapids: Kregel, 2012.

———. *Verbal Aspect Theory and the Prohibitions in the Greek New Testament*. Studies in Biblical Greek 16. New York: Peter Lang, 2014.

Huovila, Kimmo. "Towards a Theory of Aspectual Nesting for New Testament Greek." MA thesis, Department of General Linguistics, University of Helsinki, 1999.

Institute of Biblical Greek. http://www.biblicalgreek.org/links/.

Jobes, Karen H. *1 Peter*. Baker Exegetical Commentary on the New Testament. Grand Rapids: Baker Academic, 2005.

Jobes, Karen H., and Moisés Silva. *Invitation to the Septuagint*. 2nd ed. Grand Rapids: Baker Academic, 2015.

John of the Cross. "Maxims on Love." In *The Collected Works of St. John of the Cross*, translated by Kieran Kavanaugh and Otilio Rodriguez, 674–80. Washington, DC: ICS, 1973.

Joint Association of Classical Teachers' Greek Course. *Greek Vocabulary*. Cambridge: Cambridge University Press, 1980.

———. *The Intellectual Revolution: Selections from Euripides, Thucydides and Plato.* Cambridge: Cambridge University Press, 1980.

———. *A World of Heroes: Selections from Homer, Herodotus and Sophocles.* Cambridge: Cambridge University Press, 1979.

Keating, Thomas. *Open Mind, Open Heart: The Contemplative Dimension of the Gospel.* 20th anniversary ed. New York: Continuum, 2006.

Kemmer, Suzanne. *The Middle Voice.* Typological Studies in Language 23. Philadelphia: John Benjamins, 1993.

Klein, William W., Craig L. Blomberg, and Robert L. Hubbard Jr. *Introduction to Biblical Interpretation.* Dallas: Word, 1993.

Kugel, James L. *How to Read the Bible: A Guide to Scripture, Then and Now.* New York: Free Press, 2007.

Kugel, James L., and Rowan A. Greer. *Early Biblical Interpretation.* Library of Early Christianity. Philadelphia: Westminster, 1986.

Kwong, Ivan Shing Chung. *The Word Order of the Gospel of Luke: Its Foregrounded Messages.* Library of New Testament Studies 298. London: T&T Clark, 2005.

Laird, Martin. *Into the Silent Land: A Guide to the Christian Practice of Contemplation.* Oxford: Oxford University Press, 2006.

———. *A Sunlit Absence: Silence, Awareness, and Contemplation.* Oxford: Oxford University Press, 2011.

Lakoff, George, and Mark Johnson. *Metaphors We Live By.* With a new afterword. Chicago: University of Chicago Press, 2003.

Larson, Donald N. *A Structural Approach to Greek, with Special Emphasis on Learning to Read the Koine Dialect.* 5th ed. 2 vols. Lincoln, IL: Lincoln Christian College, 1971.

Leclercq, Jean. *The Love of Learning and the Desire for God: A Study of Monastic Culture.* Translated by Catharine Misrahi. Rev. ed. New York: Fordham University Press, 1974.

Lee, John. "Etymological Follies: Three Recent Lexicons of the New Testament." *Novum Testamentum* 55 (2013): 383–403. http://www.academia.edu/3700011/Etymological_Follies_Three_Recent_Lexicons_of_the_New_Testament_Novum_Testamentum_55_2013_383–403.

Levinsohn, Stephen H. *Discourse Features of New Testament Greek: A Coursebook on the Information Structure of New Testament Greek.* 2nd ed. Dallas: SIL, 2000.

Lewis, C. S. *Surprised by Joy: The Shape of My Early Life.* New York: Harcourt, Brace and World, 1955.

Liddell, Henry George, and Robert Scott. *An Intermediate Greek-English Lexicon: Founded upon the Seventh Edition of Liddell and Scott's Greek-English Lexicon.* Oxford: Clarendon, 1889. Available online at http://www.perseus.tufts.edu/hopper/search.

Liddell, Henry George, Robert Scott, and Henry Stuart Jones. *A Greek-English Lexicon.* 9th ed. with revised supplement. Oxford: Clarendon, 1996. Available online at http://www.perseus.tufts.edu/hopper/search.

"List of Middle-Earth Food and Drink." Wikipedia. http://en.wikipedia.org/wiki/List_of_Middle-earth_food_and_drink.

Long, Fredrick J. *II Corinthians: A Handbook on the Greek Text*. Baylor Handbook on the Greek New Testament. Waco: Baylor University Press, 2015.

Lorayne, Harry, and Jerry Lucas. *The Memory Book: The Classic Guide to Improving Your Memory at Work, at School, and at Play*. New York: Ballantine, 1974.

Louth, Andrew. *Discerning the Mystery: An Essay on the Nature of Theology*. Oxford: Clarendon, 1983.

Louw, Johannes P., and Eugene A. Nida. *Greek-English Lexicon of the New Testament Based on Semantic Domains*. 2nd ed. New York: United Bible Societies, 1988.

Lubac, Henri de. *The Four Senses of Scripture*. Vol. 1 of *Medieval Exegesis*. Translated by Mark Sebanc. Grand Rapids: Eerdmans, 1998.

Lukaszewski, Albert L., and Mark Dubis. *The Lexham Syntactic Greek New Testament*. Bellingham, WA: Logos Bible Software, 2009.

Lund, Nils W. *Chiasmus in the New Testament: A Study in the Form and Function of Chiastic Structures*. 1942. Reprint, Peabody, MA: Hendrickson, 1992.

Main, John. *Word into Silence: A Manual for Christian Meditation*. 1980. Reprint, Norwich, England: Canterbury, 2006.

———. *Word Made Flesh: Recovering a Sense of the Sacred through Prayer*. 1993. Reprint, Norwich, England: Canterbury, 2009.

Maloney, George. *Prayer of the Heart: The Contemplative Tradition of the Christian East*. Rev. ed. Notre Dame, IN: Ave Maria, 2008.

Mathewson, David L. *Verbal Aspect in the Book of Revelation: The Function of Greek Verb Tenses in John's Apocalypse*. Linguistic Biblical Studies 4. Leiden: Brill, 2010.

McKay, K. L. *A New Syntax of the Verb in New Testament Greek: An Aspectual Approach*. Studies in Biblical Greek 5. New York: Peter Lang, 1994.

———. "Syntax in Exegesis." *Tyndale Bulletin* 23 (1972): 39–57. http://www.tyndalehouse.com/tynbul/library/TynBull_1972_23_02_McKay_SyntaxInExegesis.pdf.

Metzger, Bruce M. *Lexical Aids for Students of New Testament Greek*. 3rd ed. 1969. Reprint, Grand Rapids: Baker 1998.

Miller, Neva F. "Appendix 2: A Theory of Deponent Verbs." In *Analytical Lexicon of the Greek New Testament*, edited by Timothy Friberg, Barbara Friberg, and Neva Miller, 423–30. Grand Rapids: Baker Academic, 2000.

Mitchell, Margaret M. *Paul, the Corinthians and the Birth of Christian Hermeneutics*. Cambridge: Cambridge University Press, 2010.

Moo, Douglas J. *The Epistle to the Romans*. New International Commentary on the New Testament. Grand Rapids: Eerdmans, 1996.

Mounce, William D. *Basics of Biblical Greek: Grammar*. 3rd ed. Grand Rapids: Zondervan, 2009.

———. *A Graded Reader of Biblical Greek*. Grand Rapids: Zondervan, 1996.

———. *Greek for the Rest of Us*. Grand Rapids: Zondervan, 2003.

———. *The Morphology of Biblical Greek*. Grand Rapids: Zondervan, 1994.

Naselli, Andrew David. "A Brief Introduction to Verbal Aspect in New Testament Greek." *Detroit Baptist Seminary Journal* 12 (2007): 17–28. http://andynaselli.com/wp-content/uploads/2007_verbal_aspect.pdf?9d7bd4.

The NET Bible. Version 1.0. n.p.: Biblical Studies Press, 1996–2006. Available at https://net.bible.org/#!bible/Matthew+1:1.

New International Dictionary of New Testament Theology and Exegesis. Edited by Moisés Silva. 2nd ed. 5 vols. Grand Rapids: Zondervan, 2014.

Newman, Barclay M. *A Concise Greek-English Dictionary of the New Testament.* Rev. ed. Stuttgart: Deutsche Bibelgesellschaft, 2010.

NT Gateway. http://www.ntgateway.com/greek-ntgateway/greek-new-testament-texts/.

O'Keefe, John J., and R. R. Reno. *Sanctified Vision: An Introduction to Early Christian Interpretation of the Bible.* Baltimore: Johns Hopkins University Press, 2005.

OpenText.org. http://opentext.org/.

Origen. *Commentary on the Gospel of John.* ANF 10:297–408.

Osborne, Grant R. *The Hermeneutical Spiral: A Comprehensive Introduction to Biblical Interpretation.* Downers Grove, IL: InterVarsity, 1991.

———. *Matthew.* Zondervan Exegetical Commentary on the New Testament. Grand Rapids: Zondervan, 2010.

Pennington, Jonathan T. "Deponency in Koine Greek: The Grammatical Question and the Lexicographical Dilemma." *Trinity Journal* 24 (2003): 55–76.

———. "Is Deponency a Valid Category for Koine Greek?" Jonathan T. Pennington. http://jonathanpennington.com/wp-content/uploads/Pennington_Middle_Voice.pdf.

———. *New Testament Greek Vocabulary.* Grand Rapids: Zondervan, 2001.

———. "Setting Aside 'Deponency': Rediscovering the Greek Middle Voice in New Testament Studies." In *The Linguist as Pedagogue: Trends in the Teaching and Linguistic Analysis of the Greek New Testament,* edited by Stanley E. Porter and Matthew Brook O'Donnell, 181–203. Sheffield: Sheffield Phoenix, 2009.

Perseus Digital Library. http://www.perseus.tufts.edu/hopper/collection?collection=Perseus:collection:Greco-Roman.

Picirilli, Robert E. "The Meaning of the Tenses in New Testament Greek: Where Are We?" *Journal of the Evangelical Theological Society* 48 (2005): 533–55. http://www.etsjets.org/files/JETS-PDFs/48/48-3/JETS_48-3_533-555.pdf.

Pietersma, Albert, and Benjamin G. Wright, eds. *A New Translation of the Septuagint and the Other Greek Translations Traditionally Included under That Title.* Oxford: Oxford University Press, 2007.

Pitts, Andrew W. "Greek Word Order and Clause Structure: A Comparative Study of Some New Testament Corpora." In *The Language of the New Testament: Context, History, and Development.* Edited by Stanley E. Porter and Andrew W. Pitts, 311–46. Early Christianity in Its Hellenistic Context 3. Leiden: Brill, 2013.

Plummer, Alfred. *An Exegetical Commentary on the Gospel according to St. Matthew.* Grand Rapids: Eerdmans, 1956.

Porter, Stanley E. *Idioms of the Greek New Testament.* Biblical Languages: Greek 2. Sheffield: Sheffield Academic Press, 1992.

———. *Linguistic Analysis of the Greek New Testament: Studies in Tools, Methods, and Practice.* Grand Rapids: Baker Academic, 2015.

———. *Verbal Aspect in the Greek of the New Testament, with Reference to Tense and Mood.* New York: Peter Lang, 1989.

Porter, Stanley E., and D. A. Carson, eds. *Biblical Greek Language and Linguistics: Open Questions in Current Research*. Journal for the Study of the New Testament: Supplement Series 80. Sheffield: Sheffield Academic Press, 1993.

Porter, Stanley E., and Matthew Brook O'Donnell, eds. *The Linguist as Pedagogue: Trends in the Teaching and Linguistic Analysis of the Greek New Testament*. Sheffield: Sheffield Phoenix, 2009.

Porter, Stanley, Matthew Brook O'Donnell, Jeffrey T. Reed, et al. *The OpenText .org Syntactically Analyzed Greek New Testament*. Bellingham, WA: Logos Bible Software, 2006.

———. *The OpenText.org Syntactically Analyzed Greek New Testament: Clause Analysis; OpenText.org Clause Analysis*. Bellingham, WA: Logos Bible Software, 2006.

Porter, Stanley E., Jeffrey T. Reed, and Matthew Brook O'Donnell. *Fundamentals of New Testament Greek*. Grand Rapids: Eerdmans, 2010.

Reed, Jeffrey T. *A Discourse Analysis of Philippians: Method and Rhetoric in the Debate over Literary Integrity*. Journal for the Study of the New Testament Supplement Series 136. Sheffield: Sheffield Academic, 1997.

Robertson, A. T. *A Grammar of the Greek New Testament in the Light of Historical Research*. Nashville: Broadman, 1934.

———. *The Minister and His Greek New Testament*. Grand Rapids: Baker, 1977.

———. *Word Pictures in the New Testament*. 6 vols. Nashville: Broadman, 1930–33.

Robie, Jonathan. "Phrasing a Greek Text." Little Greek. http://www.ibiblio.org/koine /greek/phrasing/phrasing-greek-text.html.

Robinson, Thomas A. *Mastering New Testament Greek: Essential Tools for Students*. 3rd ed. Peabody, MA: Hendrickson, 2007.

Ruhl, Charles. *On Monosemy: A Study in Linguistic Semantics*. New York: SUNY Press, 1989.

Runge, Steven E. *Discourse Grammar of the Greek New Testament: A Practical Introduction for Teaching and Exegesis*. Peabody, MA: Hendrickson, 2010.

———. *The Lexham Discourse Greek New Testament*. Bellingham, WA: Lexham, 2008.

———. "On Porter, Prominence, and Discourse." NT Discourse. http://www.ntdis course.org/on-porter-prominence-and-aspect/.

Runge, Steven E., and Christopher J. Fresch, eds. *The Greek Verb Revisited: A Fresh Approach for Biblical Exegesis*. Bellingham, WA: Lexham, forthcoming.

Schaff, Philip, and Henry Wace, eds. *A Select Library of Nicene and Post-Nicene Fathers of the Christian Church, Second Series*. 14 vols. 1890–99. Reprint, Grand Rapids: Eerdmans, 1974.

Schmidt, Daryl D. "Verbal Aspect in Greek: Two Approaches." In *Biblical Greek Language and Linguistics: Open Questions in Current Research*, edited by Stanley E. Porter and D. A. Carson, 63–73. Journal for the Study of the New Testament: Supplement Series 80. Sheffield: Sheffield Academic Press, 1993.

Shaywitz, Sally. *Overcoming Dyslexia: A New and Complete Science-Based Program for Reading Problems at Any Level*. New York: Vintage Books, 2003.

Silva, Moisés. *Biblical Words and Their Meaning: An Introduction to Lexical Semantics*. Rev. and exp. ed. Grand Rapids: Zondervan, 1995.

249

Sire, James W. *How to Read Slowly: A Christian Guide to Reading with the Mind.* Colorado Springs, CO: WaterBrook, 1978.

Smalley, Stephen S. *The Revelation to John: A Commentary on the Greek Text of the Apocalypse.* Downers Grove, IL: InterVarsity, 2005.

Smyth, Herbert Weir. *Greek Grammar.* Revised by Gordon M. Messing. Cambridge, MA: Harvard University Press, 1956. http://www.perseus.tufts.edu/hopper/text;j sessionid=D8B2B2CEC968E40F6B77C014795D1915?doc=Perseus%3atext%3a 1999.04.0007.

Spicq, Ceslas. *Theological Lexicon of the New Testament.* Translated and edited by James D. Ernest. 3 vols. Peabody, MA: Hendrickson, 1994.

Steadman, Geoffrey. *Plato's Symposium: Greek Text with Facing Vocabulary and Commentary.* Self-published, 2011.

Stehle, Matthias. *Greek Word Building.* Translated by F. Forrester Church and John S. Hanson. Missoula, MT: Scholars Press, 1976.

Story, J. Lyle. "Curriculum Resources." J. Lyle Story. http://www.greektome.biz/re sources.php.

Story, J. Lyle, and Cullen I. K. Story. *Greek to Me: Learning New Testament Greek through Memory Visualization.* Illustrated by Peter Allen Miller. Fairfax, VA: Xulon, 2002.

Student, The [Samuel H. Scudder]. "The Student, the Fish, and Agassiz." http://people .bethel.edu/~dhoward/resources/Agassizfish/Agassizfish.htm.

Taylor, Bernard A. "Deponency and Greek Lexicography." In *Biblical Greek Language and Lexicography: Essays in Honor of Frederick W. Danker,* edited by B. A. Taylor et al., 167–76. Grand Rapids: Eerdmans, 2004.

Thesaurus Linguae Graecae. http://www.tlg.uci.edu/.

Thrall, Margaret E. *Greek Particles in the New Testament: Linguistic and Exegetical Studies.* Grand Rapids: Eerdmans, 1962.

Trenchard, Warren C. *The Student's Complete Vocabulary Guide to the Greek New Testament: Complete Frequency Lists, Cognate Groupings & Principal Parts.* Rev. ed. Grand Rapids: Zondervan, 1998.

Trypanis, Constantine A., ed. *The Penguin Book of Greek Verse.* New York: Penguin, 1971.

Turner, Nigel. *Christian Words.* Edinburgh: T&T Clark, 1980.

———. *Grammatical Insights into the New Testament.* Edinburgh: T&T Clark, 1965.

———. *Style.* Vol. 4 of *A Grammar of New Testament Greek,* by James Hope Moulton, Wilbert Francis Howard, and Nigel Turner. Edinburgh: T&T Clark, 1976.

———. *Syntax.* Vol. 3 of *A Grammar of New Testament Greek,* by James Hope Moulton, Wilbert Francis Howard, and Nigel Turner. Edinburgh: T&T Clark, 1963.

The UBS *Greek New Testament: A Reader's Edition.* Stuttgart: Deutsche Bibelge-sellschaft, 2014.

Vanhoozer, Kevin J., Craig G. Bartholomew, Daniel J. Treier, and N. T. Wright, eds. *Dictionary for Theological Interpretation of the Bible.* Grand Rapids: Baker Aca-demic, 2005.

Van Voorst, Robert E. *Building Your New Testament Greek Vocabulary*. 3rd ed. Atlanta: Society of Biblical Literature, 2001.

Wallace, Daniel B. *Granville Sharp's Canon and Its Kin: Semantics and Significance*. Studies in Biblical Greek 14. New York: Peter Lang, 2009.

———. *Greek Grammar beyond the Basics: An Exegetical Syntax of the New Testament*. Grand Rapids: Zondervan, 1997.

Wallace, Daniel B., Brittany C. Burnette, and Terri Darby Moore, eds. *A Reader's Lexicon of the Apostolic Fathers*. Grand Rapids: Kregel, 2013.

Westar Institute. Resources link in "Store: A Beginning-Intermediate Grammar of Hellenistic Greek." http://www.westarinstitute.org/store/a-beginning-intermediate-grammar-of-hellenistic-greek/.

Westcott, Brooke Foss. *The Epistles of St John: The Greek Text with Notes*. 1892. Reprint, Grand Rapids: Eerdmans, 1966.

Whitacre, Rod[ney A.]. "George Herbert and Biblical Theology." *Trinity Journal for Theology and Ministry* 3, no. 1 (Spring 2009): 67–88. http://www.tsm.edu/sites/default/files/Faculty%20Writings/Whitacre%20-%20George%20Herbert.pdf.

———. *John*. IVP New Testament Commentary Series. Downers Grove, IL: InterVarsity, 1999.

———. *A Patristic Greek Reader*. Grand Rapids: Baker Academic, 2007.

Wiersbe, Warren W. *Teaching and Preaching with Imagination: The Quest for Biblical Ministry*. Grand Rapids: Baker, 1994.

Wikgren, Allen, with Ernest Cadman Colwell and Ralph Marcus. *Hellenistic Greek Texts*. Chicago: University of Chicago Press, 1947.

Wilson, Mark, with Jason Oden. *Mastering New Testament Greek Vocabulary through Semantic Domains*. Grand Rapids: Kregel, 2003.

Young, Frances M. *Biblical Exegesis and the Formation of Christian Culture*. 1997. Reprint, Peabody, MA: Hendrickson, 2002.

———. *Virtuoso Theology: The Bible and Interpretation*. Eugene, OR: Wipf & Stock, 2002. Originally published as *The Art of Performance: Towards a Theology of Holy Scripture*. London: Darton, Longman & Todd, 1990.

Young, Richard A. *Intermediate New Testament Greek: A Linguistic and Exegetical Approach*. Nashville: Broadman & Holman, 1994.

Zerwick, Maximilian. *Biblical Greek: Illustrated by Examples*. Rome: Biblical Institute Press, 1963.

Zerwick, Maximilian, and Mary Grosvenor. *An Analysis of the Greek New Testament*. 5th ed. Rome: Biblical Institute Press, 2010.

SCRIPTURE INDEX

SUBJECT AND NAME INDEX